HOLYFIRE

R.T. KENDALL

CHARISMA
HOUSE

Most CHARISMA HOUSE BOOK GROUP products are available at special quantity discounts for bulk purchase for sales promotions, premiums, fund-raising, and educational needs. For details, write Charisma House Book Group, 600 Rinehart Road, Lake Mary, Florida 32746, or telephone (407) 333-0600.

HOLY FIRE by R. T. Kendall
Published by Charisma House
Charisma Media/Charisma House Book Group
600 Rinehart Road
Lake Mary, Florida 32746
www.charismahouse.com

Unless otherwise noted, all Scripture quotations are from the Holy Bible, New International Version. Copyright © 1973, 1978, 1984, International Bible Society. Used by permission.

Scripture quotations marked ESV are from the Holy Bible, English Standard Version. Copyright © 2001 by Crossway Bibles, a division of Good News Publishers. Used by permission.

Scripture quotations marked KJV are from the King James Version of the Bible.

Scripture quotations marked NIRV are taken from the Holy Bible, New International Reader's Version®. Copyright © 1996, 1998 Biblica. All rights reserved throughout the world. Used by permission of Biblica.

Scripture quotations marked NKJV are from the New King James Version of the Bible. Copyright © 1979, 1980, 1982 by Thomas Nelson, Inc., publishers. Used by permission

Cover design by Bill Johnson

Dr. R. T. Kendall is an amazing theologian, a man with years of experience with whom I am constantly amazed by his balance and integrity. He has authored many life-changing books that teach, yes, but that also nurture the spirit and soul. *Holy Fire* is no exception. This epic work on the Holy Spirit needs to be read and ruminated by the body of Christ worldwide. Hard hitting and transparent, it will prepare you for the greatest revival ever that is almost upon us.

—JOHN ARNOTT
Catch the Fire Ministries, Toronto

Here is a book that is written for both the charismatic and the conservative evangelical. It is designed not only to make you hungry for Jesus and the ministry of the Holy Spirit but also to give a balanced theology of the Holy Spirit. In a day when there is a polarization between the excesses of the charismatic movement—strange fire—and the pessimistic outlook of those who do not believe God manifests His power—no fire, RT's book *Holy Fire* will help us to keep our heads straight while increasing a passion for God. He has a proven ministry as a brilliant theologian and a man of the Spirit. This book is a gift to the body of Christ.

—MIKE BICKLE
Founder and director, International House of Prayer

The church in our day needs *Holy Fire*. Religious sentiment will not equip believers for the end-times crisis. RT has very boldly and systematically provided scriptural truth to prepare us for that challenge. This book will help defeat the idea that God withdrew the Holy Spirit's power from the church but let the devil and his gang keep theirs.

—CHARLES CARRIN
www.CharlesCarrinMinistries.com

This man has the amazing ability to address contentious and controversial issues but cause his readers to reevaluate their own opinions in the light of Scripture. R. T. Kendall is dangerous to personal complacency. This is a must-read book. RT and I have been friends for thirty years, and I am well-acquainted with many of his books. But this is one of the most important he has written so far. It is informative, clear, and edifying. I pray it will have a wide circulation. I am sure it will be a blessing to those who read it.

—Dr. Clive Calver
Senior minister, Walnut Hill Community Church
Bethel, Connecticut

For over a decade R. T. Kendall has been part of our annual Word, Spirit, and Power Conference. The same divine life, spiritual balance, and scriptural integrity demonstrated in those conferences permeate the pages of *Holy Fire*. Pastors "have no greater joy than to hear that their children walk in truth." This book will be an invaluable aid in our discipleship process!

—Stephen Chitty
Lead pastor, Christian Life Church
Columbia, South Carolina

Having come to Christ in a county jail and experiencing the fullness of the Spirit in a Texas state prison, I felt like my experience was complete. Almost forty years later I realize that the journey had just begun, and God has given me some incredible voices to guide me on the way. R. T. Kendall has written numerous and deeply insightful books on the Holy Spirit, and I have read each one with a renewed hunger. I finish every one with a greater thirst for the anointing, the power, and the witness. Having had the distinct privilege of reading this manuscript, I can tell you this book brings fresh eyes to missed truth. I once again was captivated by the precepts, insights, and, in some cases to me, revelations I had not gleaned. I encourage you to read this book with a Bible in one hand, a notebook on the desk, and a spirit that is ready for some new wine.

—Maury Davis
Senior pastor, Cornerstone Church
Madison, Tennessee

Theologically sound, gently balanced while scripturally compelling, being clearly laid out for both student and scholar, *Holy Fire* gets the bride of Christ back on track with some very important things that were present at the start of the church way back in Acts 2. It is perfectly timed for "such a time as this." RT's words have what the apostle James calls "a gentleness of wisdom" to them that can make this book palatable to all denominational readers. Those who question the gifts of the Spirit SHOULD READ *Holy Fire*. Those who have denominational biases MUST READ *Holy Fire*. And those who are simply hungry for all that God has for them WILL READ *Holy Fire* by R. T. Kendall.

—Tim Dilena
The Brooklyn Tabernacle

As a pastor of a charismatic church, I found RT's book to be insightful, objective, and most of all, balanced. A great book about every believer's "Friend"—the Holy Spirit.

—Jeff Dollar
Senior pastor, Grace Center
Franklin, Tennessee

My longtime friend R. T. Kendall has attempted to fulfill the advice of Dr. R. T. Williams (the man he was named after) to "honor the blood…honor the Holy Spirit" by taking seriously the holistic biblical witness. He stands with one foot in the charismatic tradition and one in the Reformed with some overtones of his Wesleyan heritage, seeking to articulate what John Wesley would term a *via media*.

—H. Ray Dunning
Professor emeritus of theology, Trevecca Nazarene University

In *Holy Fire* R. T. Kendall brilliantly exposes and corrects a dangerous division that exists in contemporary Christianity. Specific claims to the immediate witness of the Spirit today should neither be uncritically embraced nor automatically dismissed. But RT's main objective is to promote hunger for the genuine Holy Fire who has enlightened and empowered generations of believers from the Book of Acts to today. A challenge both to Reformed cessationists and card-carrying charismatics.

—Colin Dye
Senior minister, Kensington Temple
London, England

Many are still confused about the Holy Spirit despite half a century of worldwide blessing. RT's book will help us to open our minds to the possibilities and might rescue us from limiting God.

—Dr. Michael Eaton
Nairobi, Kenya

I love the delightful way RT approaches difficult subjects and is not afraid to speak out cautions against excesses. This is a refreshing book on the ministry of the Holy Spirit. May the Lord spread its message far and wide. No matter who you are or how long you have walked with Jesus, you will be challenged for more of Him as you read from this reputable, recognizable Reformed theologian whom I am honored to call my friend.

—Don Finto
Caleb Ministries
Nashville, Tennessee

I have waited for years for such a theologically sound book that embraces the present-day encounter of the Holy Spirit. It is a modern-day classic you hold in your hands. R. T. Kendall is a man of unwavering truth and an apostolic teacher with unflinching character. His teachings come from many years of honoring the Word of God, history of the church, and love for historic revival. I am grateful for this treatise. May it be used in our Master's hands to ground many, challenge others, and encourage thousands to hunger for more of the Holy Spirit today.

—Dr. James W. Goll
Encounters Network, Prayer Storm, God Encounters Training
Author, *The Seer, The Lost Art of Intercession,* and *A Radical Faith*

We live in a strange time when many people—in the name of Christ—have cheapened, abused, diluted, manipulated, fabricated, and sold the Holy Spirit. And gullible audiences have been misled because we lack solid teaching about the nature of the Spirit's work. This is why I am so thankful that my friend R. T. Kendall has sounded the alarm and written this important book. At a time when so much of the church is in a backslidden state, we need to be reminded that the Holy Spirit is indeed holy—and that He desires to awaken us, purify us, and renew us.

—J. Lee Grady
Former editor, *Charisma* magazine
Author, *The Holy Spirit Is Not for Sale*

Dr. R. T. Kendall is the former pastor of one of the world's most celebrated pulpits, Westminster Chapel of London, England. His latest release, *Holy Fire,* is an incredible book bringing a fresh anointing and insightful perspectives to the adventure and warfare of the Christian life. You are holding a book that will inspire and change your life. Read it!

—John C. Hagee
Pastor and best-selling author

The biggest challenge for church leaders is to keep our congregations focused on the premise of Scripture and not be persuaded by extremes. RT has done a good job in helping us find the radical "middle" of Scripture. We cannot afford to ignore the Holy Spirit, for He has been given to the church to prepare us for the soon-returning Christ. This book is a useful tool for both saints and leaders alike.

—MARCUS HERBERT
Pastor, Cornerstone Church
Johannesburg, South Africa

Holy Fire puts a fire in your bones for the real thing, a fire in your heart to be sure you are a discerning, true, and holy fire. To me, *Holy Fire* says that Jesus is the Word made flesh, but we have taken the word and tried to make it flesh. I love the book! It is a book of simplicity and shows clearly the true fire of God, its purpose, and its power. *Holy Fire* is not only a wake-up call but also a call for the fire of God to fall.

—DR. MARILYN HICKEY
President, Marilyn Hickey Ministries

He's done it again! R. T. Kendall has provided a safe road map that allows us to chase hard after God without destroying the old landmarks of our faith. *Holy Fire* will move you out of your comfort zone regarding the ministry of the Holy Spirit without moving you away from the safety zone of doctrine, wisdom, and godly character.

—DAVID D. IRELAND, PHD
Senior pastor, Christ Church
Montclair and Rockaway, New Jersey
Author, *The Kneeling Warrior*
www.DavidIreland.org

The purpose of the Holy Spirit in the life of every Christian is to empower regular people to do extraordinary works under His influence. Unfortunately many individuals cannot discern the difference between their own appetites, preferences, and natural abilities and the divine operation of God's infinite might in our finite space. R. T. Kendall helps us dissect the truth about the workings of the Holy Spirit. In *Holy Fire* this master teacher helps us understand how to cooperate with God's purposes. This is a timely word for a tumultuous time.

—HARRY R. JACKSON JR.
Senior pastor, Hope Christian Church, Beltsville, Maryland
President, High Impact Leadership Coalition
Presiding bishop, International Communion of Evangelical Churches

If you are serious about learning to know God and His ways and not miss one nanosecond of what the Holy Spirit is doing, this is a book you must not only read but also digest. RT masterfully balances the Word of God and the manifestations of the Holy Spirit in such a way that one feels safely impassioned to pursue all that God offers. May we see all the apostle Paul wrote, "Eye has not seen, nor ear heard, nor have entered into the heart of man the things which God has prepared for those who love Him" happen today.

—JOHN PAUL JACKSON
www.streamsministries.com

Holy Fire is both timely and urgent. Author R. T. Kendall writes with wisdom and passion, showing us how this could be the church's greatest hour. While many consider all fire to be *strange fire,* he speaks with great clarity, enabling us to recognize the genuine hand and heart of God, moving in and through His people. I love reading books of great scholarship when they are laced with passion and experience. *Holy Fire* is such a book, as R. T. Kendall is truly a brilliant man fully after God's heart.

—BILL JOHNSON
Bethel Church, Redding, California
Author, *When Heaven Invades Earth*
and *Hosting the Presence*

RT has written what will become a classic on the Holy Spirit! *Holy Fire* is theologically and intellectually stimulating, biblically sound and balanced, stirring and convicting. It should be a required textbook on the subject of pneumatology in every Bible college and seminary. A must-read!

—DR. DWAIN KITCHENS
Pastor, The Tabernacle
Sarasota, Florida

This generation is rapidly becoming one that is illiterate of Scripture. The evidence is seen as nearly every imaginable "supernatural manifestation" is being heralded as genuine regardless of whether or not it is supported by the Bible. R. T. Kendall, one of the most prolific and balanced writers of our time, shares the truth about many excesses we commonly see circulate Christendom. His book *Holy Fire* will enlighten your understanding to discern the truth from error and deepen your hunger for the truth of the Holy Spirit.

—HANK AND BRENDA KUNNEMAN
Lord of Hosts Church
One Voice Ministries
Omaha, Nebraska

Holy Fire by R. T. Kendall is a great book…best I've ever read on the Holy Spirit. If I were in a confined place and told that there was only one extra-biblical book on the Holy Spirit that I could take with me, R. T. Kendall's book on the Holy Spirit would be the one. It addresses all the essential questions and issues on this subject. More importantly, it is biblically accurate and balanced. The only agenda and bias the book seems to push is a broad biblically based understanding of the Holy Spirit and an intimate relationship with Him. If that's your heart and hunger, this book is for you. I plan to recommend it to our church for all who want to know the Holy Spirit not only as a doctrine but also as a person.

—WM. DWIGHT MCKISSIC SR.
Senior pastor, Cornerstone Baptist Church
Arlington, Texas

Knowing RT as I do, I began reading *Holy Fire* confident it would be a message the church needed to hear. I never suspected how much God would use it for my own life. Once again RT has done a tremendous job with a difficult and controversial subject, staying true to biblical teaching on the Holy Spirit and calling us to do the same. This book is a much-needed resource for the entire evangelical church, both charismatics and non-charismatics.

—DAVID MCQUEEN
Senior pastor, Beltway Park Baptist Church
Abilene, Texas

R. T. Kendall's *Holy Fire* is an important book because he bridges communities that have often talked past each other—or perhaps worse, ignored each other's existence. If the Spirit's gifts are what build up the church, no part of the church can afford to ignore the way any other part of the church fosters those gifts. And as a bridge person, Kendall is also able to speak the truth in love about the way some of us distort the gifts. Faithful are the wounds of a friend.

—DAVID NEFF
Former editor-in-chief, *Christianity Today*

In his latest work, *Holy Fire*, in which he outlines the ministry of the Holy Spirit, Dr. Kendall, while standing on the lofty shoulders of those who have gone before him, has, with biblical fidelity, produced a compelling case for understanding the gifts of the Holy Spirit to be operational today. Avoiding the pitfall of continuing revelation, he has produced a work that is as pastorally sensitive as it is theologically exact. In so doing he has made us all his debtors.

—DR. ROB NORRIS
Senior pastor, Fourth Presbyterian Church
Bethesda, Maryland

Reading *Holy Fire* is like looking through bifocal glasses: my eyes are directed down at the pages as my soul longingly lifts its gaze up to the Spirit. A prayer flows from my deepest part, "Father, I long for a direct and immediate encounter with your Spirit."

—KENT REDFEARN
Lead pastor, Muldoon Community Global Church Network
Anchorage, Alaska

The pig on the tight rope said the only really hard part is balance. That is so true in everything, especially theology. R. T. Kendall has hit just the right spot. *Holy Fire* lights the way for all of us, straight into a ministry of empowerment and credibility. Kendall is noted for the very insight, balance, and readability he brings to this much-needed work on the Holy Spirit.

—MARK RUTLAND
President, Global Servants

Many books have been written on the subject of the Holy Spirit but not one like this one! This book could, when believed, change the landscape of Christianity across the world. Not one book has been written as succinctly, as directly, or more clearly than this one. It will prove immediately controversial, continuously confrontational, and ultimately transformational in the life of the serious reader and beyond.

—JACK TAYLOR
President, Dimensions Ministries
Melbourne, Florida

Balance is part of the beauty of God's kingdom. In his latest book, *Holy Fire*, Dr. Kendall masterfully shares how to ignite the needed respect for the power of God's Spirit in all of us. He also makes it clear that we can only become a holy fire of influence for God if we are empowered by the Holy Spirit.

—FRANCOIS VAN NIEKERK
Senior pastor, Hatfield Christian Church
South Africa

I've always loved and respected R. T. Kendall's forthrightness in dealing truthfully yet gracefully with "strange fire" in the Pentecostal-charismatic movement. Yet I've also appreciated his unique perspective as a Reformed charismatic who is well acquainted with both sides of the doctrinal fence when it comes to the Holy Spirit's active work in our lives today. In *Holy Fire* R. T. combines the Word and Spirit to not only set the record straight but also, more importantly, draw readers into a deeper relationship with the Holy Spirit.

—MARCUS YOARS
Editor, *Charisma* magazine

Visit the author's website at www.rtkendallministries.com.

Library of Congress Cataloging-in-Publication Data:
Kendall, R. T.
  Holy fire / R. T. Kendall. -- First edition.
      pages cm
  ISBN 978-1-62136-604-1 (trade paper) -- ISBN 978-1-62136-605-8
(e-book)
  1. Holy Spirit. I. Title.
  BT121.3.K455 2014
  231'.3--dc23
                                    2013038294

14 15 16 17 18 — 10 9 8 7 6 5
Printed in the United States of America

To

Melissa and Rex

CONTENTS

FOREWORD

I AM PRIVILEGED TO INVITE YOU TO OPEN YOUR HEART AND HAND to receive a gift. Even if you paid for this book yourself, believe me— it is still a gift because it presents you, the reader, with insight that can assist you to receive gift upon gift that proceeds from God's love and awaits your welcome.

Holy Fire is addressed to all earnest believers in Jesus, specially crafted and wrapped in words that will fan the flame of your desire to follow Jesus, obey His call, and grow in His grace and goodness by the power of the Holy Spirit. Furthermore, *Holy Fire* identifies the stepping-stones that will usher any *believer* in Jesus to become a *receiver* of power from on high—a literal clothing with the warming and abiding embrace of God's love and power. Jesus Himself is the One who calls us to allow Him to set our hearts aflame with the beauty and constancy of a life filled and overflowing with the Holy Spirit, ignited with the steadfast glow of His presence, and ablaze with the empowering ability to live as lights in the world, shining with a holy fire.

To my mind, no words could be more suited to title this book. The title *Holy Fire* is neither superficially nor arrogantly conceived. Rather, like the *content* you will find in this book, the *concept* of holy fire is derived from Scripture. Its purpose is depicted in the pillar of fire that led Israel from their post-slavery status to their predestined land of promise. Its prevailing protection and penetration are further displayed when God revealed His presence and power in actual events in both the Old and New Testaments of the Holy Bible. Thus, the words *holy fire* represent that kind and quality of God's manifest activity that not only is descriptive of His presence with power, but also bespeaks His holy nature—His excellence of person and inviolate purity. So it is entirely appropriate that *Holy Fire* titles this timely and immensely practical book. It unfolds a relationship with God that embraces everything the holy Trinity extends to us—the Father's gift of love, the Son's gift of life, and the Spirit's gift of power!

I want to affirm at the outset that every moment you spend in this book will be worth the time. You will be led and fed along a pathway of enriching truth by a friend of mine, Dr. R. T. Kendall, a known and beloved pastor-author of considerable scholarship. Still, I assure you, as well studied as RT is, his depth in "the Word and the doctrine" will only serve to assist your insight, never to intimidate. At heart he is a consummate pastor—a word and a lifestyle properly defined in the description of the Lord in Psalm 23 and in the person and nature of Jesus Christ, "that great Shepherd of the sheep" (Heb. 13:20). Dr. Kendall writes with the heart of a man tested and proven as a faithful pastor, having served congregations in both Britain and America. And of even greater importance, he is also a faithful and loving servant of abiding trustworthiness and fidelity to both his bride, Louise, and to the bride of Christ, the church.

DELIGHTED FOR THREE REASONS

I have three reasons for being delighted to write this "fore-word"— this brief "word on the front of it all" to you. My desire is to help set your appetite on edge with expectancy, to serve as a friend introducing you to another friend, believing your meeting will become helpful and productive. With that goal in mind I set about reading this book while it was still in manuscript form. As a pastor and teacher for nearly sixty years I have read innumerable books regarding Christian life and truth, and my impression of this book explains my first reason for being delighted to write to you here.

(1) I am of the opinion that *this is a landmark book.* By making that designation, I am saying I believe *Holy Fire* will, with time, become noted as more than simply a good, useful, and helpful book (which it certainly is). But beyond that, it is my studied opinion that, like a landmark, *Holy Fire* will become a point of reference for many, and

that as years pass, it will find enduring use for a generation or more. As a landmark becomes a place that provides a safe and certain guide, helping bring people to a sure destination, so also the pathway of Bible-based truth taught in these pages provides more than direction; it guides you to your destination.

I urge you to read this book and receive Jesus's call to receive the fullness of the Holy Spirit. Indeed—enter with faith, open your heart with trust, and welcome all He offers as you invite Him to baptize you with the Holy Spirit. Just as He forgave you when you invited Him as your Savior, He also will fill you as you open yourself to His promised power for service, the Holy Spirit.

But hear me carefully, please. This book is a handbook to reread and think through beyond the entry point. It processes further and deeper—beyond beginning to growing and glowing, abiding and residing! It will lead you to establish values and viewpoints for a lifetime. The elements of basic discipleship are here. They point the way to an abiding commitment to live with a power-filled life for Jesus Christ and to love with a purity-filled life under Christ's lordship, obedient to His will and ways, yielded as His servant to all He sends you and in all He leads you.

(2) The second reason I take delight in the privilege of writing you here is my gratitude for the tone and style of the author. It is both true in content and tender in delivery—a rare combination when many writers who deal with such subjects choose warring rather than winsomeness. Clearly and graciously Dr. Kendall has brought the precious message of Holy Spirit fullness with an *irenic* (pronounced "eye-rennick") tone and style. This reflects the derivation of the Greek word for "peace," *irene* (pronounced "ee-ray-nay"). By reason of the author's choice to write in this spirit, *Holy Fire* reflects the intent of God's Word in James 3:17–18:

> But the wisdom that is from above is first pure, then peaceable, gentle, willing to yield, full of mercy and good fruits, without partiality and without hypocrisy. Now the fruit of righteousness is sown in peace by those who make peace.
>
> —NKJV

This is surely the spirit one would wish to always be in evidence when the ministry of the Holy Spirit is discussed. Accordingly, even when Dr. Kendall addresses those who reject the truth of the Holy Spirit's present ministry of signs, wonders, and gifts, he repeatedly affirms those opponents as "good people who love Christ," for indeed they are. The differences of choice regarding these matters, while highly significant to both parties—and, indeed, of higher significance to our expectation regarding the presence of the Holy Spirit's ministry in the believer's life and through the church globally—is *not* an appropriate reason for loveless separatism from brotherly fellowship. While some on each side of this issue *do* fail at this point of living as peacemakers, there is a model for godly largesse of spirit here in *Holy Fire,* one manifest by the author.

Thus, you will find the truth of the baptism with the Holy Spirit—the overflowing grace and power of the Holy Spirit—clearly and biblically distinguished as a separate experience pursuant to the believer's new birth. However, you will not find the beauty of this truth blemished by a tone or a disrespect or scorn for either those denying such a grace is available or those who "hunger and thirst" for that fullness but have not yet received it.

The fullness of the Holy Spirit that Jesus promises and fulfills is the heart of the message in this book. Perhaps it is this fullness you seek, and like many, you have wished you could find a thorough handbook to guide you step by step in answering your questions and opening the door to your own experience of the Holy Spirit's presence and power. That truth is set forward here, inviting you to know and experience the same infilling, overflow, and outcome of Acts 2, when our Lord's promise of "the Comforter" was first fulfilled at Pentecost. That very day the Holy Spirit's overflowing with power occurred and was also categorically promised the same day as a continuously available blessing and resource for all who prayerfully ask, seek, and knock (Luke 11:9–13; Acts 2:38–39).

This book is designed to teach, to feed the hungry, and to satisfy the weary, nurturing hope and faith while balancing truth and love. In doing so, the tone of *Holy Fire* warmly yet passionately invites all who read to expect the Holy Spirit of Pentecost to do the same thing now as then—"for the promise is unto you" (Acts 2:39, KJV). Open your Bible and read it aloud. Then read it aloud again! Let the "promise of the Promise" fill your heart with praise and sing aloud with gratitude, thanking the Lord Jesus for His nearness, His dearness, and His readiness to fill you.

(3) The third reason for my pleasure to invite you forward into this book is because of its thoroughness and theological freshness. Dr. Kendall has an approach that gives a teacher's attentiveness to detail without becoming tedious. He also presents the Word with a theologian's awareness of history and is careful to define the lines within the revelation of God's Word in this book.

However, having mentioned theology, let me hasten to say that no one need fear becoming mired in a boring, scholastic, or wearying vain display of learning. You will not encounter any bewildering labyrinth of confusing jargon or labored theories here. Rather, *Holy Fire* provides an example of how theology appropriately serves us. Whatever else may come of its application, biblical theology is intended and ought always to arrive at the goal of helping people to know and understand God and His ways. That is the definition you will discover being fulfilled as you read.

There is nothing to drown a thirsty seeker, but there is much to provide a window through which your heart and mind can be flooded with the Holy Spirit's sweet and fruit-begetting working in your life. The purpose of this book's instruction is to reveal how you may open that window and receive the showers of blessing and rivers of grace that the Lord Jesus Christ is ready to pour into your life as you receive the fullness of His baptism in the Holy Spirit.

Having mentioned theology, permit me also to observe a refreshing surprise that will be particularly meaningful to leaders, who, like myself, might find it unlikely to have a book advancing all the best and vital principles of New Testament *charismata* written by one who embraces Reformed theology.[1] Add to this the unlikelihood of a Reformed theologian writing a complete book dedicated to bringing believers into the experience of a Book of Acts baptism with the Holy

Spirit, and the credulity of most church leaders might be stretched to the limit.

Nonetheless, God is moving in remarkable ways in the church today, and for the last twenty-five years or more one of my closest prayer partners has been another pastor-teacher of the Reformed theological tradition. This reaching beyond boundaries of human theological frameworks and joining hearts and hands around the person of Christ is not the choice of compromisers, but of leaders convinced by God's Word that His wisdom exceeds their tradition. So reason number three (the theological freshness I find in this book) is *not* the result of a *re*nunciation or *de*nunciation of a godly leader's theological tradition, but an evidence of the capacity of an honest heart and humbled mind to bow at the altar of heaven and say, "Let Your kingdom come and Your will be done—*in me!*" It evidences nothing of reduced convictions, but something beautiful of commitment to the obvious: "We know in part and we prophesy in part"; which is to say, "Father God, I bring my mind into submission with my eyes on Jesus and my heart opened to Your Holy Spirit."

Doubtless there will rise naysayers to plead, "But the Word must prevail!" To that authority I readily agree. However, when godly leaders differ, though each are committed to the authority of the Word of God, it may be time for us to cease arguing points that have become moot by reason of "irreconcilable differences" and to open ourselves up to the Holy Spirit of reconciliation around the true fountainhead of our faith—the person of Jesus our Savior and Lord! He who has occasioned our perfect justification-unto-acceptance by the almighty, all-knowing, wise, and righteous God may be calling us to be a bit more patient with the intellectual differences held between minds that, though sanctified by grace, are yet to become glorified and translated unto the eternal venue of God's throne room.

So it is that the theological refreshing I rejoice to affirm is over the fact that *Holy Fire* is written by a pastor-teacher who was trained and ordained in a theological setting that taught him to resist those who embrace charismatic or Pentecostal teaching or experience. This, of course, is terminology that discounts the biblical basis and scriptural practice of receiving Jesus's promise and ministry as the baptizer with the Holy Spirit as a distinct experience, available *after* a believer's new birth through faith in Him as Savior and Lord. And yet, as you open *Holy Fire*, you will be led in study by a remarkable teacher and writer. As you read his testimony, you will find a mind humbled by a holy God who received a baptism in the Holy Spirit's holy fire, and you will be blessed.

I found it gratifying and worthy of note how the author consistently takes time to elaborate with biblical clarity and theological precision, not only to unfold the Scriptures with a mature and patient pen, but also with a heartwarming personal candor. You will be touched as he describes his own discovery of that liberating truth revealed to him, very much in the same way Aquila and Priscilla did with Apollos: "They took him aside and explained to him the way of God more accurately" (Acts 18:24–26, NKJV).

In taking time to explain his own journey, Dr. Kendall demonstrates to every reader the need for sound, biblical theology—*not* for the purpose of theological debate, but for the sake of assisting honest seekers by introducing the liberating power of truth.[2] The Bible tells us, "You shall know the truth, and the truth shall make you free" (John 8:32, NKJV), and "Where the Spirit of the Lord is, there is liberty" (2 Cor. 3:17, NKJV). Such care for exactness and faithfulness, to assure he provides biblical support for each subject discussed throughout this book, has put solid footings under the message of *Holy Fire*. It also leads the reader beyond human opinion to God's Word to the rock of divine revelation. More writers would do well to emulate this trait of R. T. Kendall.

In Conclusion

As today's global church advances toward the end of the age, more and more former critics of charismatic teaching are recognizing that where biblical lifestyle and a biblical openness to the Holy Spirit go hand in hand, the church is thriving. This fact is increasingly drawing many believers to become open to the present works, wonders, and charismatic gifting of the Holy Spirit, acknowledging these things as continually and timelessly available to all the church from Pentecost to the Rapture.[3] Though disclaimers rise and opposition lingers among many reticent or resistant, the evidence of truth prevails: the Holy Spirit's immediate and direct ministry—bearing witness to the continuing promise at Pentecost—is forever available until Jesus comes again!

So, here is a timely handbook—a well-detailed, carefully elaborated, and biblically supported explanation and invitation. The promise *is* unto you, and the Spirit's fullness, enabling power, and Christ-glorifying presence are available!

Though this book is most certainly written to assist newer believers—offering the "pure milk of the Word," which the apostle Peter directed new believers toward for their growth (1 Pet. 2:2, NKJV), I believe its substance deserves to be studied by mature believers as well. It is *both* meat and milk, the "meat of God's Word" sliced in a way that anyone can digest. I believe that even established believers will find they are enriched and edified.

My prayer is that *Holy Fire* will be read by multitudes. It deserves a ready, restful, and receptive reading by the earnest seeker of truth whose true heart desire is to know, walk with, and follow Jesus Himself—to receive the promise He gave of the Holy Spirit as the One whose fullness in our lives would cause more of Christ's life to shine forth with the glow of biblical holy fire! And finally, it deserves to become a resourceful, instructive, and assisting source of clarifying, Bible-based answers to every earnest inquirer as to the biblical grounds and spiritual soundness of both of the ministries that John the Baptist said Jesus would bring to us, declaring: (1) "Behold! the Lamb of God who takes away the sin of the world!" (John 1:29, NKJV); and (2) "He will baptize you with the Holy Spirit and with fire" (Luke 3:16).

May the peace, power, purpose, and presence of Jesus, Lord of the church, abound unto those purposes in and through us all—according to His Word, by the power of His Holy Spirit, and unto the glory of God our Father and His Son our Savior-Messiah! Amen!

—Pastor Jack W. Hayford
Founder-Chancellor, The King's University
Dallas/Los Angeles

Note from the publisher: We encourage you to read the endnotes that are associated with this foreword because they contain additional valuable insight from Pastor Jack Hayford.

SPECIAL RECOMMENDATION FROM THE UNITED KINGDOM

S INCE AT LEAST THE MID-1960S GOD HAS GRACIOUSLY SHOWN great favor to countless individuals and churches around the world by sending sustained visitations of His Holy Spirit to bring personal vitality, seasons of renewal, the restoration of declining congregations, and indisputable authentic manifestations of His power to enable Christian leaders and people to duplicate in our day all the phenomena we see in the Gospels and Book of Acts. This has been the case on all continents and countless countries around the world.

These exciting developments have always included genuine miraculous healings, deliverance from demonic powers, accurate prophetic ministry in forth telling and fore-telling, as well as a revived, sustained practice of the spiritual disciplines such as Scripture reading, intercessory prayer, fasting, personal evangelism, fellowship, missional advance, and church planting—all greatly assisted by the emergence of mature, once ignored "Ephesians 4 ministries" of apostolic, prophetic, evangelistic, didactic, and pastoral gifts to help build and equip Christ's people for their ministry in serving Christ and His world.

Many seasons of genuine church restoration have brought vital new health, revival passion, fervent worship, God-centered living, along with widespread vocational guidance from God regarding personal destiny to millions. Beautiful clarity and ministry fruitfulness have usually followed. The result has been unprecedented advance in world mission, church growth, personal maturity, loyalty to Scripture in its entirety, and God's manifest presence among His people again—something that is often missing in periods of church decline, when unbelief and skeptical liberalism have held sway.

Nevertheless, many strong and otherwise biblical evangelicals have resisted all of these developments in prejudicial and unbiblical ways. They opt for some form of "cessationism" that renders "sign" gifts redundant and obsolete, often for less than biblical reasons. Factors such as little firsthand experience of the full range of the Holy Spirit's power, rejection of the "lunatic fringe" of renewal movements, fear of taking risks in their own ministry, and hurting their reputation or standing delay participation. Prejudiced unteachable attitudes and a refusal to read or consider the extensive theological works and narrative historical accounts that support these moves of God as authentic have also left many leaders in a state of aloof indifference or unteachable hostility toward God's greatest gift to His people, His Holy Spirit in all His fullness and charismatic power.

My dear friend and predecessor at Westminster Chapel, Dr. R. T. Kendall, has done us a great service in writing *Holy Fire*. This remarkable book addresses with clarity and accessibility many of the doubts, false arguments, misleading interpretations, and dangers of ignoring scriptural mandates designed only for our good.

RT has helpfully drawn upon a lifetime of ministry and personal accounts of his own journey in finally distancing himself from all cessationist positions on this matter, then subsequently opening his heart and mind to all that the Bible teaches concerning Christ's legacy of the Holy Spirit as Jesus's stand-in to continue His work in and through Spirit-filled believers everywhere. The result is the proper wedding of Word and Spirit in Christian spirituality, as RT takes up every issue that concerns critics of "charismatic Christianity" and answers them thoroughly from personal experience, biblical theology, historical perspectives, and accurate exegesis of relevant texts.

The result is a valuable, accessible, engaging, and informative overview of the person and work of the Holy Spirit, who like Christ who sent the Spirit is still, *"The same yesterday, today, and forever."* I am glad to say that the result is that this brief work is truly *"Theology on*

Fire!" It should hasten the death, and burial, of unbiblical and Spirit-quenching attempts to extinguish God's precious gift of *Holy Fire.*

—GREG HASLAM
MINISTER, WESTMINSTER CHAPEL, LONDON, UK

PROLOGUE

THERE HAS BEEN A SILENT DIVORCE IN THE CHURCH, SPEAKING generally, between the Word and the Spirit. When there is a divorce, sometimes the children stay with the mother, sometimes with the father. In this divorce you have those on the Word side and those on the Spirit side.

What is the difference? Those on the Word side stress earnestly contending for the faith once delivered to the saints, expository preaching, sound theology, rediscovering the doctrines of the Reformation—justification by faith, sovereignty of God. Until we get back to the Word, the honor of God's name will not be restored.

What is wrong with this emphasis? Nothing. It is exactly right, in my opinion.

Those on the Spirit side stress getting back to the Book of Acts, signs, wonders, and miracles, gifts of the Holy Spirit—with places being shaken at prayer meetings, get in Peter's shadow and you are healed, lie to the Holy Spirit and you are struck dead. Until we recover the power of the Spirit, the honor of God's name will not be restored.

What is wrong with this emphasis? Nothing. It is exactly right, in my opinion.

The problem is, neither will learn from the other. But if these two would come together, the simultaneous combination would mean spontaneous combustion. And if Smith Wigglesworth's prophecy got it right, the world will be turned upside down again.

PREFACE

I HAVE ALWAYS WANTED TO WRITE A BOOK ON THE HOLY SPIRIT but never thought I would. The main reason is this. My first editor and publisher, Edward England of Hodder & Stoughton in London, said to me more than thirty years ago, "We have fifty books on the Holy Spirit." I took that as a hint that books on the Holy Spirit were not needed! But perhaps they are today. My friends Steve and Joy Strang of Charisma House have honored me by requesting that I write a book on the Holy Spirit. So here it is. Joy had a special wish: "Write a book that will make people hungry for the Holy Spirit."

I do so wish I could fulfill that lofty goal.

Although I devoted two chapters to my relationship with my mentor, Dr. Martyn Lloyd-Jones (1899–1981), in my book *In Pursuit of His Glory* (an account of my twenty-five years at Westminster Chapel), it seems appropriate to refer to his teaching insofar as it touches on the subject matter of my present book. A medical doctor by training who gave up medicine to go into the ministry, he became the greatest preacher of the twentieth century and had one of the greatest minds of our time. So if Martin Luther and John Calvin felt a need to quote St. Augustine and St. Chrysostom to support their teaching, I have a duty to introduce *the Doctor* (as he was known by all) to those who may not know him and to quote him when so many do not realize what was dearest to his heart. He was responsible for my being in Westminster Chapel precisely *because* of the views I take in this book.

I am so honored that Dr. Jack Hayford would write the foreword to my book. He is without doubt the most esteemed leader in the Pentecostal-charismatic movement. Rev. Greg Haslam, my successor at Westminster Chapel, has also graciously provided a special recommendation from the United Kingdom. But I must mention Rob Parsons and Lyndon Bowring—closest friends and severest critics—who have helped me immeasurably once again. My thanks also to Mike Briggs, consultant to Charisma House. This is my first book with Debbie Marrie since she became executive director of Product Development of Charisma House. Her wisdom in the preparation of this book has been most significant. Also, to have my former editor with Charisma House, Barbara Dycus, back to help with this book has been a lovely providence. My thanks also to Leigh DeVore, who has had the tedious job of copy editing and doing the much-needed index for this book.

My deepest thanks is to my wife, Louise, especially for her patience during the time of my putting this book ahead of time with her. Her wisdom has been so very helpful. Furthermore, it was her idea to call this book *Holy Fire.*

This book is fondly dedicated to my daughter and son-in-law.

—R. T. KENDALL

Introduction

HE BLOWS WHERE HE WILL

The wind blows where it wishes, and you hear its sound, but you do not know where it comes from or where it goes. So it is with everyone who is born of the Spirit.

—JOHN 3:8, ESV

When the church is revived, so is the devil.

—JONATHAN EDWARDS
(1703–1758)

THE HOLY SPIRIT DOES NOT BELONG TO YOU. ARE YOU CHARIS-matic? He is bigger than your signs and wonders events. Are you Reformed? He will not be limited by your theology. The Lord Jesus said of the Holy Spirit, "He blows where he will." C. S. Lewis (1898–1963) described the lion Aslan, his central character in the Chronicles of Narnia, with the following words: "He isn't safe, but he is good."[1] Since Aslan represents Jesus in the story, it is commonly assumed that this description refers to Jesus. I personally think these words apply to all members of the Trinity, and especially to the Holy Spirit. He isn't *safe*, but you can trust Him because He is *good*.

My position is clear. I describe myself as a Reformed theologian—not only in belief but also in practice. I have to say that for some reason I have often felt last in line as far as signs and wonders are concerned. While others have been *slain in the Spirit* all around me, my body has remained resolutely upright—like the Statue of Liberty. While members of my family have seen physical healing personally, I have not. It is true that I have spoken in tongues, but you would not find an occasion of that in public. In short: if I am charismatic, I am the *least of the brethren.*

But there is more than this. In my half century of ministry I have seen the worst excesses of the charismatic movement—spurious prophecies, fake healings, fleshly speaking in tongues. I should tell you that I am "reformed" with a small *r.* I don't dot all the *i's* and cross all the *t's* as some might, although I believe in the sovereignty of God as much as anybody I know. I also think it is possible for some of us Reformed people to take ourselves a little bit too seriously—even becoming the new Sanhedrin, fancying that we alone speak for the Most Holy God. And I am also charismatic, but perhaps with a small *c.* I can't always take the party line, and yet I believe in the gifts of the Holy Spirit as much as anybody I know. I believe theologically that the Holy Spirit is as active today as He ever was because I have seen remarkable evidences of the power of His work in this world today. But above all I believe in the infallible inspiration of Holy Scripture, and try as I might, I cannot for the life of me twist the text to prove that the power of God in the supernatural gifts of the Holy Spirit was limited to the times of the early church. However, it is not just for me a matter of exegesis, but of personal experience as I will show later in this book. And here for a Reformed theologian it might get a little embarrassing.

I was brought up in the hills of Kentucky, approximately one hundred miles from Bourbon County, the seat of the Cane Ridge Revival that began in 1801. America's church historians call it America's Second Great Awakening (the first being the Great Awakening that largely featured the ministry of Jonathan Edwards from around 1735–1750). My own church in Ashland was born in the *tail end* of the momentum that came from the Cane Ridge Revival. I saw all kinds of things in my old church—the good, the bad, and the ugly. I also saw both kinds of fire—the holy fire that comes from above and the strange fire that comes from below. Call it strange fire, wild, or uncontrolled fire. I used to hear the expression, "Wild fire is better than no fire at all." In other words, if God does not send the genuine fire of the Holy Spirit, it is better to have some wild fire—with something happening—than dead orthodoxy or formalism.

Wrong. Having no fire is better than having wild fire. Having no fire is better than having strange fire. I also used to hear people say, "People will come out to see a fire," as if crowds prove something. Crowds prove nothing.

Holy fire is what is needed. Holy fire is not the main thing; it is the only thing that matters.

My heroes are John Calvin (1509–1564), Jonathan Edwards (1703–1758), and the late Dr. Martyn Lloyd-Jones. And if you were to say to me that the historic Pentecostal movement or the more recent charismatic movement has been bedeviled with strange fire, I know exactly what you mean. After all, as Jonathan Edwards used to say, "When the church is revived, so is the devil." Satan raises up the counterfeit to intimidate sincere seekers of God—to put them off so they will run in the opposite direction. Strange fire almost always shows up in any true revival or movement raised up by God. And yet I also know too much to allow the historic Pentecostal movement and the charismatic movement to be painted with one big brush—implying they are mostly characterized by strange fire—so that they can be so easily dismissed.

If you have a heart after God, Satan is unhappy with you. He will work overtime to quell that hunger. It is important to know something of his ways. Paul said of Satan, "We are not ignorant of his designs" (2 Cor. 2:11, ESV). But more important than discerning the counterfeit is to be able to recognize the genuine presence of the Holy Spirit. It is far better to be able to discern the real than the counterfeit. And yet to the degree you are able to recognize and embrace what is real and true, to that degree will you be able to detect and reject what is spurious and false.

I am not sure anyone is qualified to talk about what is false unless they are well acquainted with what is real.

If you are hungry for the Holy Spirit, this book is for you. If you are hungry for more of the Holy Spirit, this book is for you. And if the idea of being hungry for the Holy Spirit is not something that has particularly gripped you up to now, it is my prayer that as you read on, such a burning heart will emerge. Jesus said that those who hunger and thirst after righteousness will be filled (Matt. 5:6).

Walk with me now on a journey that is designed to satisfy your appetite for sound teaching and a greater measure of the Holy Spirit. We will taste both the milk of the Word and solid food—a diet that will enable us to "distinguish good from evil" (Heb. 5:14, ESV).

Chapter One

DISCERNING THE TIMES

The Spirit clearly says that in later times some will abandon the faith and follow deceiving spirits and things taught by demons....For the time will come when men will not put up with sound doctrine. Instead, to suit their own desires, they will gather around them a great number of teachers to say what their itching ears want to hear. They will turn their ears away from the truth and turn aside to myths. But you, keep your head in all situations.
                          —1 Timothy 4:1; 2 Timothy 4:3–5, niv

The worst thing that can happen to a man is to succeed before he is ready.
                          —D. Martyn Lloyd-Jones

I write this book for the young Christian, the new Christian, the theological student, the new pastor, but also the seasoned layman or minister who aspires more than ever to be jealous for the honor and glory of God. I write also for the fence straddler out there who is sincerely baffled and unsure of what to believe about the Holy Spirit. Jonathan Edwards said that the one thing Satan cannot produce in us is a love for the glory of God. So if the reading of this book results in a greater love for the honor of God and deeper reverence for the Holy Spirit, you may be sure that the devil did not put that desire and respect there. This is also why Edwards stated that when the church is revived, so is the devil! So you may count on the devil putting every obstacle in your way to rob you of the joy that comes from intimacy with the Holy Spirit. Indeed, Satan will do everything he possibly can to lure you away from tasting the genuine power of the living God.

I want to anticipate certain cautions you may face down the road. Whether your background is conservative evangelical, Reformed, charismatic, or Pentecostal, there are certain pitfalls you need to be aware of. In each of these streams you need to be armed to withstand the pressures that come from a revengeful Satan who does not want you to grow in grace and knowledge of our Lord Jesus Christ. "My people are destroyed from lack of knowledge" (Hos. 4:6). In this connection I would mention (1) lack of knowledge of God's Word and (2) lack of knowledge of God's ways.

The first thing is the reading of the Bible. The devil does not want you to read your Bible, much less spend a *lot* of time reading the Bible. How well do you know your Bible? To understand the Bible you must be on good terms with the Holy Spirit. He wrote the Bible (2 Tim. 3:15; 2 Pet. 1:21). He alone can open your mind to understand His own Word. When we grieve the Holy Spirit through bitterness or quench Him through fear, the inevitable result is an inability to focus on His Word. And yet to put it the other way around, to be on good terms with the Holy Spirit you need to know your Bible—and know it well. I fear there are ministers around who never seriously read the Bible through but only consult the Bible when it comes to preparing a sermon.

You need a Bible reading plan. For years I have recommended the plan designed by Robert Murray M'Cheyne (1813–1843), which Dr. Martyn Lloyd-Jones introduced to me the first week I was the minister of Westminster Chapel in 1977.[1] It takes you through the whole Bible in a year including the New Testament twice and Psalms twice.

This keeps you in God's Word. I heartily recommend it. You will never be sorry you started this and stayed with it. Be a Christian who knows his or her Bible. This is so pleasing to God.

Second, the way you know someone's *ways* is by spending time with them. You show your esteem of a person by how much time you give them. So I will come right to the point: *How much do you pray?* The devil does not want you to pray, much less spend a *lot* of time praying.

> And Satan trembles, when he sees
> The weakest saint upon his knees.[2]
> —WILLIAM COWPER
> (1731–1800)

I urge at least thirty minutes a day in your quiet time—including Bible reading and prayer. For the person in full-time Christian ministry, I suggest a minimum of an hour a day (two is better), and this should be for private devotions and quiet time without using any of this time for sermon preparation. Martin Luther spent two hours a day in prayer. John Wesley spent two hours a day in prayer. According to a recent poll taken on both sides of the Atlantic, the average church leader (pastor, priest, evangelist, teacher) today spends *four minutes a day in prayer.*[3] And you wonder why the church is powerless? Where are the Luthers today? Where are the Wesleys? Who is truly turning the world upside down? As for time in prayer, if you don't know how to use up that time, get a prayer list. Pray for people who will never know you prayed for them. Pray for your friends. Pray for your enemies. There will be no praying in heaven. I would lovingly plead with you: spend much time in prayer now. Get to know God and His ways by spending time with Him.

THE GOD OF THE BIBLE
VERSUS DANGEROUS TEACHINGS

I cannot predict exactly what obstacles you will face, but I will mention briefly some that are at large. For example, if you are in a charismatic or Pentecostal church, there are some strange teachings you will likely be confronted with. They come down basically to one thing: your view

3

of God. The God of the Bible is sovereign, omnipotent, omnipresent, omniscient, and holy. In my books *The God of the Bible* (CrossBooks) and *Totally Forgiving God* (Charisma House) I share these attributes of God in more detail.

1. The sovereignty of God refers to His divine right to do what He pleases. "I will have mercy on whom I will have mercy" (Exod. 33:19; Rom. 9:15). He "works out everything in conformity with the purpose of his will" (Eph. 1:11).

2. The God of the Bible is omnipotent—all powerful. There is nothing He cannot do (Luke 1:37).

3. The God of the Bible is omnipresent. He is everywhere; there is no place He is not present. Always be looking for His manifest presence. Peter called this, "times of refreshing" (Acts 3:19).

4. He is omniscient—He knows everything, past, present and future. Yes, He knows the future as perfectly as He knows the past, declaring the end from the beginning (Isa. 46:10).

5. The God of the Bible is a holy God. He demands holiness of us in our personal and private lives (1 Pet. 1:16). Never forget that you and I will stand before the judgment seat of Christ one day to receive what is "due" us for the things done "while in the body, whether good or bad" (2 Cor. 5:10).

A defective view of the God of the Bible has resulted in dangerous teachings in recent years in certain charismatic or Pentecostal circles. By Pentecostal I mainly mean a denomination—such as Assemblies of God, Pentecostal Holiness, Foursquare Gospel, Church of God, and Elim. By charismatic I refer to a movement that grew up spontaneously in the 1960s, stressing the gifts of the Holy Spirit (especially speaking in tongues) and crossed denominational lines—for example, Episcopal, Reformed, Baptist, Lutheran, and Presbyterian. I'm afraid there are a lot of strange teachings out there that have crept into these churches or movements.

One is called *hyper-grace* teaching. I will mention this heresy yet again in chapter 5—"Strange Fire." The view comes to this: since Jesus dealt with all our sin on the cross, there is no need to confess sin—it has already been dealt with. No need for repentance in the Christian life, say these people. This is tantamount to antinomianism (anti-law) and can so easily lead to ungodly living. The people who uphold this kind of thinking have actually had to eliminate certain books of the Bible, for example, Hebrews and 1 John. Imagine that! To uphold a teaching they have to cut out part of the canon of Holy Scripture! I warn you, this teaching grieves the Holy Spirit. It is a fad. It will not last. But it can do incalculable damage in the meantime.

The second teaching I mention here and again in chapter 5 is called *open theism.* This view of God brings Him down to the level of man so that such a God does not know His own mind without our input. The idea is that we actually help God know what to do next; without us He cannot move forward. This is sub-Christian teaching. It has astonishingly crept into certain charismatic circles. When one leader of this teaching was asked publicly in London, "With this view of God, is it not possible that God could lose out in the end?" The reply was: *Yes.* Imagine a God like that. The God of the Bible wins! Such a weak view of God is the ultimate consequence of denying His eternal sovereignty.

On the heels of open theism is the notion that we can virtually make God do anything. We can *decree* something, and it will come to pass. This makes man sovereign. It is sometimes a part of the *health and wealth* and *prosperity* teachings. While it is absolutely true that God promises to bless the tither (Mal. 3:10)—for we cannot outgive the Lord (2 Cor. 9:8), beware of those who pitch this point of view mainly to advance their personal ministries. Some leaders go so far as to claim that their *words of knowledge* are superior to Holy Scripture. Some deny the Bible as being the complete and final revelation of eternal truth. One leader said, "If the apostle Paul had my faith, he would not have had a thorn in the flesh." I'm sorry, but this kind of doctrine has emerged in charismatic and Pentecostal settings. Be wise to teaching that exalts any man or woman and even appeals to a person's greed. They emerge from strange fire, teachings that are alien to Holy Scripture.

However, do not let your view of the infallibility of Holy Scripture keep you from believing that God speaks to us directly today. He does. Do not believe for one moment that the God of the Bible does not perform miracles today. He does. And don't abandon your view that the Bible is God's final and complete revelation of eternal truth. It is. My prayer is that you will uphold Holy Scripture as God's infallible Word while simultaneously believing that God is unchanging in His willingness to manifest His power (Mal. 3:6; Heb. 13:8). It would therefore be a great pity—and a victory for Satan—if you let strange teachings disillusion you. I write this book to encourage you to wait for and expect the conscious and manifest presence of the third person of the Godhead—the Holy Spirit.

THEOLOGY AND WORSHIP

Having had one foot in the Reformed camp and the other in the charismatic-Pentecostal camp, I have been increasingly alarmed at the trend in some of the worship among the latter camp. The early Methodists got their theology mostly from their hymns. This made them theologically minded—a trait you and I must never lose. Whose hymns did the early Methodists sing? They sang those written by such people as Isaac Watts (1674–1748), Charles Wesley (1707–1788), William Cowper, and John Newton (1725–1807). Read them. Sing them. Have you had a look lately at the words of hymns such as, "And can it be that I should gain an int'rest in my Savior's blood?,"[4] "When I survey the wondrous cross on which the Prince of glory died,"[5] "God moves in a mysterious way His wonders to perform,"[6] "How sweet the name of Jesus sounds,"[7] or "O for a heart to praise my God, a heart from sin set free"[8]? I would plead for the present generation of all Christians to sing the new as well as the old. Jesus spoke a parable about "the owner of a house who brings out of his storeroom new treasures as well as old" (Matt. 13:52), a truth that could readily apply to new and old hymns.

What worries me most about some contemporary worship is its lack of good theology. Some seem to have almost no theology at all! This is not good. I fear that we are producing a generation of people who are vulnerable to heretical movements partly because of a lack of good grounding in the truth. That said, I thank God for hymns such as Chris Bowater's "Jesus Shall Take the Highest Honour"; Graham Kendrick's "Restore, O Lord," "Knowing You, Jesus," and "Such Love"; Stuart Townend's "How Deep the Father's Love For Us" and "In Christ Alone"; Matt Redman's "Blessed Be Your Name" and "10,000 Reasons"; Stephen Fry's "Oh the Glory of His Presence"; Darlene Zschech's "Shout to the Lord"; and others.

But there are pitfalls in conservative Evangelicalism too. One teaching that is common in Reformed theology is called *cessationism*. The idea is that the miraculous *ceased* sometime after the last apostle died or when the canon of Scripture was complete. This concept is so important I will devote both chapters 8 and 9 to it. Cessationism is not a fad. It has been around for a long time. Those who uphold this are not heretics. They are good people. But cessationism quenches the Holy Spirit as much as the previously mentioned teachings that displease Him. You will not likely convince a cessationist to believe that the living God heals supernaturally today. A man convinced against his will is of the same opinion still! I just don't want some of these people to convince *you*! So do not let those who hold to their views that God will not manifest His power today deter *you* from seeing the God of glory show Himself in our generation. That is why I write this book.

As I said, my own theological stable is Reformed. But I came into it not by reading Reformed theology. My purpose in writing this book, however, is not to change your theology but to make you hungry for the Holy Spirit. If you walk in the Spirit, know your Bible, and spend sufficient time alone with God, your theology will take care of itself. My greatest mentor was Dr. Martyn Lloyd-Jones. Through this book I want to make him better known and a blessing to you as much as he was to me. The greatest thing he ever said to me was this: "The worst thing that can happen to a man is to succeed before he is ready." This statement is what helped me *keep my head* when God did not manifest His power in my own ministry as quickly as I hoped. But I never gave up. I don't want you to give up!

Chapter Two

WHAT EVERY CHRISTIAN SHOULD KNOW ABOUT THE HOLY SPIRIT

I will ask the Father, and he will give you another Helper, to be with you forever, even the Spirit of truth...he dwells with you and will be in you.

—JOHN 14:16–17, ESV

If the Holy Spirit was withdrawn from the church today, 95 percent of what we do would go on and no one would know the difference.

—A. W. TOZER
(1897–1963)

THE DISCIPLES OF JESUS DID NOT ENJOY HEARING ABOUT THE Holy Spirit. It made them uneasy, as we will see below. Today some Christians feel much the same way. The mention of Him makes them uneasy. There can be many reasons for this. In the case of conservative evangelicals, they sometimes think that charismatics talk more about the Holy Spirit than they do about Jesus or the gospel. In my own experience I have often observed that there are a surprising number of charismatics who have little or no assurance of why they are saved.

The proof of this is when I preach the gospel in some of their churches. I often ask these questions, borrowing from the late D. James Kennedy's *Evangelism Explosion*[1] (the best soul-winning program I have come across):

1. Do you know for sure that if you were to die today you would go to heaven?

2. If you were to stand before God (and you will) and He were to ask you (and He might), "Why should I let you into My heaven?," what would you say?

I have been shocked how many of them (all over the world) admit that their hope of heaven is not in the blood of Jesus but their own efforts. This is worrisome. It makes me feel many of them have not heard the gospel at all! And yet this lack of assurance would also be true in some conservative evangelical churches when they are taught that it is not looking to Christ alone but to your good works as being the only way you can be sure you have been converted, as we will see further in chapter 3.

There are also conservative evangelicals who feel at times that they are being judged as being unspiritual by overly zealous people—especially if they do not speak in tongues. Rightly or wrongly, some are made to feel they are not even Christians or are—at best—second class. However, any reference to the Holy Spirit in some situations can be almost counterproductive.

The reason the Twelve did not like the idea of the Holy Spirit—at least at first—was because it sent a signal to them about Jesus's departure. To the Twelve, the Holy Spirit meant losing Jesus. The initial reference to the Holy Spirit came simultaneously with the mention of Jesus's going away. This was upsetting. After all, the Twelve felt they were at long last getting to understand Jesus Himself. They were slowly getting to know some of His ways. They had followed Him for three years. They knew what He looked like. They knew His height, the color of His eyes, hair, and skin. They knew the sound of His voice. They heard His sermons, the parables, the dialogues with Pharisees and Sadducees. They saw the miracles, the healings. They saw Him walk on water. They were convinced He was the long-awaited Messiah who would come. They anticipated Him setting up His kingdom and overthrowing Rome at any moment.

But Jesus began to talk about going away. The notion of Him going away was puzzling. I wonder if they listened very carefully at all. The reason I say that is because even after He was raised from the dead—and was around for forty days—the only thing on their minds was: When would Jesus restore the kingdom (Acts 1:6)? Had they truly taken in what Jesus taught, they would not have asked that question. In any case, Jesus did all He could to spoon-feed them and break to them gently as possible that He was going away. Jesus's task was to help them to make the transition from the level of nature to the realm of the Spirit. It would not be easy. Any thought of a transition was nowhere in their thinking.

THE HOLY SPIRIT WOULD TAKE JESUS'S PLACE

Jesus introduced the Holy Spirit to them by carefully telling them it was in their interest that He depart. "It is for your good that I am going away" (John 16:7). He talked about "another" Comforter or Counselor coming along (John 14:16). But the very idea of "another" person did not interest them in the slightest. The Greek word is *parakletos*—a word impossible to translate into one word so that it is fully meaningful—whether it be comforter, advocate, helper, or counselor. The word literally means, "one who comes alongside"—which Jesus in fact was to the Twelve at the natural level. He had indeed come alongside them during those three years. They were very happy with Jesus, Jesus in the flesh. The thought of Him leaving them was confusing, upsetting, and very painful. So the notion of "another" Paraclete did not bless them at the time. The whole concept of the Holy Spirit was threatening to them.

Do you feel threatened by the Holy Spirit? The disciples of Jesus

11

were threatened by the thought of the Spirit because they liked things just as they were—except for waiting for Jesus to overthrow Rome. They were at ease with the idea of Him setting up His kingdom. The word *kingdom* to them had a good sound. By the end of three years with Jesus these disciples were firmly in their comfort zones. After all, they were quite convinced they would be right *in* on the new regime. James and John even hoped to sit at Jesus's right hand and left hand in this kingdom. In any case, they looked forward to His kingdom. But they could only think at a natural level, even though Jesus clearly said that His kingdom was not something you can see with your naked eye (Luke 17:20–21).

So if you feel threatened by the Holy Spirit, is it because you are happily in your comfort zone? Are you afraid of what the Holy Spirit might do to you? What He would require of you? What He might ask you to do? Do you think you will lose something if you make yourself vulnerable and totally open to Him? Are you afraid He will embarrass you? Do you think you will lose your identity? Do you think you might have to change?

Whether the disciples listened carefully to Jesus, we only know that He kept on speaking. One of the things Jesus said was that the Holy Spirit would *remind* them of what He had taught them. It was indeed the Holy Spirit who enabled them to go back to those sermons and discourses—remembering them all by the help of the Spirit. And not only the words but also the very meaning.

TWENTY-ONE THINGS

There are twenty-one things every Christian should know about the Holy Spirit. These twenty-one principles, built upon what I have said up to now, summarize the things the Bible says about the Holy Spirit generally and what Jesus said about the Holy Spirit particularly.

1. The Holy Spirit is God.

When Ananias lied to the Spirit, he lied to God (Acts 5:4). "The Lord is the Spirit" (2 Cor. 3:17). We may speak of the deity of Jesus Christ—that

He is God—because He is. And yet we don't feel a need to speak of the deity of the Father—it would be redundant. Sometimes I think I would like to preach on the Godhood of God! The most neglected member of the Trinity these days is God the Father. That said, I would like to talk about the deity of the Holy Spirit. The Holy Spirit is God—every bit as much as Jesus being God or the Father being God.

That said, never underestimate or take for granted the deity of the Holy Spirit. The Holy Spirit in you is God in you. You can worship the Holy Spirit; you can pray to the Holy Spirit; you can sing to the Holy Spirit. And yet there are some sincere Christians who are reluctant to pray or sing to the Holy Spirit. This is because of a faulty translation of John 16:13, which I will examine below. Such well-meaning Christians don't mind singing the first two verses of a well-known chorus that speaks of glorifying the Father and the Son, but when it comes to glorifying the Spirit, some are afraid to continue singing! As if the Spirit does not want to be worshipped and adored! Or as if the Father and the Son would not want this!

Such Christians feel uncomfortable about worshipping and adoring the Spirit because the Authorized Version (King James) translated John 16:13—referring to the Holy Spirit—"He shall not speak of himself," a verse that should be translated, "He will not speak *on his own*," as I show further below. I actually sympathize with them. I know where they are coming from. I used to have the same problem until I saw what the Greek literally said. And yet traditional church hymnals for many years have included hymns with lyrics such as "Holy Spirit, Truth divine, dawn upon this soul of mine,"[2] "Holy Ghost, dispel our sadness,"[3] "Lord God, the Holy Ghost, in this accepted hour, as on the day of Pentecost, descend in all Thy power,"[4] or "Spirit of God, descend upon my heart."[5] You could not address the Holy Spirit like that if He were not God. Do not be afraid to talk directly to the Holy Spirit. There is no jealousy or rivalry in the Trinity. The Father is happy and the Son is happy when you address the Holy Spirit in prayer. After all, the Spirit of

God is God the Spirit. What is more, the Trinity is not God the Father, God the Son, and God the Holy Bible!

Just remember: the Holy Spirit is God.

2. The Holy Spirit is a person.

Jesus referred to the Holy Spirit as "he" (John 14:16; 16:8) and introduced Him as being "another" *paracletos* (which is what Jesus was). Never think of the Holy Spirit as an "it," an "attitude," or an "influence." He is a *person* and has very definite ways. Call them peculiar, eccentric, or unique if you like; He has His *ways*. You may or may not like His ways. But get over it! He is the only Holy Spirit you have! He won't adjust to you; you must adjust to Him.

The Holy Spirit Himself spoke of ancient Israel as not knowing God's "ways" (Heb. 3:7–10). God was grieved because His own covenant people did not know His ways. They should have. But they didn't. God has His own "ways" and wants us to know them. And so too it is when it comes to the person of the Holy Spirit. He wants us to know His ways. As we will see below, the Spirit can be grieved, He can be quenched, and He can be blasphemed.

The Holy Spirit can also have *joy*. In Romans 14:17 Paul talked about "joy *in* the Holy Spirit" (emphasis added), whereas Paul referred to the "joy *of* the Holy Spirit" in 1 Thessalonians 1:6 (ESV, emphasis added). It is His own joy. This joy is not necessarily what *we* feel; it is what *He* feels. And yet sometimes He invites us to feel what He feels! It is called "gladness" in Acts 2:28 (ESV). That is exactly what I experienced years ago driving in my car, an event to which I will return later.

We need therefore to learn the difference between feeling happy because of circumstances and feeling the very "joy of the LORD" (Neh. 8:10). There is certainly nothing wrong with our feeling happy because things are working out for us. Indeed, there was "joy in that city" when many who had been paralyzed were healed (Acts 8:7–8). Good news about Gentiles being converted made the disciples "very glad" (Acts 15:3). But the highest level of joy on this planet is when we are allowed to experience the very joy *of* the Spirit—feeling what He feels. For when the Spirit lets us feel His joy, it is truly "inexpressible" (1 Pet. 1:8).

3. The Holy Spirit is eternal.

"How much more, then, will the blood of Christ, who through *the eternal Spirit* offered himself unblemished to God, cleanse our consciences from acts that lead to death, so that we may serve the living God!" (Heb. 9:14, emphasis added). The Father, the Son, and the Word existed in eternity before God chose to create the heavens and the earth (Gen. 1:1). "Before the mountains were born or you brought forth the whole world, from everlasting to everlasting you are God" (Ps. 90:2). God the Father is eternal, and so is the Holy Spirit. When Paul said that in the fullness of time God "sent his Son" (Gal. 4:4), it is because the Father already had a Son. Jesus Christ is the eternal Son. He was the Word until the moment He became "flesh" (John 1:14). That did not happen in Bethlehem but at His conception in Nazareth the moment the Word entered the womb of the Virgin Mary.

The Holy Spirit is equally eternal with the Father and the Word. This is the same Holy Spirit whom Jesus talked about and introduced to His disciples. It is also easy to find mention of the Holy Spirit in the Old Testament. He was, in fact, present all the time. Pharaoh discerned the Spirit of God was in Joseph (Gen. 41:38). Bezalel was filled "with the Spirit of God" (Exod. 31:3). The "Spirit of the LORD" was upon Othniel (Judg. 3:9–10), Gideon (Judg. 6:34), Jephthah (Judg. 11:29), Saul (1 Sam. 10:10), and David (1 Sam. 16:13). The Holy Spirit lay behind the ministry of Elijah (1 Kings 18:12; 2 Kings 2:16). The Spirit of God came upon Azariah (2 Chron. 15:1) and Zechariah (2 Chron. 24:20). The references to the Holy Spirit go on and on. One of the greatest of all is this: "'Not by might nor by power, but by my Spirit,' says the LORD of hosts" (Zech. 4:6, NKJV).

As we will see again below, Jesus said that the Holy Spirit spoke through David in Psalm 110:1 (Matt. 22:43). It was the testimony of the early church that God spoke "through the mouth of…David, your servant, said by the Holy Spirit" (Acts 4:25, ESV). Indeed, as we will see below, the Holy Spirit had a role in Creation and was the author of all Scripture.

4. The Holy Spirit is the Spirit of truth (John 14:17; 16:13).

Jesus said of Himself that He is the "way and the *truth* and the life" (John 14:6, emphasis added), and so equally the Holy Spirit is truth. As it is impossible for God to lie (Heb. 6:18), never forget that the Holy Spirit is *incapable* of lying to you. He will never deceive you.

Jesus Himself was full of grace and "truth" (John 1:14). Truth means fact. It means what is reliable. What Jesus does can be proved and will not let you be ashamed. When a miracle was performed, the enemy of truth was forced to say, "We cannot deny it" (Acts 4:16). Jesus is transparent integrity. Today we sometimes use the expression "the real deal." It is what people want to see in leaders, what people long for in relationships—no deceit, no infidelity, but honesty and trustworthiness. That is what we want in a friend—pure gold, the real thing.

Jesus is that. The God of the Bible is that—His words are "trustworthy" (2 Sam. 7:28), "true, and righteous altogether" (Ps. 19:9, ESV). And so virtually the first thing Jesus said about the Holy Spirit was that He is "the Spirit of truth" (John 14:17). This means genuineness, trustworthiness, faithfulness, and integrity. It also means theological truth. The Holy Spirit will never lead you to error. What He reveals you can believe and stake your life on.

To put it another way, the Holy Spirit is the opposite of the devil. Jesus said of Satan: "There is no truth in him…for he is a liar and the father of lies" (John 8:44, ESV). He is incapable of telling the truth. He lives to deceive. Do you know the feeling of being deceived? To know what it is to embrace a person, recommend them, put your ministry on the line for them—then find out you were deceived! It can be very painful.

The Holy Spirit, however, will never mislead you. You don't need to be afraid of Him. He may not be "safe," but He is "good."

5. The Holy Spirit was involved in Creation.

"The Spirit of God was hovering over the waters" (Gen. 1:2). We know that Jesus is depicted as Creator. "Through him all things were made; without him nothing was made that has been made" (John 1:3). "For by him all things were created: things in heaven and on earth, visible and invisible, whether thrones or powers or rulers or authorities; all things have been created by him and for him. He is before all things, and in him all things hold together" (Col. 1:16–17). Some of these lines could describe the Holy Spirit—for example, that He is before all things. The Holy Spirit had a hand in Creation, as Jesus did.

6. The Holy Spirit, using people, wrote the Bible.

"All Scripture is God-breathed and is useful for teaching, rebuking, correcting and training in righteousness" (2 Tim. 3:16). "For prophecy never had its origin in the human will of man, but prophets, but men spoke from God as they were carried along by the Holy Spirit" (2 Pet. 1:21).

Jesus had the same view of Scripture that Paul and Peter held to, namely, that the Holy Spirit wrote the Old Testament. Jesus asked the Pharisees (a question they could not answer), "How is it then that David, *speaking by the Spirit*, calls him [Christ] 'Lord'? For he says, 'The Lord said to my Lord: "Sit at my right hand until I put your enemies under your feet."' If then David calls him 'Lord,' how can he be his son?" (Matt. 22:43–45, emphasis added). My point is, Jesus said that David was able to write as he did because the *Holy Spirit*—in 1,000 BC—enabled him to do so. And, as we also saw earlier, it was the testimony of the early church. When being persecuted, they turned to the Lord and said, "You *spoke by the Holy Spirit* through the mouth of your servant, our father David: 'Why do the nations rage and the peoples plot in vain?'" (Acts 4:25, emphasis added).

One more thing in this connection. The canon of Holy Scripture is closed. It is final. Absolute. Incontrovertible. It is God's complete and final revelation. No word that will come in the future will be equal to the Bible in level of inspiration. This means that any *leading, prophetic word, word of knowledge,* or *vision* one may have today *must cohere with Holy Scripture.* If it doesn't, it must be rejected. The main reason that King Saul became yesterday's man and rejected by God was because he thought he was above the Word of God. When he offered the burnt offerings, he knew he was going right against Moses's mandate that only the person called of God could offer burnt offerings.

And yet he claimed to have been "compelled" to do it (1 Sam. 13:12). Whenever a person claims to speak for God, claiming "The Lord told me"—and it goes against Scripture, you may safely, comfortably, and most assuredly reject that person's word, no matter how credible that person may seem!

The Holy Spirit takes the responsibility for the authorship of the Bible. He used people of course. But the *buck* stops with the Holy Spirit. The same Holy Spirit may speak today at various levels. But no level of inspiration will equal the inspiration of the Bible—ever.

7. The Holy Spirit is our teacher.

"He will teach you all things" (John 14:26, ESV). "You do not need anyone to teach you. But as his anointing teaches you about all things and as that anointing is real, not counterfeit...remain in him" (1 John 2:27).

The Holy Spirit is our teacher in basically two ways: directly and indirectly—a most important concept, which I will unpack in detail later. If He teaches us directly, then, "you do not need anyone to teach you." The Holy Spirit is very capable of teaching us in that fashion, and it is a wonderful thing to have happen. The things I was taught directly had been alien to me—for example, that I was eternally saved and chosen from the foundation of the world. I could not have thought that up in my own mind. I was taught the opposite—that such teaching was actually "born in hell" (I am not joking). So how did I come to it? By the direct teaching of the Holy Spirit.

The indirect teaching refers to the way the Holy Spirit *applies* what we read or hear. It is when the Spirit applies the Word of God when we read it. It is when the Spirit applies preaching, teaching, a blog, a poem, a loving word of encouragement from a friend, or when singing a hymn or chorus. As it happens, this very morning in my quiet time I sang the hymn, "Be Still, My Soul" to the tune "Finlandia." Only God (and Louise, who was with me) knew what those words meant to me on this particular day. It was as though they were penned for me! The Holy Spirit was at work applying this great hymn.

The Holy Spirit is our best and only reliable teacher. In fact, He is the only teacher who matters. Whatever teaching you hear or read (including this book)—whoever the preacher or teacher, if the Spirit does not apply it and witness it to your heart (which He is most capable of doing), you should learn to hold that teaching in abeyance—if not dismiss it.

Caution: the Holy Spirit only witnesses to the *truth*. Remember too that the best of teachers make mistakes; they are not infallible. You must be like the people of Berea who "examined the Scriptures [the Old Testament in this case] every day to see if what Paul said was true" (Acts 17:11). In those days Paul was a *nobody*; he did not have the stature then he has today. Anyone who says to you, "Believe it because I say it," is doing you no favor and is probably insecure in himself.

8. The Holy Spirit can be grieved.

"Do not grieve the Holy Spirit of God, with whom you were sealed for the day of redemption" (Eph. 4:30). You will recall that the Holy Spirit is a person. He can be *grieved*. The Greek word *lupeo* can mean, "get your feelings hurt." What hurts the Holy Spirit's feelings? Chiefly, bitterness. The next thing Paul says is: "Get rid of all bitterness, rage and anger, brawling and slander, along with every form of malice. Be kind and compassionate to one another, forgiving each other, just as in Christ God forgave you" (Eph. 4:31–32).

I have written an entire book on this subject, called *The Sensitivity of the Spirit*. Not sensitivity *to* the Spirit, important though that is; the issue is how sensitive the *person* of the Holy Spirit Himself is. How easy it is to grieve Him, to hurt His feelings. When you think about this—anger, losing your temper, shouting when you get frustrated, speaking impatiently or unkindly of a person, holding a grudge, or pointing the finger—these things grieve the Holy Spirit! But it doesn't seem to bother us! It should. If we are conscious of the sensitivity *of* the Holy Spirit, we will develop an acute sensitivity *to* Him—and be able (in ever-increasing measure) to hear His voice. This comes by living in love—keeping no record of wrongs (1 Cor. 13:5).

In 1974 my family and I visited Corrie ten Boom (1892–1983) in Holland. I asked her, "Is it true that you are a charismatic?" Without saying yes or no she bluntly replied: "First Corinthians 12 and 1 Corinthians 14. But don't forget 1 Corinthians 13." It was a shrewd way of saying we need both the gifts and the fruit of the Holy Spirit.

9. The Holy Spirit can be quenched.

"Do not quench the Spirit" (1 Thess. 5:19, ESV). "Do not put out the Spirit's fire." What is the difference between grieving the Spirit and quenching the Spirit? They almost certainly overlap. But if there is a difference, it is probably this: we grieve the Spirit by our relationships with one another—like judging and unforgiveness; we quench the Spirit when we are prejudiced toward the way the Spirit may be manifesting Himself and by not respecting His presence. It is usually fear that lies behind quenching the Holy Spirit.

Whether we hold that the Holy Spirit does not, will not, or cannot manifest today through the gifts of the Spirit or the miraculous, by adhering to cessationism, the Holy Spirit is put to one side before He is given an opportunity to show His power.

Don't be threatened by the Holy Spirit. Some would say that, "The Holy Spirit is a gentleman." I'm not sure I agree with that! Whereas I am sure you don't need to be threatened by Him, He may not be so "nice" as some might hope. Dr. Lloyd-Jones said often that the problem with the ministry today is that it has "too many nice men" in it. The Holy Spirit may require something of you that was not on your radar screen. Back in 1982 I made the decision to give up my aspiration of being a great theologian—and instead be willing to take to the streets, give out tracts—not that I am suggesting they are mutually exclusive! I began to talk to complete strangers and passers-by about the Lord. It was so embarrassing! But I never looked back.

So I do not say God will not require something of you that leads you out of your comfort zone. You may indeed have to leave your comfort zone. But I can promise this: follow the Holy Spirit by being totally open to Him; you will be forever thankful.

10. The Holy Spirit will be the One who convicts.

"He will convict the world concerning sin and righteousness and judgment" (John 16:8, ESV). Only the Holy Spirit can make us see our sin, show us the need for righteousness, and the urgency of the gospel—that there is judgment. A person cannot feel convicted of these things on his or her own. It takes the Spirit to shake us rigid.

This is true before and after our conversion. We cannot see our sin or the seriousness of unbelief before our conversion—we are all so self-righteous. It requires the Holy Spirit to make us see the painful truth—that we have grieved Him by self-righteousness and unbelief and are going to have to give an account of our lives at the judgment seat of Christ. Even after conversion we must beware of self-righteousness. This is why John said—writing to Christians, "If we claim to be without sin, we deceive ourselves and the truth is not in us" (1 John 1:8). It is also why it is good to pray the Lord's Prayer daily—recalling the petition, "Forgive us our sins, for we also forgive everyone who sins against us" (Luke 11:4).

The Spirit shows us our sin but also leads us to see the need for righteousness—of which there are two sorts:

1. Righteousness imputed to us when we believe the gospel (called saving faith)

2. Righteousness imparted to us when we "continue to live in him" (called persistent faith—Col. 2:6)

Righteousness is connected to Jesus's ascension ("I am going to the Father, where you can see me no longer," John 16:10) partly because the preaching of the gospel did not begin until Jesus died, rose from the grave, and ascended to the Father's right hand.

But what is the "judgment" of which the Spirit promises to convict us? It is a reference to the final day—when the Judge of all the earth shall do right (Gen. 18:25). Satan is the cause of all the evil and injustice in this world. The death of Jesus took Satan by surprise (1 Cor. 2:8) and not only spelled his downfall but also forecast the day of his judgment. Death was defeated by Jesus's death (Heb. 2:14), which is why Jesus said, "The prince of this world now stands condemned" (John 16:11). People often ask, "Is there no justice in this world?" Answer: sometimes there is. But don't count on it. "Life's not fair," said John

F. Kennedy. But one day God will openly bring about Satan's demise. God will explain the reason for evil and suffering. Everything will be put under Jesus's feet. Satan himself will be "thrown into the lake of burning sulfur" (Rev. 20:10). The Holy Spirit convicts of this truth, testifying that Satan stands condemned but also that judgment is coming.

For this reason, we "all" must stand before the judgment seat of Christ and give an account of the things done in the body, whether good or bad (2 Cor. 5:10). The Holy Spirit therefore convicts of the final judgment. The affect this should have on us is godly fear. As soon as Paul mentioned standing before the judgment, he mentioned the "fear" of the Lord ("knowing therefore the terror of the Lord," 2 Cor. 5:11, KJV). The reference to judgment also points to the neglected teaching of eternal punishment. When Paul witnessed before Felix, he spoke of "judgment to come" (Acts 24:25). Felix was afraid. He trembled. In times of great revival there is often a revival of the teaching of judgment and eternal punishment. And yet only the Holy Spirit can make this truth terrifying. If He does not come alongside when such is preached, people will be unaffected.

11. The Holy Spirit is our guide.

"He will guide you into all the truth" (John 16:13). Unless you are led to see truth by the Spirit, you will never see it. "The man without the Spirit does not accept the things that come from the Spirit of God, for they are foolishness to him, and he cannot understand them, because they are spiritually discerned" (1 Cor. 2:14). Without the Spirit we will likely think it is our great brain that keeps us from seeing what is there. Only by the Holy Spirit guiding us can we understand the Bible and then experience the joy of the Spirit.

My hobby for many years was bonefishing in the Florida Keys. A bonefish (called that because they are bony and virtually inedible) is a wily, skittish, hard-to-see, fast-as-lightning, shallow-water fish that is great fun to catch. They average in size around six to eight pounds. But if you have never tried it, you are unwise to do so the first time without a professional guide. When I first heard this, I refused to hire a guide. First, I didn't want to pay his fee. Second, I didn't want to admit I *needed* a guide. But after repeated failures on my own I gave in—and hired a guide. The funny thing was, he took me to the exact spots in Largo Sound where I had fished for months—without seeing any! With this kind of fishing—which requires stalking them and seeing them before they see you—it is imperative to see them before you cast to them. But I hadn't even seen the first one! But with the guide I saw them in no time! I will never forget it. I was eventually able to see them. And yet I would never have seen one on my own without a guide.

The Spirit "guides" us into truth—showing what is *there* but what cannot be seen without Him opening our eyes. It is humbling for prideful people to admit to the need of the Holy Spirit. The cost? Our pride being shattered. But once we are broken and enabled to see our stubbornness, the Spirit will show us amazing things—in Scripture.

As it happens, I was recently in Bimini, Bahamas, to do some bonefishing. I hired a wonderful guide—"Bonefish Tommy." Despite knowing how to see them (in the past), I realize how much I had forgotten on how to spot them, even in crystal-clear water only a foot or so deep. As a matter of fact, most of the fish I caught I had not seen at all; Tommy would usually tell me where to cast—and I would then catch them. I felt so dumb!

Sometimes we experienced Christians—who know sound theology—need to humble ourselves and admit our need for further illumination by the Spirit. I need the Holy Spirit more than ever. I have been reading the Bible for some seventy years. I have read it through about forty times. But sometimes I feel I've barely begun to know God and His Word. We never outgrow our need for the heavenly guide to lead us to truth we had never seen before—but which has always been there.

12. The Holy Spirit speaks only what the Father gives Him to say.

"He will not speak on his own; he will speak only what he hears" (John 16:13). The Authorized Version (King James) is sadly famous for translating this verse "he shall not speak of himself," which is one of the more unfortunate translations in biblical translation history. As we saw above, it has led good people to infer that they should barely (if at all) mention the Holy Spirit lest they say what the Spirit Himself would never allow. This is a mistake. After all, the Holy Spirit wrote the New Testament! This is how we know about the Holy Spirit! The correct translation is *not* that He would not speak of Himself but that he will not speak "on his own" or "on his own authority" (ESV). This means He passes on what the Father tells Him to say. That is what the verse means. Never be afraid to talk about the Holy Spirit. It is exactly what the Father and Son want you to do.

The Holy Spirit, in fact, continued the same pattern Jesus followed. Jesus said, "I tell you the truth, the Son can do nothing by himself; he can do only what he sees his Father doing, because whatever the Father does the Son also does" (John 5:19). This means Jesus took His cue from the Father—what to say, where to go, when to heal, when to reply. He did *nothing* without receiving the green light from the Father. Everything Jesus did had been orchestrated in heaven by the Father. Everything. The Son did nothing on His own. Ever.

That is exactly what the Holy Spirit is saying about Himself. The Spirit does nothing without the green light from the throne of grace— what to say, where to go, when to heal, when to reply. Concerning where to go, the disciples were once forbidden by the Holy Spirit to go into Asia—or Bithynia (Acts 16:7). The Spirit was doing what the Father ordered; it was the will of the Father that they not go. God the Father orchestrated from heaven all that the Holy Spirit would say or do here on Planet Earth. That is the meaning of these words. Jesus never said that the Holy Spirit would not speak of Himself. In fact, He *does* speak of Himself.

13. The Holy Spirit will predict the future.

"He will tell you what is yet to come" (John 16:13, emphasis added). This is the basis for prophecy. We saw earlier some references to the Holy Spirit in the Old Testament. *All* prophecies in the Old Testament— from Moses to Elijah, from Samuel to Malachi—were borne by the Holy Spirit. I wrote a book based on Isaiah 53 called *Why Jesus Died.*[6] Isaiah 53 is written in such a manner that one is amazed that Jews today could read that chapter and not see how Jesus and His death

were perfectly predicted and fulfilled. "I make known the end from the beginning, from ancient times, what is still to come. I say: My purpose will stand, and I will do all that I please'" (Isa. 46:10).

This is how Agabus knew a famine would be coming (Acts 11:28). This is how Paul knew the ship he was on would be shipwrecked (Acts 27:23–26).

Never forget: God knows the end from the beginning. He knows the future as perfectly as He knows the past.

14. The Holy Spirit will glorify Jesus Christ.

"He will bring glory to me by taking from what is mine and making it known to you" (John 16:14). One of the interesting characteristics of the Trinity is that the persons of the Godhead heap praise on one another. As I said, there is no jealousy or rivalry in the Godhead. This is hard for some to grasp. The Father does not mind if you pray to Jesus or the Holy Spirit. The Father honors the Spirit and the Son. The Son honors the Father and the Spirit. The Spirit glorifies Christ and speaks only what He hears from the Father.

Glorifying Christ is honoring Him for:

1. Who He is

2. What He said

3. What He did for us

4. What He continues to do for us

5. What He will do

It is giving Him the honor *now* that He will receive openly on the last day—when every knee shall bow and every tongue confess that Jesus Christ is Lord to the glory of God the Father (Phil. 2:9–11). *You cannot praise Jesus too much. It is impossible to heap too much praise on the Lord Jesus Christ.* The Holy Spirit leads us to praise the Lord Jesus as He deserves, although we all wish we could do better. This is why Charles Wesley wrote, "Oh, for a thousand tongues to sing my great Redeemer's praise."[7]

Jesus said that the Holy Spirit would take "what is mine." What is *His*, and what is made known to us? Answer: (1) His work as Redeemer, and (2) the glory and praise Jesus Christ deserves—what belongs to Him. Jesus is the focus. He is the one who was *to be* glorified—and who *was* glorified. Jesus prayed, "Father, the time has come. Glorify your Son, that your Son may glorify you....Glorify me in your presence with the glory I had with you before the world began" (John 17:1–5). The glory of Christ is the focus. He is our Redeemer. He is the God-man. It is not the Spirit who is to be focused on when it comes to glory. You may ask: Is not the Holy Spirit God? Yes. But it was not the Holy Spirit who died. It is not the Holy Spirit to whom every knee shall bow one day. So when Jesus said that the Holy Spirit would take what is "mine," He was stating that the focus would be on the Redeemer and Savior of the world who would be glorified and made known to us.

15. The Holy Spirit can be blasphemed.

"Blasphemy against the Spirit will not be forgiven" (Matt. 12:31). This is arguably the scariest passage in the New Testament. It is called the unpardonable sin because there is no forgiveness if one blasphemes the Holy Spirit. Many pastors have someone in their church who fears he or she may have committed this sin. What is it? First, it is not any sin against the moral law (Ten Commandments). It is not committing murder or adultery. King David committed both murder and adultery, and he was forgiven. The unpardonable sin is committed when one's *final verdict* regarding the gospel is to show contempt for the Spirit's testimony—which is to glorify Christ—revealing His deity. One blasphemes the Holy Spirit by finally denying that Jesus is God in the flesh—or saying that Jesus has an evil spirit (Mark 3:29–30). How can you know you have not committed the unpardonable sin? If you can testify from your heart that Jesus is God, worry no more.

In my old church in Ashland, Kentucky, we had evangelists come in two or three times a year to hold *revivals*—missions usually lasting two weeks each. It was common for the minister to preach on blaspheming the Holy Spirit at least once—usually on the last evening—scaring everybody nearly to death. However, I cannot recall ever hearing a minister explain exactly what the unpardonable sin was—or how it could be committed. It was used sometimes as a ploy to get people to run to the altar, lest they commit this sin and inevitably go to hell.

And yet I have had people in London come to see me, worrying that they had blasphemed the Spirit. One dear man—who was solid in his faith—remembers a time before he was converted that he said, "Damn you, Holy Ghost." After he was converted, he heard the teaching about the blasphemy of the Spirit. Although he was serving the Lord faithfully, this incident haunted him. When I showed him that blaspheming the Spirit is showing contempt for the testimony of the Spirit, which pointed to the person of Jesus, He was set free and never troubled again. I repeat: if you can say from your *heart* that Jesus Christ is God, you have not committed this sin. Paul said that no person can say "Jesus is Lord" but by the Holy Spirit (1 Cor. 12:3).

16. The Holy Spirit is our reminder.

He will "remind you of everything I have said to you" (John 14:26). He will "bring to your remembrance all that I have said to you" (ESV). If you fear you have forgotten what you heard, don't worry! The Holy Spirit will remind you of what you were taught.

Picture this. The disciples have just heard the Sermon on the Mount. They may have said among themselves, "If only I could remember this!" Or when they heard Jesus's parables. Or His confrontation with the Sadducees and Pharisees. In John 14:26 Jesus is virtually saying, "Don't worry if you can't remember what I said. The Holy Spirit will remind you of what I taught."

This is so relevant today. People ask: "Why should I read my Bible? I don't understand it. Why should I memorize Scripture? Why should I go listen to teaching—it is often so boring."

I reply: even if you don't understand it and think you won't remember it, you are taking in more than you consciously realize at the time. In an appropriate moment—possibly at a time you least expect—the Spirit will remind you of what you heard.

You may say, "I need the Holy Spirit to fall on me. I need the power of God to make me fall on the floor."

I reply: if you are empty-headed when you fall, you will be empty-headed when you get up! The Holy Spirit promises to remind you of *what is there.* If there is nothing there to be reminded of, whatever do you expect the Holy Spirit to do?

17. The Holy Spirit gives power.

"You will receive power when the Holy Spirit comes on you; and you will be my witnesses in Jerusalem, and in all Judea and Samaria, and to the ends of the earth" (Acts 1:8). I don't think this promise about the Spirit interested the disciples as much as it should have. They had something else on their minds. They really wanted to know if Jesus would at long last be restoring the kingdom to Israel (Acts 1:6). Jesus evaded the question and promised them power that would come when the Spirit came on them. This promise was fulfilled on the Day of Pentecost.

The power of the Holy Spirit was experienced basically in three areas. First, there came a demonstration of supernatural power—that which defied a natural explanation. Mind you, not a high level of faith was needed for what they heard, saw, and felt. It was heard by their ears, seen with their eyes, and felt in their bodies. Although Jesus said the kingdom of God would not be visible (meaning an earthly government), ironically the initial evidences of the Holy Spirit were physical! The first sensation was hearing. Suddenly there came from heaven a *sound* like a "mighty rushing wind." The 120 disciples sitting (not standing, not kneeling) inside the house were given power to hear and see and feel what was unprecedented in Israel's history. They looked at one another and saw "tongues of fire" resting upon each one's head! It was a visible display of holy fire. This came with being "filled with the Holy Spirit." They began to speak "in other tongues as the Spirit gave them utterance" (Acts 2:1–4, ESV). Although Mark 16:17 (a passage in dispute by some scholars since it was not apparently in the earliest manuscripts we have} indicated that Jesus's followers would speak "in new tongues," I don't believe they were prepared for this.

They were enabled to do this as the Spirit gave them "utterance." They didn't work it up. The tongues on the Day of Pentecost were recognizable languages. The multitude that had gathered heard each one speaking "in his own language" (Acts 2:6).

Second, they were given inner power to grasp what had previously been dark or mysterious. It was not until the Holy Spirit came on them that the disciples came to see the real purpose of Jesus coming to the earth. They now understood that (1) the falling of the Spirit was a fulfillment of Joel 2:28–32; (2) Jesus's death on the cross was no accident but was purposed for our salvation; (3) His resurrection demonstrated who Jesus was—that He was the Son of God; (4) Jesus was now at the right hand of God; (5) the ascension took place to make way for the Holy Spirit; (6) people needed to be forgiven of their sins; and (7) all those who heard Peter's sermon could be forgiven and could receive the Holy Spirit if they repented and were baptized (Acts 2:14–39). It all fell in place for Peter.

Third, this power meant power to witness. Acts 1:8 connects two things, making them virtually inseparable—power and witnessing. The power was not merely for their enjoyment—although it must have been thrilling for them all. It is what enabled Peter to confront thousands of Jews with utter fearlessness. The same Peter who cowardly denied knowing Jesus to a Galilean servant girl only seven weeks before was now telling the powerful Jews of the day what *they* needed to do. In fact, Peter's preaching was so effective that the hearers were "cut to the heart"—something that only the Holy Spirit can do—and asked, "What shall we do?" (Acts 2:37). They were scoffing at first, dismissing the 120 who were filled with the Spirit as having "too much wine" (Acts 2:13). I personally doubt that they were poking fun at them over the tongues—hearing what was said but understood in their own language would have sobered them. When we get to heaven and see a DVD of the entire episode, I predict we will see that many of these Spirit-filled disciples were laughing their heads off with extreme joy. But after hearing Peter, the scoffers were now begging to know what to do next! The explanation: power, a supernatural energy that defies a natural explanation.

Paul said that the kingdom of God consists not in talk but in "power" (1 Cor. 4:20). I have no doubt that the power of the Holy Spirit is relevant and available not only for insight and witnessing but also for holy living and other demonstrations of the supernatural.

18. The Holy Spirit manifests through various spiritual gifts.

"Now to each one the manifestation of the Spirit is given for the common good," these including: wisdom, words of knowledge, faith, healing, miraculous powers, prophecy, discernment of spirits, different kinds of tongues, and interpretation of tongues (1 Cor. 12:7–10). A recondite issue among some Christians—including Pentecostals and charismatics—is whether the evidence of the baptism of the Holy Spirit is always and necessarily speaking in tongues. Is the gift of tongues or praying in tongues (1 Cor. 14:2, 14) the same phenomenon as the 120 received on the Day of Pentecost (Acts 2:4)? Possibly not. It may have been something different. The best scholars among Pentecostals and charismatics differ on this, and I see no need to make an issue of this.

19. The Holy Spirit directs people to Jesus and makes Him real.

"He will testify about me" (John 15:26). What makes people want to turn to Jesus? The Holy Spirit. What makes Jesus real? The Holy Spirit. What makes what He did for us—dying on the cross and being raised from the dead—real? The Holy Spirit.

This is why Jesus said, "No one can come to me unless the Father who sent me draws him" (John 6:44). We are all born "dead"—"dead in your transgressions and sins" (Eph. 2:1). Can a dead man speak? Can a dead man hear? Can a dead man move? Can a dead man make a choice? Jesus's statement in John 6:44 came in the midst of what Bible teachers call *the hard teachings of Jesus*. At the beginning of this discourse Jesus had a following of five thousand (John 6:10). At the end "many of his disciples turned back and no longer followed him" (v. 66). Jesus elaborated on His various *hard* sayings: "The Spirit gives life; the flesh counts for nothing.... This is why I told you that no one can come to me unless the Father has enabled them" (vv. 63, 65).

What is the aim of the Holy Spirit's witness? Jesus Christ. The Holy

Spirit directs people to Jesus. "He will testify about me." It is the Spirit who makes people see *why* Jesus died and rose again. Remember that the eleven [now that Judas Iscariot is out of the picture] did not know *why* Jesus died or rose from the dead even after they saw His resurrected body. It was not until the Holy Spirit fell on them on the Day of Pentecost that it all came together for them.

20. The Holy Spirit manifests through various fruit.

"The fruit of the Spirit is love, joy, peace, patience, kindness, goodness, faithfulness, gentleness and self-control" (Gal. 5:22–23). I think it is possible for one to have the gifts of the Spirit without the fruit of the Spirit. I think too one can have the fruit of the Spirit without the gifts of the Spirit. Charismatics and Pentecostals tend to emphasize the gifts; conservative evangelicals and Reformed Christians tend to stress the fruit.

I don't mean to be unfair, but I have long suspected that, were it not for the gift of tongues, many evangelicals (many of whom are *not* cessationists) would have no objection to the gifts of the Spirit. The stigma (offense) is not with regard to wisdom; who doesn't want and need wisdom? It is not with regard to having words of knowledge, the gift of faith, prophecy, discerning of spirits, the miraculous, or healing. The offense is invariably speaking in tongues. Why? As my friend Charles Carrin has put it, tongues is the only gift of the Spirit that challenges our *pride.* There is no stigma attached to *any* of the other gifts. Only tongues.

That said, when it comes to gifts and fruit of the Holy Spirit, I ask: Why not both?

21. The Holy Spirit gives renewed power.

"After they prayed, the place where they were meeting was shaken. And they were all filled with the Holy Spirit and spoke the word of God boldly" (Acts 4:31). This event was some time after Pentecost, possibly weeks later. It shows that the same people who were filled on the Day of Pentecost were filled again—and were thus enabled to speak with renewed power.

What happened was this. A forty-year-old man who had never

31

walked was suddenly and miraculously healed by Peter and John. Everybody in Jerusalem knew who this crippled man was. After thousands saw him "walking and praising God," Peter (again) took advantage of this opportunity to preach the gospel. At least two thousand were converted as a result (Acts 3:1–4:4). Instead of the elders and teachers of the Law being thrilled, they were indignant. They warned Peter and the other disciples "to speak no longer to anyone in this name" (Acts 4:17). Peter and John reported this to the disciples who began to pray. It is an amazing prayer. (See Acts 4:24–30.) This is when the place was shaken and they were all filled with the Holy Spirit.

My point is this. What happened once can happen twice. Or three times. Many times. This is why Paul wrote, "Be filled with the Spirit" (Eph. 5:18). We need to be filled—again and again.

Chapter Three

THE IMMEDIATE AND DIRECT
TESTIMONY OF THE HOLY SPIRIT

We are witnesses of these things, and so is the Holy Spirit,
whom God has given to those who obey him.

—ACTS 5:32

The Trinity of some evangelicals today is God the Father,
God the Son, and God the Holy Bible.[1]

—JACK TAYLOR

ONE OF THE LAST SERMONS DR. MARTYN LLOYD-JONES DELIV-
ered before he became ill and had to give up preaching was on
the Operation Mobilization (OM) ship *Doulos* when it was anchored
for a few days in East London. Dr. Lloyd-Jones was invited to speak
to those young people (mostly in their twenties) who felt the call to
join OM. He took his text from Acts 5:32: "We are his witnesses of
these things; and so is also the Holy Ghost, whom God hath given to
them that obey him" (KJV) The Doctor focused on the words "*and so
is also the Holy Ghost*," using the Authorized (King James) Version
as he always did. The tape of that sermon is available today. He had
been burdened for some time that the next generation should not only

understand but also experience the Holy Spirit directly for themselves. In this sermon he emphasized that the witness of the Spirit in Acts 5:32 was the Holy Spirit's *own direct* witness—not merely indirectly through the Word, but coming *immediately and directly* to the disciples. The person of the Holy Spirit was therefore *in* them and making Jesus's resurrection and ascension real as Peter spoke. Dr. Lloyd-Jones believed that this was both the disciples' theological understanding and also their experience. The phrase, "and so is also the Holy Ghost," may seem to some as an incidental or a throwaway comment. But not to the Doctor.

What Acts 5:32 further meant to him was this. Not only had the disciples seen the crucifixion and the risen Lord, but the *Holy Spirit also* witnessed to it. You might say, "Of course the Holy Spirit saw this. So what? Furthermore, that would have meant utterly nothing to the Jews." But it meant everything to Peter. The Holy Spirit was witnessing to Peter at that moment as he spoke! The Spirit's witness was so real that the disciples would have believed in Jesus's resurrection had they not seen Him alive at all! Moreover, Peter and John affirmed that Jesus was at the right hand of God (Acts 5:31)—something no one could have seen. When the Holy Spirit told them that Christ ascended to the right hand of God, they knew it had literally happened!

But you ask, "Why waste this information on the Jews who didn't believe the disciples' testimony or that of the Holy Spirit?" First, Peter knew that the Holy Spirit could convict these Jews there on the spot—telling them they could be given repentance and forgiveness of sins. But there is more: God will give the Holy Spirit to those who obey Him! They could have the Spirit too. This was part of Peter's sermon on the Day of Pentecost. His hearers that day wanted what Peter and the 120 disciples had. So Peter told them: "Repent and be baptized...and *you* will receive the gift of the Holy Spirit" (Acts 2:38, emphasis added).

Every Jew knew that Peter had something they did not have, and they wanted it! Now Peter speaks again to Jews, asserting: the Holy Spirit will be given to those who obey Him. What made Peter's word attractive was the thought of having what Peter had—to have the Spirit make things real as they were real to the disciples; to give them power, boldness, and authority as Peter had before all these high-ranking Jews. How could Peter speak as he did? The answer is: he had the Holy Spirit Himself in him—immediately and directly. I will return to this below, but I now need to relate an incident that should make this chapter easy to grasp.

During my three years I was studying at Oxford University, I became the pastor of the Calvary Southern Baptist Church in Lower Heyford, Oxfordshire. It was made up largely of US military and their families, although a few local English people came along as well. Louise and I and our children lived in Headington, Oxford. Dr. and Mrs. Lloyd-Jones visited us regularly, and he preached for me several times. He also was keenly interested in the thesis I was writing to earn the DPhil,[2] keeping up to date on my progress right to the end. On one of those visits I shared with him a catechism I wrote for our church. A young lady aged fourteen had memorized the answers. On one of the occasions the Doctor was to preach, I asked her all the questions of my catechism in front of the congregation of about one hundred people. One of the questions was: How do you know that the Bible is the Word of God? Answer: by the inner testimony of the Holy Spirit. My answer was the exact answer—verbatim—John Calvin would give; it came right out of his *Institutes of the Christian Religion.*[3] It was quite an honor for that girl to get to answer my catechism questions in front of Dr. and Mrs. Lloyd-Jones. They listened carefully.

After the service on our way back to Headington the Doctor said, "That catechism of yours. I need to talk to you about that. You should add the words *immediate and direct* to your answer of how we know the Bible is the Word of God." It was a critical moment in my time at Oxford. "Immediate and direct," words I will never forget as long as I live. This helped me as much as anything to understand the English Puritans I had been studying and struggling with. He said it again: "It is not enough merely to say 'testimony of the Holy Spirit.' You need to put in the words 'immediate and direct,'" driving the point home. I knew exactly what he meant by that. It was what had happened to me in October 1955, an event to which I shall return later. It was something that, sadly, had apparently *not* happened to most of the Puritans.

In the highlighted section of text immediately following this paragraph, I am providing some bonus material that takes a closer look at the theological position of a majority of the English Puritans who believed a person could be assured of his or her predestination to salvation *only by reflecting on their consciences.* This became known as *the practical syllogism of the Holy Ghost* or the *reflex act.* As a result of this belief, and the teachings that followed as they tried to further define their position, nearly every one of these Puritans died without any assurance of salvation. If you choose to dig into this deeper teaching, it is worth the effort it may take to understand their concept of assurance of salvation. As we will see in more detail, Dr. Lloyd-Jones frequently employed the word "sealing" for assurance.

The English Puritans and the "Reflex Act" or "Practical Syllogism"

Almost without exception the English Puritans that I studied could not conceive of assurance of salvation except through the *conscience*—and that by "reflection." They knew nothing of an immediate and direct witness of the Spirit, but only what could be *reasoned.* From William Perkins (1558–1602) to the formation of the Westminster Confession of Faith (1648), these men believed a person could be assured of his predestination to salvation, *but only by reflecting on his conscience.* Their assurance was therefore "indirect." Using Aristotelian logic, they came up with a syllogism—a kind of reasoning that led to a conclusion. In fact, Perkins called it, "the practical syllogism of the Holy Ghost"— which he applied more than one way: (1) assurance by reasoning, and (2) assurance by good works. It came down to this: a major premise followed by a minor premise led to a conclusion. So the major premise was this: *All who believe in Jesus Christ are saved.* The minor premise: *I believe in Jesus Christ.* Conclusion: *Therefore I am saved.* That was it. That was the main way they could know they were genuinely converted.

Now there is nothing wrong with this—not at all. It is a perfectly valid way to know you are saved. I am merely saying "reflecting" was the *only* way they could conceive of having assurance of salvation.

Perkins and his followers called it the "reflex act"—a mental exercise by which you reflected on knowing you have believed. To them *there was no assurance in faith itself.* You came to assurance by reflecting on the fact that you *have* believed. From this you deduce you have been saved.

They also called it the "indirect" act of faith. You therefore come to assurance *indirectly* not directly. It is mediated, or applied, to you by the Word. They did not speak of an immediate coming of the Holy Spirit. In other words, you "reflect" on the fact that you have trusted Jesus Christ. One could say: *I know I am saved because I have believed.* It was a cerebral, intellectual but subjective exercise. Perkins even called this "full assurance." It was to him the highest level of faith to which a person could attain. The reason it was called "the practical syllogism of the Holy Ghost" was because that was God's way of bringing His elect people to assurance of salvation.

I repeat: there is nothing wrong with a person coming to the knowledge that he or she is saved by this indirect act of faith. The problem was, it was the only way they could think. This is why Dr. Lloyd-Jones wanted me to insert those words "immediate and direct" witness of the Holy Spirit when it came to how you know the Bible is true.

A SAD TURN

Whereas the practical syllogism as I have just described is a valid way to know you are saved, Perkins did not leave it at that. It is at this point we see (in my opinion) one of the most melancholy aspects of Puritan thinking. It was not enough to know you are saved because you *believe.* They then asked: How do you *know you have truly believed?* The Puritans were always worried about the possibility of a counterfeit faith.

This is where their doctrine of assurance was undermined by sheer legalism. It is why virtually none of them (including their hearers) had the assurance they themselves taught. They brought in a teaching that you only know you are really and truly saved by godly living. Sanctification. Good works. So Perkins and those after him showed another way by which this syllogism was applied. You know you are one of

God's elect by your personal holiness. This too meant reflection by the conscience. Whereas the previously mentioned syllogism was reflecting on whether or not you truly believed, the ultimate way you *know* you have truly believed is by your good works, or sanctification. They called it "universal obedience" (keeping all the Ten Commandments, not just some of them). Sanctification, the process of being made holy—or "universal obedience"—meant endeavoring to keep *all* the Ten Commandments, doing your best to keep the *whole* of the moral law of God. So if you keep the Ten Commandments, if you love God's ministers, if you love sound teaching and are faithful in worship on the Sabbath, you may conclude that you are saved.

In a word: *All who are living godly lives are saved. I am living a godly life. Therefore I am saved.*

This, then, was another way the "reflex act" was applied, that is, this "indirect act" of faith. Assurance was only mediated indirectly— by the experimental knowledge you have truly believed. In my DPhil thesis—"The Nature of Saving Faith From William Perkins (1558–1602) to the Westminster Assembly (1648)"—I gave the Puritans the name "experimental predestinarians." They knew they were saved by these experiments—reflecting on whether or not they had truly believed. If they could conclude that they *truly* believed, they were assured they were not reprobate but elected of God. The saddest thing of all is, nearly every one of these Puritans died without any assurance of salvation. Perkins himself went to his grave in great agony—not knowing whether he was saved. For those wanting to go into this in more detail, see my *Calvin and English Calvinism to 1648*.

JOHN COTTON AND THOMAS GOODWIN

I said above that these Puritans were almost totally agreed on the way of coming to assurance of salvation. But there were two exceptions: John Cotton (1584–1652) and Thomas Goodwin (1600–1680). Dr. Lloyd-Jones did not know about Cotton's views, but he knew Goodwin's view backward and forward. When at first I explained to him what Cotton believed, he thought it was too good to be true. I will never forget it. While Louise and Mrs. Lloyd-Jones spent time together, the Doctor and I went into our dining room in our house in Headington. It was when I read that Cotton *rejected* the view, "We have no revelation but the Word," that Dr. Lloyd-Jones became intrigued. It was as though Cotton had been confronted with a twenty-first-century cessationist—as if a cessationist said to Cotton, "We have no revelation but the Bible." In the early seventeenth century Cotton was thus rejecting the notion that God does not speak directly today. The Doctor then said to me, "Read that again. Did Cotton really say that?" I handed to him my copy of *A Treatise of the Covenant of Grace*.[4] He had to read it for himself! "This is marvelous," he said to me and wondered how we could get this word out. Shortly after that he asked me to bring a paper on John Cotton at the Westminster Conference in December 1976.

In a word: Cotton believed that a person came to assurance of salvation *not* by the indirect route (as he once believed before he left Boston in England to found Boston in Massachusetts) but by a direct witness of the Holy Spirit. Cotton argued that coming to assurance by good works is a "papist" position. You know you are justified by *faith alone,* Cotton insisted; sanctification is no proof of justification. There was assurance *in* faith alone. One did not need to add to it. He regarded it as a huge mistake to derive assurance of salvation by the conscience. He even disdained the idea that "we have no revelation but the Word," thus stating that the Spirit's witness is *immediate*—the sentence in Cotton's book that thrilled Dr. Lloyd-Jones the most. Cotton rejected the notion of reflex act and believed that the immediate witness of the Holy Spirit assures one of his salvation. Furthermore, this is for "all ordinary Christians" not merely "men of renown." Moreover, no one should be afraid of the word *revelation*, which comes by the "immediate" witness of the Holy Spirit. When the Spirit comes, He speaks "peace to the soul." By the Spirit's immediate testimony we have "full assurance" of our spiritual state. When John Cotton lay dying in 1652, his pastor, John Wilson (c. 1591–1667), prayed that God would lift His countenance on Cotton and shed love into his soul. Cotton's last words were: "He hath done it already, brother."[5]

The truth is, coming to assurance of faith by one's good works, or sanctification, is a shaky foundation when it comes to dying. But the immediate work of the Spirit removes all doubt.

I must add a word about Cotton not accepting the view "we have no revelation but the Word." He was certainly *not* espousing the view of continuing revelation, that God is still revealing new truth apart from the Bible. That would have been the furthest thing from his mind. Dr. Lloyd-Jones moreover would abominate such a thought, which, sadly, some charismatics apparently endorse. What John Cotton was rejecting was the common view that the Holy Spirit can speak *only* through the Word. He believed the Spirit may reveal Himself *as though* apart from the Word. When the Holy Spirit spoke to Philip, it was immediate and direct (Acts 8:29). It was apart from the Word. But it not only did not go against Scripture—Philip was on his way to lead a man to Christ!

SEALING OF THE SPIRIT

The word *seal*, or *sealing*, has basically five meanings. First, it refers to that which authenticates or conveys authority. It establishes the validity or authenticity of a document or statement. A seal will indicate whether a document, or signature, is real or counterfeit. Second, it is a mark of ownership. It indicates that something belongs to another, that it is someone's property. The seal has a particular image on it, showing it belongs to one person only. In the Wild West ranchers would brand their own seal on cattle to show their proper ownership. Third, a seal is also used for the purpose of security. A seal may be put on a parcel, for example. But if that seal is broken you know it has been tampered with. Fourth, a seal may indicate approval. We speak of "seal of approval." This means we approve of a person on whom we put our seal. Fifth, we sometimes speak of one's fate being sealed. We may say that a person "sealed his fate" by a comment he made. It refers to the possibility of an unchangeable destiny—once a seal has been put on it.

All of God's children have God's seal on them. In a word: *all who have saving faith are sealed with the Holy Spirit*. "God's solid foundation stands firm, sealed with this inscription: 'The Lord knows those who are his'" (2 Tim. 2:19). First, He authenticates us. We have been given authority to become sons of God (John 1:12). Second, He owns us. We are not our own; we are bought with a price (1 Cor. 6:20). Indeed, God "set his seal of ownership on us" (2 Cor. 1:22). Third, the seal of God on us guarantees our safety. "He will command his angels concerning you to guard you in all your ways" (Ps. 91:11). Fourth, there is nothing greater than having the approval of one whose power, authority, and integrity matters. Timothy had Paul's approval. "I have no one else like him"…he "proved himself" (Phil. 2:20, 22). Finally, our eternal destiny is sealed. Paul said, "Do not grieve the Holy Spirit of God, with whom you were sealed for the day of redemption" (Eph. 4:30).

A CRUCIAL DISTINCTION

However, there is a crucial distinction at stake here. Do not miss this: Although all who are saved are objectively sealed with the Holy Spirit, not all who are saved have experienced the *conscious seal* of the Holy Spirit. This distinction is equally relevant when it comes to the baptism with the Holy Spirit.

A very relevant verse in this connection is Ephesians 1:13: "And you also were included in Christ when you heard the word of truth, the gospel of your salvation. Having believed, you were marked in him with a seal, the promised Holy Spirit." Whereas the Authorized King James Version, as we will see below, says that the sealing of the Spirit came to them "after" they believed—indicating the sealing is subsequent to faith, most versions read so that all Christians have the seal of the Holy Spirit *when* they believe.

There are, therefore, two ways of looking at this seal: objectively and subjectively. Objectively, all Christians are sealed with the Spirit. But not all Christians are subjectively—consciously—sealed with the Holy Spirit. The same question could be asked: Are all Christians baptized with the Holy Spirit? Objectively, yes. (See 1 Corinthians 12:13.) But do all Christians automatically experience the baptism with the Spirit as described by Luke in Acts?

Immediately after I became the minister of Westminster Chapel, the Doctor and I agreed that I would go see him every Thursday between 11:00 a.m. and 1:00 p.m. It was set in our diaries. Mrs. Lloyd-Jones would serve coffee and give us KitKats. She would talk with us five minutes or so, then leave us to ourselves. One Thursday Dr. Lloyd-Jones asked me to read fifty pages of Dr. Thomas Goodwin's commentary on Ephesians 1:13 the following week. I told him I had already read it and knew Thomas Goodwin's position very well. "Would you read it again?" he asked. Certainly. I happened to own Thomas Goodwin's entire works. I spent an hour or more reading Goodwin's comments on Ephesians 1:13: "In whom ye also trusted, after that ye heard the word of truth, the gospel of your salvation: in whom also after that ye believed, ye were sealed with that holy Spirit of promise" (KJV). Thomas Goodwin and his contemporary Dr. John Owen (1616–1683) were not in total agreement on how that passage should be interpreted— like many interpreters today. John Owen was in the tradition of William Perkins and those who formed the Westminster Confession of Faith, upholding the idea of the Spirit *indirectly* applying the Word to one's conscience. Thomas Goodwin's views were very similar to those of John Cotton. Goodwin's point is that the Holy Spirit's seal is the Spirit's *own* witness—and that it came *after* one's conversion. It was real—that is, conscious and immediate. It did not require any accompaniment (such as good works) to assure one of his salvation.

When I went to see Dr. Lloyd-Jones the following week, he, for some reason, seemed very keen to discuss this as soon as I arrived. He wanted to know what I thought of Thomas Goodwin's view of Ephesians 1:13 even while we still were having coffee, before I shared my sermon preparation for the following weekend. "Well, what did you think?"

I replied: "It's exactly what I believe, Doctor."

Tears filled his eyes. I will never forget his response as long as I live: "That's the greatest thing I ever heard you say."

My point in bringing in Dr. Lloyd-Jones into this present book is obvious and straightforward. I know how much conservative evangelicals revere Dr. Lloyd-Jones. If you are Reformed or regard yourself as a conservative evangelical, I am sure you admire Dr. Martyn Lloyd-Jones. But are you aware of his view of the Holy Spirit? I hope that knowing exactly what he believed will help you to be more open to the immediate and direct witness of the Holy Spirit. I know many Reformed people are unhappy with his view of the Holy Spirit. Some would rather you did not know about this! I want to convey as best and honestly as I know how what the Doctor truly believed about the Holy Spirit. I am not saying he was a "Charismatic." But he certainly was such with a small *c*. He believed that the gifts of the Spirit are available today and was categorically on the side of those who were open to the immediate and direct witness of the Holy Spirit. This is why his regular publisher would not publish his books on the Holy Spirit—a fact that is well known among those who live in Great Britain.

Countless Pentecostal and charismatic leaders in Britain have testified to the way the Doctor went out of his way to encourage and affirm them. It was an ache in his heart that so many Reformed people—who believed in his theology generally—did not embrace what he believed about the Holy Spirit. He said publicly and privately again and again, "I'm an eighteenth-century man [the age of Whitefield and Wesley], not a seventeenth-century man [the age of the Puritans]." If you asked him what label he would give himself, it was "Calvinistic Methodist" (which is what Whitefield was). If the Doctor could speak from heaven today, he would not only testify that I have been absolutely accurate and faithful to his teaching, but he also would be pleased to no end that I am upholding his view of the Spirit.

Many conservative evangelicals hold only to a soteriological (meaning salvation) doctrine of the Holy Spirit. This means that the Holy Spirit can only speak through the Bible and *apply* it when the gospel is preached. And yet they rightly believe that the Holy Spirit makes the Bible come alive and makes Jesus Christ real. This is what we all believe! But according to them, the Holy Spirit would not speak directly today as He did to Philip—"Go to that chariot and stay near it" (Acts 8:29). In other words, most conservative evangelicals only have on their radar screen the thought that the Holy Spirit will *apply* the Word when it is preached. They have no concept of an immediate and direct witness of the Holy Spirit Himself. The Spirit "applies" the gospel to the mind and heart when it is preached. What is wrong with this? Nothing! This is the normal, necessary, and needed witness of the Holy Spirit when the Bible is preached. The Holy Spirit reaching the hearts of men and women *through* the Word is absolutely essential to the preservation of historic truth. It is what I lean on when I myself preach.

But there is more to be had. Either we believe that God the Holy Spirit is alive and well today—or our Trinity is merely God the Father, God the Son, and God the Holy Bible. It is this undoubted anointing of the Holy Spirit at work directly and immediately that is needed today! It is what was going on when Peter preached on the Day of Pentecost (Acts 2:37). It is what happened to the disciples in Acts 4:31. It is what Peter preached and experienced as we saw in Acts 5:31. It is what happened when Peter preached in the house of Cornelius. As he spoke, the Holy Spirit "fell" on all who heard the message (Acts 10:44, ESV). It was the immediate and direct witness of the Holy Spirit that "fell" on them. Incidentally, this event in Acts 10 led Dr. Lloyd-Jones to accept that the immediate and direct witness may come to a person at conversion, suggesting that it was an exception. He, however, believed that Ephesians 1:13—the sealing of the Spirit that comes *after* a person believes—was the norm.

If I knew that every reader would read Dr. Lloyd-Jones's view of Ephesians 1:13 in his exposition *God's Ultimate Purpose: An Exposition of Ephesians 1*, I would spare you of much of the following.[6] But you may not have access to this volume. In the exact same manner that Dr. Lloyd-Jones felt he was largely alone in the Reformed world when he preached on Ephesians 1:13 at Westminster Chapel, little has changed. Reformed people love his doctrine of election. They love his teaching of the sovereignty of God. They love his oratory and manner of exposition of the New Testament. But when it comes to the Doctor's teaching of the immediate and direct witness of the Spirit, they all seem to go quiet. I sometimes think that the Reformed world does not want to know his view—or to know his *heart.* Are they embarrassed by it? He himself quoted Thomas Goodwin, Charles Hodge, Charles

Simeon, John Wesley, and George Whitefield because he wanted the people to know what was on record in church history when it came to his view of the Spirit.[7] So that is why I quote the Doctor in my book, this time to take a glimpse of his exposition of Ephesians 1:13. A lot of people may not realize that he actually spent three Sunday mornings on this verse. I begin by a reference he made to John Wesley:

> Now listen to John Wesley: "It is something immediate and direct, not the result of reflection or argumentation." Note that Wesley emphasizes the same elements of immediacy and directness as Goodwin. The blessing is not the result of reflection or argumentation.... According to Wesley's teaching you can be a good Christian, and you can have experienced the operations of the Spirit in many ways even including foretastes of joy and peace and of love from God Himself, long before you have this direct witness of the Spirit, this overwhelming experience.[8]

Dr. Lloyd-Jones devoted several pages to reject the idea that the sealing or baptism of the Spirit is unconscious. He says over and over again that the sealing of the Spirit is a "conscious experience." He emphasized this because "most of the books which have been written on the Holy Spirit during this present [twentieth] century go out of their way to emphasize that the sealing of the Holy Spirit is not experiential, and has nothing to do with experience as such."[9] And yet, "If it is right to say that that this sealing with the Spirit is something outside the realm of our consciousness, and that it is entirely nonexperiential, then in a sense it is something about which we should not be very much concerned."[10]

The Doctor stressed not only that the sealing of the Holy Spirit (which he used interchangeably with baptism of the Spirit) is a conscious experience, but also that it *follows* conversion. "The sealing with the Spirit and the baptism with the Spirit are the same," such being subsequent to regeneration.[11] He always stressed, however, that the baptism with the Holy Spirit is not an experience of sanctification, nor is it connected necessarily to speaking in tongues. Although he preferred the label "Calvinistic Methodist" for himself, he added that this experience referred mainly to joy, assurance, and intimacy with God. He felt it was a mistake of the Wesleyan tradition to attach this experience to the doctrine of sanctification. The sealing of the Spirit is "not sanctification, but it has an inevitable effect on it." Sanctification is not "an experience to be received," and yet the sealing of the Holy Spirit promotes sanctification.

In any case, this experience was normally not given when a person is granted saving faith. It comes "after" a person has believed. I quote again the King James translation of Ephesians 1:13:

> In whom ye also trusted, after that ye heard the word of truth, the gospel of your salvation: in whom also after that ye believed, ye were sealed with that holy Spirit of promise.

The word *after* is found twice. The Doctor focused on the second word *after* in the Authorized Version of Ephesians 1:13. The sealing with the Spirit is "something which follows believing," Dr. Lloyd-Jones insisted. It is "different from, separated from, distinct from believing, and not a part of believing." Not only that, but he also categorically rejected the common teaching among conservative evangelicals that the sealing of the Spirit "is something that happens inevitably, inexorably to all who believe."[12] Not true. Such men are "so afraid of excesses," he went on, so afraid of being labeled in a certain way that they claim the baptism of the Spirit to be "something unconscious, non-experiential, a happening that does not affect a man's feelings. Such an argument is utterly unscriptural. Not conscious!... [The apostles were, in fact] in a state of ecstasy," he noted.[13] They were accused of drinking "new wine." Moreover, "In our fear of excesses that some who claim this experience may be guilty of we often become guilty of 'quenching the Spirit,' and robbing ourselves of the richest blessings."[14]

He believed that the Galatians had experienced this coming of the Spirit subsequent to their conversion. He interprets Galatians 3:2 in this fashion. Paul said, "I would like to learn just one thing from you: Did you receive the Spirit by the works of the law, or by believing what you heard?" The Doctor made this observation: "How can anyone answer that question if this is something outside the realm of experience? How can I know whether I have or have not received the Spirit if it is not something experiential?"[15]

To conclude: Dr. Lloyd-Jones regarded the "sealing" or "baptism of the Spirit" as being the "highest form of assurance." It was a conscious experience and something that follows saving faith. He would be *unhappy* with calling it a second work of grace—that is, connecting it to sanctification. This immediate and direct testimony of the Holy Spirit was the optimum level of assurance of salvation. As for those who have not experienced this—but eagerly want it—Dr. Lloyd-Jones had this to say (quoting Thomas Goodwin): "Sue him." This word in the seventeenth century meant: *Don't give up. Hold God to His own Word.* One should remind God of His own promise: Don't give up "until you know you have the life of God in your soul," Dr. Lloyd-Jones would say. Or, to put it as I shall explain in the next chapter, don't give up until God swears an oath to you.

Chapter Four

THE OATH AND THE STIGMA

So when God desired to show more convincingly to the heirs of the promise the unchangeable character of his purpose, he guaranteed it with an oath, so that by two unchangeable things, in which it is impossible for God to lie, we who have fled for refuge might have strong encouragement to hold fast to the hope set before us.

—HEBREWS 6:17–18, ESV

Hardships often prepare ordinary people for extraordinary destiny.

—C. S. LEWIS

T HERE IS ANOTHER WAY OF DESCRIBING THE IMMEDIATE AND direct witness of the Holy Spirit and the way it may come to us. It is when God swears an oath to you. God graciously swearing an oath to us is a derivative of the immediate and direct work of the Holy Spirit.

The oath is a conscious witness of the Holy Spirit that leaves you virtually without doubt. Whereas nothing God may do for us in this life will replace faith, the oath comes close!

God swearing an oath to us often comes after a period of hardship and suffering. Like it or not, a stigma of some kind will almost always be linked to God speaking to us in this extraordinary manner. It will very probably mean moving outside your comfort zone. Abraham had to go outside his comfort zone before experiencing God swearing an oath to him:

> I swear by myself, declares the LORD, that because you have done this and have not withheld your son, your only son, I will surely bless you and make your descendants as numerous as the stars in the sky and as the sand on the seashore.
>
> —GENESIS 22:16–17

God had asked Abraham to do what seemed utterly unreasonable: to offer his son Isaac as a sacrifice (Gen. 22:2). There is a predictable pattern throughout the history of God's dealing with His own: He often *asks us to do what makes no sense at the time.*

In this chapter I am explaining one of the most wonderful experiences of the Holy Spirit that a person can receive. If the sealing of the Holy Spirit is the highest form of assurance, having God swear an oath to you is the highest form of *knowing you have it right* when it comes to hearing from God. But the oath is usually linked to suffering—possibly persecution, and almost certainly a stigma.

Have you ever had God to swear an oath to you?

What is it like when God swears an oath to you? I answer: Have you ever wondered how Peter could have so much power and authority on the Day of Pentecost when—only six weeks before—he was disgracefully weak and cowardly by denying he knew Jesus of Nazareth before a Galilean servant girl (Luke 22:54–62)? Have you ever wondered how Elijah could say to King Ahab, "It won't rain unless I say so"? (See 1 Kings 17:1.) Did Elijah spend the following three years biting his fingernails, worrying day and night that it might rain? Have you ever wondered how Elijah could be so at ease and even comical when poking fun at the prophets of Baal on Mount Carmel? "Shout louder!…Maybe he is sleeping and must be awakened" (1 Kings 18:27).

Shortly after that Elijah calmly prayed, and "the fire of the LORD fell" (v. 38). Elijah knew the fire would fall.

How did he know? God had sworn an oath to him. I explain this in some detail in my book *These Are the Days of Elijah*.[1]

How did Moses know to order those who refused to follow Korah? "Move back from the tents of these wicked men!...This is how you will know that the LORD has sent me...if these men die a natural death and experience only what usually happens to men, then the LORD has not sent me." Immediately afterward "the ground under them split apart and the earth opened its mouth and swallowed them, with their households and all Korah's men and all their possessions. They went down alive into the grave, with everything they owned" (Num. 16:26, 28–33).

How could Moses have been so sure this would happen immediately? Answer: God had sworn an oath to him.

This, then, is the explanation for how real the resurrection of Jesus was to the early church. It was as clear to them as if they were physically present at the tomb of Jesus on Easter morning and had seen the entire event with their very eyes.

I am saying in this chapter that the Holy Spirit is capable of making truth so clear to the mind that a fact does not need to be proved to you. This is how Moses, Elijah, and Peter could be so sure of what they believed and said.

Two Levels

There are therefore two levels by which God generally communicates to us: the promise level and the oath level. Both are equally true. But a promise sometimes implies a condition; it implies an *if*. For example, take John 3:16—the Bible in a nutshell. It is a promise. It says, "For God so loved the world that he gave his one and only Son, that whoever believes in him shall not perish but have eternal life." There is an implied *if* in John 3:16—*if you believe, you will have eternal life.* But if you don't believe, you will perish.

At the oath level, however, there is no *if*; when God swears an oath it is as good as done.

There are likewise basically two ways of convincing another person you are telling the truth: (1) you simply promise; (2) you swear an oath. You normally would not swear an oath unless it becomes necessary. But if someone should bother to say, "I swear I will do this," you would even be *more certain* that the person would keep his word. At the end of the day, however—when it comes to human relationships—"It is not the oath that makes us believe the man, but the man the oath," said Aeschylus (d. 456 BC).

But when it is *God Himself swearing an oath*, you can stake your soul on it a thousand times! As for a promise from God, you can believe it because it is impossible for God to lie. But should God swear an oath to us, it is much easier to believe!

God dealt with Abraham at both levels. He initially began communicating to Abraham by promise: "I will make you into a great nation and I will bless you; I will make your name great" (Gen. 12:2). Then came another promise: "Look up at the heavens and count the stars....So shall your offspring be" (Gen. 15:5). Then another—saying much the same thing: "I will make you very fruitful; I will make nations of you, and kings will come from you" (Gen. 17:6).

But one day God swore an *oath* to Abraham: "I swear by myself...I will surely bless you and make your descendants as numerous as the stars in the sky and as the sand on the seashore" (Gen. 22:16–17). The promise and the oath contained the same truth! But the oath was given so that Abraham would likely never doubt again.

The writer to the Hebrews refers to "two unchangeable things": the promise and the oath. But the oath is "more convincing" and so much easier to believe. Why? It is because God is pleased to pour out *a greater measure of His Spirit* into us when He swears an oath to us. He condescends to our level. It is the highest level of encouragement that can be given to us by the Holy Spirit.

GOD'S OATH IN WRATH

The sobering thing is that God can swear an oath in wrath. And when He did that, nothing could stop it. Once He swore that the people would not enter His rest, they couldn't—no matter how hard they tried. (See Numbers 14:21–45; Hebrews 3:10–11.) *Before* God swears an oath, then, you might, just maybe—through your repentance and intercessions—twist His arm and get Him to change His mind. The king of Nineveh found this to be true. Although Jonah the prophet said, "Forty more days and Nineveh will be overturned" (Jon. 3:4), the king said, "Who knows? God may yet relent and with compassion turn from his fierce anger so that we will not perish?" And what happened? "When God saw what they did and how they turned from their evil ways, he had compassion and did not bring upon them the destruction he had threatened" (vv. 9–10).

This shows that Jonah's prophecy and preaching had been communicated at promise level. But the king stepped in, and God changed His mind. But when God swears an oath, nothing—ever—will get Him to change His mind. You can try twisting God's arm, but if He swears an oath, it's over. Yogi Berra used to say, "It ain't over 'til it's over." But if God swears an oath—whether in mercy or in wrath—it's over.

The oath may come regarding a number of things, for example:

- Assurance of salvation (Heb. 4:10; 10:22)
- Advanced notice of answered prayer (Mark 11:24; 1 John 5:15)
- Knowing you have it right theologically (Col. 2:2)
- The "prayer of faith" for healing (James 5:15, ESV)
- A prophetic word

BEARING THE STIGMA

One day Josif Tson asked me out of the blue, "RT, how far are you prepared to go in your commitment to Jesus Christ?" Good question. I thought about that question for days...and months. I asked myself, "How far am I really and truly prepared to go in my commitment to Christ? Haven't I done enough already?"

So I ask you: How far are *you* prepared to go in your commitment to Jesus Christ? Are you willing to suffer? Could you bear a stigma that He may well ask you to undergo?

The oath and a stigma of some kind are usually linked together. Paul and Barnabas concluded that, "We must go through many *hardships* to enter the kingdom of God" (Acts 14:22, emphasis added; "much tribulation," KJV). Paul is not saying we are born again by hardships. He is not saying we are justified by tribulation or saved by bearing a stigma. He is referring to coming to know Christ at a very intimate level. Some do; some don't. It is coming to know Christ in a manner that, sadly, few experience. It was the apostle Paul's greatest ambition: "That I may know him" (Phil. 3:10, ESV). Is Paul saying that he doesn't know the Lord? Of course not. He is saying that he *yearns* to know Christ and the power of His resurrection and fellowship of His sufferings in a way that he had not yet experienced. Those who do pursue such a relationship with Jesus Christ invariably find that they are faced with hardships. It is partly God's way of testing us to see how much we really do care. That then is what Paul and Barnabas were talking about in Acts 14:22. Tribulation. Trouble. Stigma. Going outside one's comfort zone. As C. S. Lewis put it, "Hardships often prepare ordinary people for an extraordinary destiny." You will say, "But Paul was extraordinary." No doubt. So were Moses and Elijah. But the kind of relationship he wanted with Christ is on offer to *all* Christians.

That means you and me. But if we are going to have a similar relationship with God that the famous people of Scripture had, we must be willing to suffer as they did. God therefore extends this extraordinary experience to ordinary people, but we must be willing to bear the stigma.

The word *stigma* means, "offense, disgrace, shame, embarrassment." *Stigma* is a pure Greek word. In Hellenistic literature it referred to a mark on the body—like a tattoo—usually put on a runaway slave. Paul said that he bore in his body the "marks" (*stigmata*) of Jesus. He was not ashamed of the stigma.

At one stage Peter ran from a stigma—when he denied knowing the Lord. But the day came when he *embraced* it. Sometime later Peter and John could hardly believe how blessed they were that they were *privileged* to bear the stigma of Jesus. Having been warned and flogged by the Sanhedrin, they left the Sanhedrin "rejoicing because they had been counted worthy of suffering disgrace ["shame," KJV; "dishonor," ESV] for the Name" (Acts 5:41). Shame. Dishonor. "Hardships" (Acts 14:22).

Would you call yourself ordinary? What if God is using hardships to give you an extraordinary destiny?

Have you run from a stigma? Avoided persecution? Embarrassment?

Paul said we are "destined" for afflictions (1 Thess. 3:3, ESV). "For it has been granted to you on behalf of Christ not only to believe on him, but also to suffer for him" (Phil. 1:29). In other words, this is part of our calling. It is part of our destiny as believers. What is more, when we will count it "pure joy," as James exhorted (James 1:2), we dignify the trial God sets for us. Dignifying the trial shows we can be trusted with a greater anointing. The greater the suffering, the greater the anointing.

Part of the suffering is accepting from God what sometimes seems utterly unreasonable. Consider what Abraham faced when God told him to sacrifice his son Isaac—the only link to the very promise that his seed would be as numerable as the stars in the heavens. It made no sense. But, as I said, God sometimes calls us to do what makes no sense at the time. What a stigma Abraham accepted! It gave God great pleasure. "Now I know that you fear God," the Lord said to Abraham (Gen. 22:12).

The oath followed.

Could it be that God is calling you to bear a stigma—all for a greater measure of the Holy Spirit? How far are you willing to go in your commitment to Jesus Christ? Yes, God often uses hardships to prepare ordinary Christians for an extraordinary destiny.

You may recall from the previous chapter that the Puritan John

Cotton said that the witness of the Holy Spirit is not merely for the people of "renown" in Scripture and church history—by which he meant people of high profile; it was also for ordinary Christians. This is because God has offered the immediate and direct witness of the Holy Spirit to all believers. It is not only what persuades you that the Bible is the infallible Word of God, but also that God is on His throne! God is willing to be as real today as He was to the patriarchs, to Moses, to David, and the prophets. He is as real today as He was to the earliest church. Jesus Christ is the same yesterday and today and forever (Heb. 13:8). Don't come short of discovering how real God is because some well-meaning person says this kind of relationship with God is not possible today. For it is possible.

Randy Wall, a close friend of mine, tells how his own father on his deathbed lamented how cessationist teaching governed his life and robbed him of something he could have had all along. But in the days of his illness, he poured his heart out to God. Lo and behold, the Holy Spirit filled him from the crown of his head to the soles of his feet. God was absolutely real to him. He said to his son Randy, "We have been taught wrong." Randy never forgot that, and later he experienced exactly the same relationship to God that his dad got only before he died.

Some used to call it "dying grace." They thought that there was no use seeking this or expecting this until just before you die. The only problem was, some of them lived! And they lived to tell how real God can be. Call it God's rest. Call it the oath. Call it the immediate and direct witness of the Spirit. Call it the "sealing of the Holy Spirit." Whatever you call it, get it. Wait before the Lord. Don't give up. You won't have to work it up. Just wait.

Chapter Five

STRANGE FIRE

The names of the sons of Aaron were Nadab the firstborn and Abihu, Eleazar and Ithamar. Those were the names of Aaron's sons, the anointed priests, who were ordained to serve as priests. Nadab and Abihu, however, fell dead before the LORD when they made an offering with unauthorized fire before him in the Desert of Sinai. They had no sons, so only Eleazar and Ithamar served as priests during the lifetime of their father Aaron.

—NUMBERS 3:2–5

The simple meaning is that they were "doing their own thing."

—RABBI SIR DAVID ROSEN

A NUMBER OF YEARS AGO I WENT TO A TENT MEETING IN FORT Lauderdale. Many of my friends were claiming miraculous healings from an ostentatious faith healer who also told people amazing details about their backgrounds. One old friend of mine had thrown his hearing aid away, having been *totally healed* of deafness. So I consented to go. As we walked into the tent, I noticed a book for sale that denied the eternal deity of Jesus Christ. That told me all I needed to know. We took our seats in the back of the tent. After the singing the preacher began to speak. He shortly left the platform and went into the audience, going up to people.

"Have you and I met before?"

"No."

"Do you believe I am God's prophet?"

"Yes," they always replied.

"Do you believe God has told me something about you?"

"Yes."

And then he would tell them something that (supposedly) nobody knew but the people themselves. After a half hour I whispered to Louise, "He's coming back to me." How did I know? I just knew. Seconds later he came all the way to the back of the tent and singled me out. He asked me to stand. I did. Holding the microphone to my lips he asked:

"Have you and I ever met before?"

"No."

"Do you believe I am God's prophet?"

"No."

"Do you believe God has shown me something about you?"

"No, sir."

"Have you and I ever met before?"

"No, sir."

"Do you believe I am God's prophet?"

"No, sir."

"Do you believe God has shown me something about you?"

"No, sir." I reached for his microphone to say more. He backed away and shouted to the crowd, "There, ladies and gentlemen, is a man on his way to hell." The people hissed at us as we left after the service.

This man is still holding meetings around the country. You can watch him on television. He has been in and out of court over the years for financial fraud. He maintains a following. And, by the way, after struggling with his deafness, my old friend put his hearing aid on two weeks later. He had not been healed after all.

A more recent event was in one of our Word, Spirit, Power conferences in a western state. The kind man who drove Louise and me to our hotel from the airport began telling us of gold dust that settled on his church; some of it was imbedded into the carpet, he said. Indeed, after they took the carpet up when they remodeled the church, they took pieces of gold and put them in a frame where it hung on the wall in the auditorium. They showed it to me as soon as we arrived at the church later on. The pastor and the people were obsessed with gold. Gold, gold, gold. It dominated the meeting. However, they had not seen gold for a good while. It reportedly happened years before. But they were still fixated on it and were hoping for its return any day now, hopefully while we were there.

On the second evening, moments before it was my time to speak, I noticed a piece of gold in front of me on the carpet. I picked it up. It was a piece of a gold bracelet. My spirit stirred in me like I had not experienced in years. I will *not* say I heard an audible voice. No. It could have been my own voice. But this voice said to me, "RT, if you have any integrity at all and really believe what you do about the gospel and the Word of God, you will speak to this church what you know is true." I turned to my two colleagues Jack Taylor and Charles Carrin and told them I was changing my sermon from what I had previously agreed to deliver. "Go for it," they said to me.

I went to the pulpit, then showed everyone the piece of gold I just picked up from the carpet. I asked, "How many of you believe this is gold that God put there supernaturally?" Many hands went up. I pointed out that it was only a piece of gold from a bracelet. I then proceeded to deliver my soul. I don't have the tape recording of my eighteen-minute talk, so I can only from memory give the gist of what I said. I took my text from Psalm 138:2 (KJV, which correctly translates the Hebrew): "Thou hast magnified thy word above all thy name." I proceeded:

> God cares more about His Word than even His own name. The Word is His integrity put on the line. He regards His integrity more highly than He does His reputation or even His power. People are not saved by seeing miracles. They are saved

by hearing the gospel. Let me tell you why, in my opinion, you dear people are not seeing the miraculous in your church. The supernatural and the extraordinary are all you seem to think about. You are consumed with gold and the supernatural. My advice to you: start emphasizing the gospel and the Word and, maybe, God will manifest His presence. The great Charles Spurgeon said: "I looked to Christ, and the Dove flew in; I looked to the Dove, and He disappeared."

I sat down. The reaction to my talk was mixed, but I felt sure we would not be invited back to that church.

Nadab and Abihu

The single but never to be forgotten occasion of strange fire is described as follows: "Aaron's sons Nadab and Abihu took their censers, put fire in them and added incense; and they offered unauthorized fire before the Lord, contrary to his command. So fire came out from the presence of the Lord and consumed them, and they died before the Lord" (Lev. 10:1–2). They were not following divinely mandated instructions. They were "doing their own thing," as Rabbi David Rosen put it. God told Israel explicitly in the ceremonial law how He wants to be worshipped. God wrote the ceremony; He prescribed the order of worship. He knew what He wanted. Trying to do one better than His Word was not pleasing to Him. There is no reward for uncommanded work; doing only what God commands pleases Him.

God is Spirit; those who worship Him must do so in "spirit and in truth" (John 4:24). Some hastily think only of worshipping Him *in the spirit*—and forget the truth. God is Spirit; He is also truth (Ps. 31:5).

"Strange fire" is the King James Version of what the NIV translates as "unauthorized fire." The Hebrew word means "foreign" or "profane" fire. Not only was the fire not commanded; indeed, it was "contrary to his command" (Lev. 10:1).

It might seem to some of us that the moral law—the Ten Commandments—is all that mattered in those days. But God wrote the moral law, the civil law, and also the ceremonial law (although these distinctions are what theologians have made in order to clarify their application). It was the ceremonial law that was being violated in this account.

KING SAUL

King Saul later became "yesterday's man" because he did not respect the explicit command regarding who is qualified to offer the burnt offering (part of the ceremonial law). He was to wait for Samuel but didn't. "Bring me the burnt offering," Saul commanded. Someone should have stopped him or at least cautioned him. No one did. He then offered the burnt offering. When Samuel arrived, Saul explained that he felt "compelled" to do this (1 Sam. 13:8–12).

Imagine that. Going against the plain teaching of the Word because he felt "compelled" to do so! Is this not like those who say, "I know it's not in the Bible, but God told me to do it," or "I felt led to do it"—going right against Holy Scripture? One of the quickest ways to become an irrelevance—and become yesterday's man or woman—is to put yourself above Holy Scripture. Saul did that. Samuel told him that he had "acted foolishly" and would forfeit his kingdom and legacy (1 Sam. 13:13–14). That is exactly what happened—all because he took lightly the Lord's command regarding how God wanted to be worshipped. Although he became "yesterday's man" in that moment, he wore the crown for another twenty years. Twenty years without God's favor, but the people had no idea of this. Only Samuel (1 Sam. 16:1).

It was so sad that Aaron's very own sons Nadab and Abihu did this. The event of this strange fire incident would no doubt have been recorded in Holy Writ even if these two men had not been such high profile. But being the sons of none other than Aaron—God's number two in those days—heightened their sin. Nadab was actually Aaron's *firstborn* son—a most prestigious and respected place in ancient Israel. The firstborn had double the rights when it came to inheritance. You may recall that Esau was Isaac's firstborn but forfeited it all to Jacob by his folly (Gen. 25:31–34).

Sometimes those who are brought up in a holy environment develop an over-familiarity with God and holy things, and they take privilege for granted. It is an inestimable privilege to be brought up in a godly home. I had godly parents. My father was a layman but had a commitment to the Lord that (in my opinion) exceeded many who are in the ministry. I was therefore given a head start. I would be without excuse if I showed the slightest ingratitude for my background. Children being brought up in a minister's home too are sometimes guilty of taking holy things lightly. There is sometimes a propensity for *preacher's kids* to become smug and act as though they are exceptional. Sometimes pastors themselves are guilty of this. They begin to feel they have some sort of a *claim* upon God because of their heritage or calling. Big mistake.

We learn from this ancient episode that God is no respecter of persons. Therefore Nadab and Abihu would not be exempt because they were Aaron's sons. And yet these two brothers would have known of their father's own idolatry when Aaron was directly involved in making a golden calf (Exod. 32:2–35). Children imitate their parents. It is possible that these two sons never truly saw the seriousness of their father's grievous sin. They may have even developed an absence of reverence by Aaron's rebellion.

The Kind of Sins That Lay Behind Strange Fire

What are we to learn from this incident of unauthorized fire? First, we must remember that the use of fire itself in the old sacrificial system was God's idea. So whether it was natural fire used in the sacrificial system or supernatural fire when God manifested His glory, God had a reason for fire. The use of fire therefore was never man's idea. Moreover, everything in the Mosaic Law was a shadow of good things to come (Heb. 10:1). The fire of the Old Testament pointed to the divided tongues of fire at Pentecost. It pointed to the baptism of the Holy Spirit and fire. God Himself would always be a consuming fire. Fire itself therefore would be sacred when it came to God's prescription of how He would be worshipped. Only holy fire was acceptable. And yet man has a way of imitating God's ideal. What Nadab and Abihu did by offering strange fire set a pattern for subsequent generations to follow. Too many became either rebellious, prideful, impatient, or faithless— and took God's own Word lightly.

Rebellion

If Aaron's legacy was partly planting the seed of rebellion in his two sons, so the example of Nadab and Abihu set the stage for rebellion in subsequent generations. Referring to the golden calf incident, Moses said to the Israelites, "From the day you left Egypt until you arrived here, you have been rebellious against the LORD" (Deut. 9:7). Rebellion became one of the chief sins in ancient Israel. "If you have been rebellious against the LORD while I am still alive and with you, how much more will you rebel after I die!" (Deut. 31:27). "Rebellion is like the sin of divination" (1 Sam. 15:23). The false prophet Hananiah said that Jeremiah had "preached rebellion against the LORD" (Jer. 28:16). The Lord said to Ezekiel, "Son of man, I am sending you to the Israelites, to a rebellious nation that has rebelled against me; they and their fathers have been in revolt against me to this very day" (Ezek. 2:3). What Nadab and Abihu had done by offering their unauthorized fire was to rebel against God's prescription of worship.

The offering of strange fire therefore was not merely a sin of weakness or ignorance; it was sin with a high hand. Not adhering to Scripture is rebellion.

Rivalry

Another way of getting into the minds of the two men that lay behind this unauthorized fire was that a rival spirit set itself up in their hearts. A competitive spirit. It was *their* fire versus the fire of God.

But there was even more going on here. They showed no respect for their elders and those whom God appointed. Nadab and Abihu were insubordinate. In the New Testament we are commanded never to rebuke an elder but entreat him as a father (1 Tim. 5:1). Whether elder means an older man or an official position, one is to show respect for those over them. Sometimes young people—or those new in ministry—get impatient for their day to come and consequently become their own authority. As Dr. Lloyd-Jones used to say, "The worst thing that can happen to a man is to succeed before he is ready." Nadab and Abihu could not wait for their time to come; they wanted to show themselves equal to their elders.

A rival spirit is also what motivates people to reject God's way of salvation. God says: salvation is by grace through faith—not of works (Eph. 2:8–9). A rival spirit says: I can save myself by what I do. In other words, people by nature want to compete with what Jesus Christ has done on the cross. They cannot bear the thought of giving total glory to God for their salvation; they want to feel they have a hand in it. So with the strange fire of Nadab and Abihu, they wanted to do their own thing.

Pride

This is a feeling of pleasure from one's own achievements. This equally lay at the bottom of this unauthorized fire. They wanted to show what they could do without following God's prescribed way. Their egos got involved. They wanted to make a statement. They knew exactly what they were doing. They were not doing this in a corner so that no one would know. Quite the contrary; they wanted to make sure *everyone* witnessed what they did. They wanted to be the first to do this. Perhaps people with less profile would not have thought of such a thing. But they wanted to set a precedent, to go down in history. They certainly would be known in history, but not as they envisaged. They were so sure they could get away with it.

THE FAITH HEALING MOVEMENT

I began following the faith healing movement when I was a teenager. But even then I was surprised, and not a little disappointed, when the healing evangelist was introduced as if he were in show business: "And now, ladies and gentlemen, welcome God's man of faith and power!" The people enthusiastically applauded. This must have had the approval of the evangelist or such would not continue. I can't imagine the early apostles allowing this sort of thing. "Why do you stare at us," asked

Peter when the forty-year-old crippled man was suddenly healed, "as if by our own power or godliness we had made this man walk?" (Acts 3:12). Few seem to notice how so many of today's healers and evangelists quite openly encourage you to focus on them. They are stars. And yet the strangest coincidence I ever witnessed in this connection was when, in a large auditorium in a major city—after a long time of singing, the famous preacher dressed in white came out as they sang "How Great Thou Art." If it was not a coincidence, it must have made the angels blush.

Signs and Wonders Replaced by Prosperity Teaching

Arguably the worst development in our generation, however, is the way the prosperity message has taken over. Appealing to the rich and poor, the message of "name it and claim it," "believe it and receive it" has been the main reason for the financial blessing of many ministries. Instead of teaching people how to pray and find out for themselves how God answers prayer, they say, "Send in your requests, and I will pray for you"—as if the preacher's prayers are more effectual than those of ordinary people. But it's the money they are after.

The old Pentecostal movement was born in the belief of God's manifest presence and power. They saw wonderful things. These early Pentecostals, being largely at the bottom of the socioeconomic level, were scoffed at by traditional Christians, neglected if not rejected by the middle class of American Christianity. They were really and truly outside the camp! And yet are not Christians told to go "outside the camp," bearing Christ's reproach (Heb. 13:13)? Yes. Some would even say, "The farther out the better." I am not sure I would agree with the latter statement, but I do know that the older Pentecostals were *way* outside the camp. They carried on as God blessed them more and more. They began to grow—faster than all others. They saw healings. Signs and wonders. Gifts of the Spirit in operation.

In the 1960s Pentecostals were joined by people of other denominations—Episcopalians, Catholics, Lutherans, Reformed, and

Baptists. As we know, the latter were called charismatics. They too saw the miraculous and were also "outside the camp" of their denominations. They are still largely seen by conservative evangelicals as the "lunatic fringe" of American Christianity. But they too have grown. The blessings of the manifest presence of the Holy Spirit were the undoubted common denominator—the thread that held these movements together.

But no more. According to a recent poll, the common thread has changed. Was it because there was a sudden diminishing of real miracles? Was it because the American economy improved? Was it because people wanted to stay in their comfort zones? Was it the emergence of Christian television? I only know that the common denominator of these movements today is no longer the manifest power of God but the in-your-face promise of financial blessing if you give generously to one's ministry—their ministry. I sincerely question whether some Christian television networks would survive if the appeal to money with the promise of God's blessing suddenly ceased. I wonder if some of them would fold overnight.

It's All About Money

A prominent leader of the charismatic movement in Britain told me candidly that when he watches Christian television nowadays—as if listening through the ears of the unsaved—he would undoubtedly get the impression that Christianity is "all about money." If Jesus showed up today, would it surprise you if He would head immediately for today's equivalent of the money changers in the temple and drive them out? Our own family *so* hoped to attend a particular church when coming to America until they found it unbearable to endure the pastor taking an hour or more every Sunday just to raise the offering.

And yet the ultimate shame is how some television preachers manage to make certain passages of Scripture explain supposedly the *real* meaning of and reason for God sending His Son into the world to shed His precious blood: your financial blessing and healing. Some actually make prosperity teaching to be the essence of the very gospel of Jesus Christ. There is therefore no need for sickness or suffering. None. Paul may have had his "thorn in the flesh" (2 Cor. 12:7, NKJV), but he was not as spiritual as we can be today! If we are to believe some of these people, the reason Jesus died on the cross was mainly for us to have a prosperous and healthy life here on earth. Some of these people never mention that Jesus really died on the cross that we might go to heaven and not to hell when we die. That message does not sell well. So it is all about the here and now. Existentialism. Money. Strange fire.

Not all Pentecostals and charismatics are happy with these things. The preponderance of these people are godly and sound who love their Bibles and want it preached. They welcome leadership that will focus on Scripture, solid teaching, and Christ-exalting worship. I write this book to preserve this very thing and, if possible, help to stop the present trend. The day has come that false teaching has abounded. True. But you don't have to embrace it!

Arrogance

This might be defined as overbearing pride indicated by a superior manner toward inferiors. Nadab and Abihu, knowing they were the sons of Aaron, felt they were a "cut above" the rest of the priests of the day. They wanted to show that they could get away with their revolt against the prescribed way.

King David conceived of the noble idea to bring the ark of the covenant to Jerusalem. He thought this was a righteous thing to do. It was. And that God would reward him. Perhaps. But there in David also, sadly, was an unconscious arrogance, a feeling that he was doing a most wonderful thing for God, something that had never been done. It apparently did not cross his mind to consult Scripture or the priests first. So when he first arranged to bring the ark into Jerusalem, Uzzah reached out and took hold of it because the oxen that carried it stumbled. The Lord's anger burned against Uzzah "because of his irreverent act," and he was struck dead.

This made David himself "angry" because of the Lord's wrath; it seemed so unfair (2 Sam. 6:6–8). Then he humbled himself. He later recognized that God was perfectly just in doing what He did. "We did not inquire of him how to do it in the prescribed way"—namely, that the ark should be carried with poles on the shoulders of the priests, "as Moses had commanded in accordance with the word of the LORD" (1 Chron. 15:13–15). This shows how seriously God takes His own Word and will not bend the rules for anyone—even the man after God's own heart!

Impatience

We noted that Nadab and Abihu could not wait for their time to come. The sons of Aaron were thus impatient with the Lord. Instead of waiting before God and waiting upon God—giving Him opportunity to pour out holy fire as He had just done, the two men went ahead of the Lord and offered their own fire. Never forget the context of this heinous sin in Leviticus. Immediately prior to this fateful event, when Moses and Aaron entered the Tent of Meeting, the glory of the Lord appeared to all the people. "Fire came out from the presence of the LORD and consumed the burnt offering." When all the people saw it, "they shouted for joy and fell facedown" (Lev. 9:23–24). Immediately after that glorious moment was when Nabib and Abihu brought their own fire. They did not wait for God to do it.

As I indicated above, this was the kind of impatience that led to King Saul's downfall. If only Saul had waited for Samuel. "But now your kingdom will not endure," Samuel said to Saul, "the LORD has sought out a man after his own heart...because you have not kept the LORD's command" (1 Sam. 13:14).

Unbelief

All the previously mentioned depictions of sin can be traced to unbelief. Unbelief is the essential cause of rebellion, rivalry, pride, arrogance, and impatience. Unbelief is doubt that degenerates to a conscious act of the will. It is one thing to be tempted to unbelief. We all face this. Unbelief was at the heart of Satan's appeal to Eve in the Garden of Eden. "Did God really say, 'You must not eat from any tree in the garden?'" (Gen. 3:1), instilling doubt in Eve by that very question. Satan said to Jesus, "If you are the Son of God, tell these stones to become bread" (Matt. 4:3), implying that Jesus was not really the Son of God. We all face temptation to doubt.

But when we consciously *decide* that God did not say what He did— and we can do it better; or that He is not going to keep His word—or manifest Himself, and then put ourselves above His Word, we cross over a line. This is dangerous stuff.

Nadab and Abihu did not really believe in the prescribed way. They did not do what they did with fear and trembling but with the smug persuasion they were doing the right thing. Their unbelief led to their highhanded revolt. They opted for their own way of worshipping God—offering their own fire before Moses and Aaron and all the priests. They believed that their fire was as good as any fire.

FLORIDA

Shortly after Louise and I moved to Nashville, having lived in the Florida Keys, I began to get e-mails about a revival that had broken out in Florida. It was being regarded as "last day ministries," the great revival before the Second Coming. It was being carried "live" around the world on GOD TV night after night. We started watching it immediately. People were coming to Florida from all over the world, especially from England, to see what was happening. They even filled the local stadium one evening. One well-known prophetic man claimed on live TV that this was a fulfillment of his own visions of stadiums being filled in last day ministries before the end.

Never in my lifetime have I known of such an opportunity to reach the world with the gospel. It was amazing. It was being carried even into countries where the gospel had not truly penetrated, including Middle Eastern nations. What a wonderful opportunity for the lost to hear the gospel of Jesus Christ.

But I was troubled. I watched and listened carefully night after night after night. I was waiting for one thing: the preaching of the gospel. Question: How many times do you suppose the evangelist who was the main speaker preach the gospel? Answer: not once. It was entirely "word of knowledge" and claims of people being healed. I do not say the words of knowledge were inaccurate. Perhaps they were accurate. I only know one thing: the gospel was never—ever—preached. There was no sense of conviction of sin. True revival includes conviction of sin. This Florida meeting instead was all people falling backward when the evangelist gave a word of knowledge and shouted "Bam!" Such people were supposedly healed. Perhaps they were. But there was one thing on my heart if this phenomenon was truly of God. "Am I to believe," I asked myself, "if this is the great revival before the end—and these meetings are being seen all over the world—that God would not raise up a person to preach the gospel of His Son?" Never *once* did the evangelist say that Jesus Christ died on the cross for our sins that we might go to heaven when we die.

High-profile charismatic leaders came from all over America, laying hands on this man and uttering most extraordinary prophecies about him. I had been given the opportunity to join them but turned it down.

I said that this "revival" was not of God. "Don't say that it is not of God," people lovingly cautioned me. I stuck to my guns—even wrote about it in *Ministry Today*. After a few months, when it turned out that the man was living in immorality during the very time of the "revival," some changed their minds. I said, "Why did it take his immorality to convince you? Even if he had been clean as a pin morally, you should still have seen it was not of God." Why? *The gospel was not preached.* No conviction of sin. He also inserted "Bam!" for the Holy Spirit when he baptized people—in the name of God the Father, God the Son, and "Bam!" And yet there was no outrage. How many of these charismatic leaders have publicly repented and said they had gotten it wrong? Jesus said that preachers like this man would deceive the very elect (Matt. 24:24). After all, Satan masquerades as an "angel of light" (2 Cor. 11:14).

There is, however, another interpretation of why Nadab and Abihu did what they did. Because the passage in Leviticus that follows this event prohibits drinking wine when going into the Tent of Meeting—"or you will die" (Lev. 10:9), some interpreters—including some Rabbinic sages—believe the two sons of Aaron were drunk. If they were intoxicated—and this was the cause of their irreverence, two other explanations for their conduct are worth considering. First, what they did was so serious that it may indeed prove they were intoxicated—or they would not be so foolish. In other words, in their right minds they would not tempt God like that. Second, if the axiom is true *in vino veritas* ("in wine you have the truth"), the wine may have removed their inhibitions and let surface what was in their hearts, namely, the rebellion, pride, and arrogance toward God.

At any rate, God stepped in when Nadab and Abihu offered their unauthorized fire. After the strange fire came the holy fire. "So fire came out from the presence of the LORD and consumed them, and they died before the LORD. Moses then said to Aaron, 'This is what the LORD spoke of when he said: "Among those who approach me I will show myself holy; in the sight of all the people I will be honored"'" (Lev. 10:3). It was a horrible, horrible moment for Aaron. "Aaron remained silent" (v. 3). The dead sons were carried by their cousins—"still in their tunics, outside the camp, as Moses ordered" (vv. 4–5). There followed further instructions concerning the worship of God. Moses made sure that the Tent of Meeting would always be reverenced. He wanted to make sure that the fear of God was always present. "The LORD's anointing oil is on you," Moses said to those who were to carry on the worship of God (v. 7).

Some thirteen hundred years later Ananias and Sapphira lied to the Holy Spirit. This happened while the Spirit of the Lord was present in the early church at an optimum level. They too were struck dead on the spot. Part of the fallout of this notable moment was "great fear" (Acts 5:1–11).

Here's the sobering thing. Aaron's sons were not the last to do "their own thing" in the work of the Lord. And yet God for some reason does not always send supernatural fire to show His displeasure. Moreover, there have been many people since Ananias and Sapphira to lie to the Holy Spirit. But they are not struck dead. Why? Perhaps because this happens only in what I might call "a revival situation"—when a maximum level of the Holy Spirit's power is present.

STRANGE TEACHING TODAY

As I said in the introduction, I do not believe that the historic Pentecostal movement or the more recent charismatic movement should be painted with one big brush so as to accuse these as modern examples of strange fire. There is some strange fire, as we have seen. But what troubles me equally is strange teaching in some quarters. I pray that these teachings will soon be rejected. I wish my book might help. But I do warn you, be aware of them. I must address two of these teachings again in a little more detail. I hate to say it, but some respected charismatic leaders have sadly embraced strange teaching. I would kiss integrity good-bye if I did not say something about this. I wish it weren't necessary.

The apostle Paul gave us advanced notice that in the last days some would abandon the faith and follow deceiving spirits and things "taught by demons" (1 Tim. 4:1). Indeed, "the time will come when men will not put up with sound doctrine" (2 Tim. 4:3). Coupled with this is the melancholy fact that too many church members don't know for sure what to believe!

GOD-CENTERED WORSHIP
CAN HELP PREVENT HERESY

Heresy is a word not often mentioned in many circles today. *Heresy* means "false doctrine." Some people do not think that upholding sound doctrine and avoiding heresy matters all that much. Wrong. Huge mistake. It is crucial. The people of God are always being destroyed from "lack of knowledge" (Hos. 4:6). One could say that God's people are destroyed from lack of knowledge yesterday and today. Hopefully, not forever. But the knowledge of God's *Word* and His *ways* is essential to God's favor on us. If we lose His favor we are finished—and God will raise someone else to uphold His honor.

We all love the verse: "Jesus Christ is the same yesterday and today and forever" (Heb. 13:8). Charismatics use that verse to prove that God's *power* today is the same as it was in Jesus's day, and we are absolutely right to do so. But conservative evangelicals can use that verse too—for the preservation of sound teaching. After all, do you know the context of Hebrews 13:8? Verses 7 and 9 point to one thing: sound teaching. Hebrews 13:7 says: "Remember your leaders, *who spoke the word of God* to you. Consider the outcome of their way of life and *imitate their faith*" (emphasis added). Then came the beautiful truth that Jesus is the same—but by that phrase the writer also meant *upholding the Word* so that teaching does not change! For Hebrews 13:9 says: "Do not be carried away by all kinds of strange teachings." Whereas we have a perfect right to apply Hebrews 13:8 against cessationist teaching, the *immediate context* refers to doctrine. Sound theology. The writer wanted the teaching of Jesus to remain the same yesterday and today and forever. Knowing His Word and His ways.

How is solid teaching to be maintained? First, leaders must teach the truth as found only in Scripture. The Word of God does not change. Our mandate is to uphold the teaching of the apostles—who emphasized the Word *and* the Spirit (1 Thess. 1:5); indeed, the Scriptures *and* the power of God (Matt. 22:29). Paul's last letter to Timothy included the mandate: "Preach the Word" (2 Tim. 4:2). That is our job. We must therefore continually contend for the faith that was "once for all" given to the saints (Jude 3). It is imperative that ministers teach sound doctrine. It begins in the pulpit. This kind of preaching will not only edify people but also enable them to smell heresy when it shows up.

But there is more. With worship being more popular these days— and with this at times being the central item in church services— someone needs to blow a trumpet that will be heard all over the world! Like it or not, agree or disagree with it, often the worship lasts longer than the preaching. And yet what is often disturbing are the *words that are sung.* We have never had better talent. The best vocalists. The best musicians. The best tunes and melodies. Fantastic. But the words? If the early Methodists learned their theology from their hymns, what kind of theology are many charismatics imbibing today? The "what's in it for me?" generation has infiltrated so much of the modern songs. A lack of God-centeredness lays the groundwork for heresy that is creeping into the church. That is what worries me most.

The Welsh Revival (1904–1905) was unusual partly because it was characterized largely by congregational singing. But those in the middle of it were sound theologically. They had been converted in churches that preached the gospel. Moreover, this phenomenon emptied pubs and jails for a time because so many people were converted. And yet it was rejected by some people as not being authentic revival, owing to its lack of preaching. There is no doubt in my mind that the Welsh Revival was a sovereign movement of the Holy Spirit. But when it comes to the type of worship often carried out nowadays, one sometimes suspects it can be more of a performance than focusing on the pure worship of God. I think we should pray that God will raise up talented men and women who are superb musicians and singers but also theologically minded to restore the preservation of the Word in the church. As a preacher must forfeit "words of eloquent wisdom" lest the cross be emptied of its power (1 Cor. 1:17, ESV), so worship leaders need to guard against the need to perform lest the worship time appear more like a concert. One can obviously go from one extreme to another. We don't want people up front leading worship who, frankly, cannot sing. We don't want musicians playing who don't know their stuff.

But if the honor of God is the supreme focus in the words and the singing, it will help prevent false teaching from seeping in. People will recognize the false because they have become acquainted with the real. We must thank God for those hymn writers who show great theological insight. We do have them, as I indicated at the beginning of this book. With God-centered hymns and Spirit-filled worship leaders the people will not as likely be tossed to and fro by every wind of doctrine. They won't be so gullible. If they hear an authority figure say things—sometimes heretical things—they will learn not to accept them and not be swayed because of the personality or high profile of the preacher.

Strange fire brings strange teaching with it. This is why the Word is paramount. Theology matters. Dr. Lloyd-Jones often referred to those evangelicals who were "perfectly orthodox, perfectly useless." But I still want to be perfectly orthodox. There is admittedly a lot of strange fire around these days. I regret this. And there is not nearly enough holy fire in my own life and ministry and in the places where I go. I am not all that I want to be, but I am not giving up.

Is the relative absence of holy fire generally today the reason for so much strange teaching? Almost certainly. I am writing this book (1) to introduce the Holy Spirit as if you did not know very much about Him, (2) to show the inconsistency of the teaching of some evangelicals, but (3) also to warn you of strange fire that is about. So I am not going to stick my head in the sand like an ostrich and gloss over the weird and bizarre things that are sometimes reported from various charismatic leaders.

There is no need to give credibility to the notion held largely by conservative evangelicals that the charismatic movement is the "lunatic fringe" of American Christianity. In Great Britain it is mainstream. If enough of us pour the pure water of the Holy Spirit on strange fire, we will not only extinguish it, but we also find ourselves joined by people from all over the world that are hungry and thirsty for holy fire.

False Teaching

By and large the Pentecostal and charismatic movements have been sound theologically over the years. The anti-Trinitarian teaching ("Jesus only") is fairly remote nowadays. The people I write for and preach for are orthodox. Not all are Reformed in their theology as I am, but they are solid nonetheless on the essential issues of the Christian faith. If Dr. Martyn Lloyd-Jones could embrace the John Wesleys of this world, so can I. However, in recent years I have been saddened over the way certain teaching has been welcomed in certain parts. I mentioned two of these teachings in my introduction but want now to say a bit more about each, then add two that you must be warned about.

1. Open theism

This is process theology in evangelical dress. Process theology denies the immutability of God and the infallibility of Scripture. The idea of open theism comes to this: God does not know the future. He certainly does *not* know the end from the beginning. He does not know what will happen one year from now and can only guess what might happen day after tomorrow. This kind of God needs our assistance and cooperation to make things happen now and in the future. He does not have a mind of His own. What He thinks is linked to us. He cannot move without us. The God of open theism could not save a Saul of Tarsus; that God isn't strong enough. I'm sorry, but there are open theists among some charismatic leaders who actually believe such sub-Christian views. If open theism were true, it would mean that God could actually lose in the end.

I have been astonished at the number of leaders who have accepted this teaching. It is of Satan. It should be rejected categorically. Please don't go near it. Imagine praying to a God who says, "I can only help you if you help Me." Imagine a God who does not know for sure what is going to happen next. Who waits for input from us before He can decide what to do.

The God of the Bible is all-powerful—can do anything—and knows the end from the beginning (Isa. 46:10). What is more, victory is assured! I don't fully understand the Book of Revelation, but I know three things: (1) God wins, (2) Satan loses, and (3) one day every knee shall bow and every tongue confess that Jesus Christ is Lord to the glory of God the Father. Yes. God will win.

2. Hyper-grace

This is a phrase given to the teaching that the blood of Jesus covers all sin once we become Christians. So far, so good. That is where they hook you. But now for the unthinkable: once we are saved, we don't need to confess sin if we sin. The sin has already been paid for on the cross. No need to confess, no need to repent. Never mind that *Christians* are told that if we confess our sins God is faithful and just to forgive us our sin and to purify us from all unrighteousness (1 John 1:9). You would show you don't really believe in Jesus's atonement if you confessed sin that isn't there since He has washed them all away forever. Not only is this antinomianism (anti-law, lawlessness); there is no motivation for a Christian to obey the Word of God, to walk in the light, and prepare to face God at the judgment seat of Christ. Those who hold to this dangerous teaching dismiss the need for a Christian to acknowledge his or her sin. And yet if we say we have no sin, "we deceive ourselves and the truth is not in us" (1 John 1:8). Not only that, the proponents of this teaching also actually dismiss a huge part of the New Testament as irrelevant—including 1 John and the Epistle to the Hebrews. Hebrews warns Christians severely who do not persist in faith. First John does the same thing. The Holy Spirit did not inspire these books, say these people. So the hyper-grace people have their own canon of Scripture. Whereas cessationism makes certain passages irrelevant for today, hyper-grace teaching rejects entire New Testament books—such as Hebrews and 1 John. These two books categorically dismiss what the hyper-grace people teach.

Christians believe that "all" Scripture is God-breathed—every book in the Old Testament and New Testament—and is profitable for teaching, rebuking, correcting, and training in righteousness so that the man or woman of God may be thoroughly equipped for every good work (2 Tim. 3:16).

3. Universalism

This is not new except that it has sadly emerged among some Pentecostals and charismatics. It is the belief that all people will be saved. None will go to hell; all will go to heaven. I wish it were true. But it isn't. There would be no need to preach the gospel if it were true. The Bible teaches that people need to be saved, and we need to get the gospel to them or they will be lost. This is why Jesus died: that we might not perish but have eternal life (John 3:16).

When I was in seminary, I became temporarily enamored with the teaching of Karl Barth (1886–1968). I believe the thinking of Karl Barth is what lay behind hyper-grace teaching. Barth also gave the best rationale for universalism you will find anywhere. It is very attractive and so convincing. That is not all. I watched students take this in. Unless they came to their senses soon, they largely ended up as Bible-denying liberals. Eventually Barth became too conservative for them. Many of them ended up leaving the ministry—and their ministries.

4. Character versus gifts

Fourth, the notion that *gifts are more important than character*. Of all the strange teachings I have come across in recent years, this one flummoxes me the most. I find it incredible. But there are those who unashamedly state that having the gifts of the Holy Spirit—whether healing, prophecy, or word of knowledge—should take priority over one's personal character. No wonder the ever-increasing outbreak of scandals among charismatic and Pentecostal leaders in recent years. Sadly you can expect more. And yet one can see why this teaching would be attractive. People generally are far more fascinated by seeing a display of spectacular words of knowledge—or a healing—than hearing the exposition of the Word. No doubt about that. I have watched ministers who have genuine gifts of word of knowledge or prophecy and have noted how those in the congregation seem to endure or barely tolerate preaching in order to get to the "good stuff"— the miracles. They make better television watching for sure! For this reason the notion that gifts are more important than one's personal life has trumped the need for godliness.

The gifts are without repentance—irrevocable (Rom. 11:29). This explains why a person's gift continues to flourish despite their personal morality. Never forget that King Saul prophesied on his way to kill David (1 Sam. 19:21–24). It is assumed by some sincere but gullible people that if a person is able to perform miracles, it can only be because God's seal of approval is on them. Wrong. Very wrong. The gifts are irrevocable; God lets you keep them. This is why prophesying proves nothing. Speaking in tongues proves nothing. Performing a miracle proves nothing.

You ask: How can people uphold such a teaching? I'm sorry, but it is because they are biblically and theologically ignorant. They are not immersed in the Word of God but in the practice of getting "words" for people. This is what they thrive on. This is what their followers live for. Some of them end up in the most bizarre type of thinking. One well-known prophetic person stated that their personal angel was "Emma"—a two-foot-tall angel that floated around above the ground. Emma said that the church does not need to keep mentioning

Jesus—"everybody knows about Him"; we should talk about angels. These strange ideas are in the public domain. I just heard of one well-known preacher who—so it was revealed to him—has Bob Hope for his guardian angel.

When I first returned to America in 2002 and began preaching in all sorts of churches, I was sobered instantly by the absence of prayer that often preceded services and the lack of prayer in the services. I have been in many services when there is no public praying at all. I have also discovered that most pastors and church leaders don't have a Bible-reading plan (they turn to the Bible mostly to get a sermon)—and have almost no personal, private payer life. No wonder that Bob Hope is welcomed.

Listen to me. When you and I are not grounded in the Word and disciplined by regular time alone with God, we are going to be vulnerable to all sorts of weird notions in these days when people are carried along by every wind of doctrine.

Character should always—*always*—govern a person's life and ministry. Far better to have transparent character and no gifts than to have power to call fire down from heaven when one's personal life is immoral.

Each of these four teachings—open theism, hyper-grace, universalism, and character versus gifts—no doubt deserve more attention than I can give in this book. I would go on bended knee to any person who is attracted to these heresies and say: *Please don't go there.* Intellectual temptation is like sexual temptation; you never know how strong you will be. Whenever you flirt with a heresy, you have Satan breathing down your neck to make you fall for it. It will destroy you.

God judged the original strange fire instantly. But since that ancient event found in the Book of Leviticus, He has allowed strange fire to flourish and apparently keeps quiet about it. The same is true with strange teaching. But I cannot keep quiet about it.

Chapter Six

THE DOVE

Then John [the Baptist] told them, "I saw the Spirit come down from heaven like a dove. The Spirit remained on Jesus. I would not have known him. But the One who sent me to baptize with water told me, 'You will see the Spirit come down and remain on someone. He is the One who will baptize with the Holy Spirit.'"

—JOHN 1:32–33, NIRV

I looked to Christ, and the Dove flew in. I looked to the Dove, and he disappeared.

—CHARLES H. SPURGEON
(1834–1892)

IF YOU HAVE READ MY BOOK *THE SENSITIVITY OF THE SPIRIT*, YOU may recall this story.[1] A British couple were sent by their denomination to be missionaries in Israel some years ago. They were given a home to live in near Jerusalem. After being there a few weeks, they noticed that a dove had come to live in the eave of the roof of their home. They were thrilled. They took it as a seal from God on their being in Israel. But they also noticed that the dove would fly away every time they would slam a door or get into an argument with each other.

"How do you feel about the dove?" Sandy asked Bernice.

"It is like a seal from the Lord on our being in Israel," she replied.

"But have you noticed that every time we slam a door or start shouting at each other, the dove flies away?"

"Yes, and I am so afraid the dove will fly away and not come back," she said.

"Either the dove adjusts to us, or we adjust to the dove," Sandy concluded.

They both knew that the dove was not going to adjust to them. They mutually agreed: they would adjust to the dove. This decision changed their lives. Just to keep a bird at their home!

The dove is a shy, sensitive bird. But the Holy Spirit, depicted as a dove in each of the four Gospels (Matt. 3:16; Mark 1:10; Luke 3:22; John 1:32) is a thousand times more sensitive than a turtle dove.

The dove is not the only way the Holy Spirit is depicted in the New Testament. He can be seen, described, or symbolized as fire, wind, water, and possibly oil. But why the dove? The dove is, in fact, a wild bird; it cannot be trained or domesticated even though it is a gentle bird.

This book is about holy fire. Many people understandably and rightly pray that the "fire will fall" on them. I pray for this too. But after you read this chapter, you may wonder if our most urgent need is for the Dove to come down on us. Could it be that the order of the day is: the Dove first, then the fire?

John the Baptist knew that Jesus was the Messiah because he had been told to look for the dove to come down on a particular man. There is more. He was not only to see the Spirit come down as a dove; this dove would "remain" on Him. In fact, the word *remain* is mentioned two times in John 1:32–33. I myself had read John 1:32–33 hundreds of times without noticing the word *remain*. But one Sunday evening at Westminster Chapel I asked Dr. Hwell Jones to read the Scripture lesson. It may have been the anointing of the Spirit—or his lovely Welsh accent; I only remember being gripped by the way he emphasized "and remain" as he read. "The man on whom you see the Spirit come down *and remain* is he who will baptize with the Holy Spirit."

You may know what it is like for the Holy Spirit to come down on you. The problem is, He doesn't stay. He doesn't remain. He apparently flies away. When the Holy Spirit comes down on you, there is literally nothing like it in the world. The peace. The joy. You want time to stop. You don't want to hear a phone ring, a knock at the door. If only it would last forever. While it lasts, you find yourself calm and instilled with a deep holy peace. You find yourself pleased with God just as He is without any complaints about the times He hides His face. While the Spirit comes on you, you will find yourself saying, "Lord, I love You just as You are. I would not change a single thing about You even if I could."

But that sense of His presence doesn't seem to last. It is not that the Holy Spirit leaves us. He doesn't. Jesus promised that He would abide "forever" (John 14:16). So let's be clear about this: the Holy Spirit never leaves us. I am using the Dove illustration as a metaphor. The Dove only *seems* to leave. He merely *seems* to fly away. He *seems* to lift. It is therefore the *sense of God* that appears to lift from us.

With Jesus, the Dove *remained.* He stayed. He never flew away.

Why? It is because Jesus never grieved the Holy Spirit. When the heavenly Dove came down on Jesus of Nazareth, He felt completely at home. It is as though the Dove said, "I like it here. I'm staying here." The Holy Spirit was at home with the Lord Jesus.

We saw earlier that the Holy Spirit can be grieved. Paul said, "Do not grieve the Holy Spirit of God, by whom you were sealed for the day of redemption" (Eph. 4:30, ESV). When you look at this important verse, you see good news and bad news. The good news: the Holy Spirit never leaves us. We are "sealed for the day of redemption." Nothing can be clearer than that. Grieving the Holy Spirit does not cause us to lose our salvation. We can thank God for this, or we would have been lost long ago—and many times at that! The bad news: when the Dove lifts—although the Spirit never leaves you, the anointing diminishes. That is, the sense of His presence is gone.

Grieving the Holy Spirit is the easiest thing in the world to do. To put it another way, the hardest thing in the world is to keep from grieving the Holy Spirit. Why? Because He is so sensitive. Indeed, we can say reverently that He is hypersensitive. When we speak of a person being hypersensitive, it is *not* a compliment. You may say, "Well, the Holy Spirit ought not be like that. He shouldn't be so sensitive." Remember: He's the only Holy Spirit you have. He will not adjust to you; you must adjust to Him. I wish it weren't true: the hardest thing in the world is not grieving the Holy Spirit.

Where I was preaching once, just before the service the minister asked me, "What does a veteran like you have to say to a young whippersnapper like me?"

I replied to him: "Find out what grieves the Holy Spirit and don't do that."

Believe me, make it your goal sixty seconds a minute, sixty minutes an hour, twenty-four hours a day, seven days a week *not to grieve the Holy Spirit,* and you will have your work cut out for you.

When I wrote the book *The Sensitivity of the Spirit,* I asked the publisher if I could call the book *Hypersensitivity of the Spirit.* The reply was that this would not work; it would be misunderstood. I agreed. But that's the idea. It is impossible to exaggerate how sensitive the person of the Holy Spirit is. Some people think that my book is called *Sensitivity* to *the Holy Spirit.* No. It is *The Sensitivity* of *the Spirit.* It is a description of an important facet of the *personality* of the third person of the Godhead. In a word: the Holy Spirit is a very, very, very sensitive person.

Can I put it another way? The Holy Spirit gets His feelings hurt easily. Again, this is not a compliment to any human being. But like it or not, that is the way God the Holy Spirit is. He gets His feelings hurt *so easily.*

When I completed the manuscript for my book *The Sensitivity of the Spirit,* I sent it to my friend Dr. Michael Eaton, who is the most learned person I know. He has read virtually every book in the history of the Christian church—from the Apostolic Fathers, the Church Fathers, the Medieval Scholastics, the Reformers, the Anabaptists, the

Puritans, the early Methodists, the nineteenth-century German theologians, the neo-orthodox theologians of the twentieth century, and whatever came out last week! I asked him, "Has anything been written on the sensitivity of the Holy Spirit?" His answer: no. I was surprised and yet not surprised. I suspect this is the most neglected aspect of the person of the Holy Spirit. It is known—but only just—to conservative evangelicals and charismatics. We know the word *grieve* but haven't thought a lot about it.

This aspect of the person of the Holy Spirit came up in my early days at Westminster Chapel when I had Dr. Martyn Lloyd-Jones at my side every week. I not only became acquainted with the phrase—grieving the Spirit—but also sought to live in such a manner that I never grieve Him. I found it impossible.

There are many ways to grieve the Holy Spirit—many. But at the head of the list is *bitterness*. As soon as Paul said, "Do not grieve the Holy Spirit of God, with whom you were sealed for the day of redemption," he immediately added, "Get rid of all bitterness" (Eph. 4:30–31).

Bitterness. It is a word that encapsulates resentment, anger, annoyance, being irritable, even impatience. It can spring forth in a second without notice. You were calm, happy, at peace. Then suddenly the Dove flies away. It can happen when you are driving. The car in front of you is going too slow. You show your irritation. You are in a hurry at a supermarket when you are in a line to be checked out. The person in front of you is in no hurry. He or she is counting the change and chatting with the person at the cash register. You sigh (out loud). You wanted the person to know you are in a hurry. They got it. But so did the Dove. He just flew away.

You may say, "God does not expect us to worry about things like that. RT, you are being too legalistic, too detailed, too careful, and holding to a ridiculously high standard that God does not expect of us."

If you wondered this, I know what you mean. That is the way I used to look at losing my temper. Until I came upon this teaching; it changed my life. My marriage. My relationship with my children. My deacons at Westminster Chapel (ask them). My friends. My enemies.

I was never to be the same again.

What is more, I began to see things in the Bible I had not seen before. I began to understand Old Testament characters. New Testament doctrine. The teachings of Jesus. The parables. Galatians. First Corinthians. Second Corinthians. I could go on and on. It has little to do with my intelligence or education. It has *everything* to do with the anointing.

So what is the bad news? The good news: we don't lose our salvation when we grieve the Spirit. The bad news: we lose the anointing. Not permanently, but as long as we remain in a state of irritability, defensiveness, and resentment, the Dove will invariably be some distance away.

When the anointing is on you, you will see things in the Bible you had not seen before. You will feel God near as you had not felt Him. You will be easier to live with!

But when the anointing lifts, you will get little or no fresh insight when you read the Bible. Your mind will seriously wander when you pray. You will not be so easy to live with.

The reason for the connection between the ungrieved Spirit and the Bible is easily explained. The Holy Spirit wrote the Bible. It is His Word. If you want to know His Word, get on good terms with Him. He knows His own Word inside and out, backward and forward. When He indwells in you *ungrieved,* He makes His Word come alive to you. You see things you hadn't seen before.

To put it another way: the Holy Spirit is in you if you are a Christian (Rom. 8:9). But it does not follow that He is always in you *ungrieved.*

The Holy Spirit won't bend the rules for any of us. He is no respecter of persons. He will not adjust to any of us. He favors no human being. We must adjust to *Him.* We must adjust to His ways.

At Westminster Chapel I began my Sunday morning sermon preparation on Monday mornings. But there was one time—only once—when I was so busy all week that I had no time to prepare. I had not cracked a book. It was now Saturday morning, and I had *nothing* for Sunday morning. I asked the Lord to compensate by unusual help from Him, and I prayed there would be no interruptions all day long. At nine o'clock that morning Louise and I got into an argument. It was a dandy. I slammed the door and rushed to my desk. There was my open Bible and a blank sheet of paper. "Lord, please do help me. Deal with Louise. Give me my sermon for tomorrow."

Nothing came. Nothing. At eleven o'clock I began to pray more earnestly. "Lord, please, please help me." Nothing came. Nothing. Twelve o'clock. One o'clock. Nothing. At two o'clock I said, "Lord, You've got to help me. You know that every word of my sermon tomorrow will be tape recorded and may go around the world. You've got to help me." Nothing came. Nothing. All I had was a Bible and a blank sheet of paper.

At four o'clock I finally went into the kitchen (I had been waiting for her to come to me). There was Louise standing by the refrigerator, tearful. I said, "Honey, I am *so* sorry. It is *all my fault.*" We kissed, we hugged. I went back to my desk and Bible and blank sheet of paper. I promise you, in forty-five minutes I had *everything* I needed for Sunday morning. Everything. Thoughts came faster than I could write them down. Why? The Dove came. We can accomplish more in five minutes when the Dove comes down on us than we can achieve in a lifetime trying to work something up.

God lamented of ancient Israel, "They have not known my ways" (Heb. 3:10). You might also sense a tear in God's voice, feeling sad that His own people did not know His *ways.* God wants us to know His *ways.* That He is a most holy God. That He is sovereign. He is all-powerful. That He knows everything. And that He can be grieved.

"My people are destroyed for lack of knowledge," as we have seen (Hos. 4:6). I remind you: there are two areas of knowledge God has in mind in particular—His Word and His ways. His Word is the Bible— His integrity put on the line. He wants you to know His Word. So how much do you really read the Bible? Do forgive me for saying again that you need the discipline of reading His Word with a good Bible-reading plan every day. As I said, you get to know a person's ways by spending time with them. So how much do you actually pray? I repeat: there will be no praying in heaven. The last verse of that lovely hymn, "Sweet Hour of Prayer," points precisely to this:

> Sweet hour of prayer! sweet hour of prayer!
> May I Thy consolation share,
> Till, from Mount Pisgah's lofty height,

I view my home and take my flight:
This robe of flesh I'll drop, and rise
To seize the everlasting prize;
And shout, while passing through the air,
"Farewell, farewell, sweet hour of prayer!"[2]

—WILLIAM WALFORD
(1772–1850)

Hour of prayer? A whole hour? How much time do you give to God in your daily quiet time? Just before I retired from Westminster, I was asked to address one hundred ministers in London at Holy Trinity Church, Brompton. I was given ten minutes to speak on the subject of prayer. I used the ten minutes to urge every minister there to spend at least one hour a day in prayer. Two hours is better.

HOW MUCH DO YOU PRAY?

Here is the point: when you spend time with God, you get to know His ways as well as His Word (assuming you are reading His Word). More than that, you develop a sensitivity *to* the Holy Spirit. You eventually get to know His ways to the extent that you sense when you are about to grieve Him. The problem is, when we grieve Him, we almost never know we did it! We find out later. But you rarely know at the precise moment. Samson told his secret to Delilah and didn't feel a thing. But he found moments later that his prodigious strength had gone. (See Judges 16:20–21.)

I would define *spirituality* as the time gap between sin and repentance. In other words, how long does it take before you realize—or admit—that you sinned? That you were wrong. Some take years. They say, "I'll *never* admit I was wrong." And they are true to their word. Some, however, after a long time cool off or come to themselves and say, "Well, perhaps I got it wrong after all." But what a pity that it took so long! Some narrow the time gap to months. Some to weeks. Some to hours (that's better). Some to minutes. Some to seconds. And if you can narrow the time gap to *seconds,* you are often able to sense the wings of the Dove flapping and ready to fly off—and you stop yourself!

Don't finish that sentence! Don't write that letter! Don't make that phone call!

Nothing is worth grieving the Holy Spirit.

So if you want to have a lively, real, unfeigned, and constant relationship with God, His Son, and the Holy Spirit, you must get to know God's ways. One of the ways of the Holy Spirit is that He is sensitive. Like the dove.

Did you know that pigeons and doves are in the same family? But they are not the same! You can train a pigeon. You cannot train a dove. The pigeon can be domesticated. The dove is a wild bird. A pigeon is belligerent. The dove is loving. A pigeon is boisterous. A dove is gentle. A pigeon will mate with more than one pigeon. The dove mates with only one dove for life.

The pigeon represents the counterfeit spirit. Strange fire. The dove represents the Holy Spirit. Holy fire. I reckon there are services where people imagine that "the Holy Ghost came on our church," but when you get to the bottom of it, you discern it may have been *pigeon religion.* Strange fire. Personally I think it is an absolutely wonderful but probably rare moment when the authentic Holy Spirit comes down in great measure. Holy fire.

It is so easy to grieve the Spirit. It happens to people on the way to church. They shout to each other as they drive into the parking lot. Then they worship as if nothing is wrong and wonder why there is no sense of God. It happens to a minister as he prepares his sermon. It can happen at any moment. Although we have only ourselves to blame when we lose our tempers, point the finger, or speak of another person in an unflattering manner, it is also true that our adversary the devil lurks about looking for an opportunity to seize our weak spot. We all have them.

The ungrieved Spirit in me will connect to the ungrieved Spirit in you. If you get two or three people together when all have been walking in the ungrieved Holy Spirit, there is richness of fellowship. That doesn't mean everybody is in total agreement theologically or politically. But the sweetness is there. Imagine what it would be like when a congregation of a dozen—or twelve hundred—or twelve thousand are all—*everyone*—walking in the same ungrieved Holy Spirit! Who knows what would happen when marriages are healed, people start forgiving their parents, Christians start speaking to one another, ministers finally begin speaking to one another, and everybody truly loves each other!

First the Dove, then the fire.

WHAT GRIEVES THE HOLY SPIRIT?

I wonder how many people pray for the fire to fall but take no notice of their personal attitudes. I wonder how many pray for revival but do not think of examining themselves. I wonder how many go to church to worship God and hear a sermon but have no awareness of personal issues that cause the Dove to stay at bay. I wonder how many times we grieve the Spirit and feel no conviction of sin whatever.

If therefore you want to know what grieves the Holy Spirit, read Ephesians 4:30–32.

Bitterness

I return to this. It is one of the most natural feelings in the world. It also seems right! We all are prone to feel justified in having a feeling of bitterness. It comes from being mistreated, maligned, hurt, betrayed, lied about—and especially when we feel we are upholding what is fair and true! There is one other ingredient in bitterness: self-righteousness. This is so often the cause. Because we feel so right, we may feel no conviction of sin—*unless*, that is, we develop an acute sensitivity to the Spirit's ways.

Bitterness is the result of unforgiveness. At the conclusion of this section on grieving the Spirit, Paul exhorts: "Be kind and compassionate to one another, forgiving each other, just as in Christ God forgave you" (Eph. 4:32). Totally forgiving those who have hurt us eradicates one of bitterness. This comes when you resolve and carry out:

1. Never telling anybody what "they" did.

2. Not letting them be afraid of you or feeling nervous around you.

3. Not letting them feel guilty but overlooking what they did, even if they don't know what they have done (remember how Jesus forgave on the cross, Luke 23:34).

4. Letting them save face as opposed to rubbing their noses in it (as Joseph forgave his brothers, Genesis 45:8).

5. Accept this matter of total forgiveness as a permanent lifestyle—you do it today and a year from now and ten years from now.

6. You bless them. When you can sincerely pray for them to be blessed (to be successful and not punished)—and do this from your heart, there will almost certainly be no bitterness left.

Total forgiveness and the indwelling ungrieved Spirit are virtually the same thing. It ensures that the Dove remains and feels at home with us.

Always pray for conviction of sin. Why? Because the heart is deceitful above all things and desperately wicked (Jer. 17:9). To be sure that you have totally forgiven, ask the Lord to show you when you haven't totally forgiven others. I hope you would want to know if you haven't totally forgiven! When there is conviction of sin, it is a good sign that God is on your case, especially if you are truly sorry before God for your self-pity and feeling of entitlement. Once you are convicted, the next step is appealing to good old 1 John 1:9 (primarily for Christians): "If we confess our sins, he is faithful and just and will forgive us our sins and purify us from all unrighteousness."

Keep short accounts with the Lord. As soon as you sense bitterness— and the Dove lifting from you—turn to the Lord. Remember 1 John 1:9. He is faithful.

The goal is to enjoy unbroken fellowship with the Holy Spirit so that there is no discontinuity in sensing His smile and presence. After all, you want the Dove to remain.

Rage and anger

God can show His wrath, but we cannot! Seems unfair, doesn't it? But that's the way it is. No matter how right you and I may be—even theologically—when we lose our tempers, we are the ones in the wrong, even if we are right! The Holy Spirit's fruit is love, joy, peace, patience, kindness, goodness, faithfulness, gentleness, and self-control (Gal. 5:22–23). All that I am saying about the Dove in this chapter can be summed up: it is the fruit of the Holy Spirit.

If I am filled with rage and anger and claim that the Holy Spirit has come down on me in power, mark it down: it is strange fire.

Brawling and slander

The ESV has "clamor and slander" (Eph. 4:31). Clamor means shouting. The wisdom that comes from "below," said James 3:13–15, is "earthly" and "of the devil." A shouting match shows that the devil got in.

Slander is making false and damaging statements about someone. You may ask, "But what if it's true?" I would only say, be very careful. You may be telling the truth, but what would be your motive in hurting someone's name or reputation?

Every form of malice

This basically means ill will. Far from wishing a person well, you want to see him punished. Caught. Exposed. A motivation like this has its origin in the flesh and the devil. The Holy Spirit will not lead you to wish bad things for a person. Vengeance belongs to God (Rom. 12:19). If the person you may hope will get their *comeuppance* has been truly evil, leave it to God. Don't touch it. Don't deprive God of what He does best, namely, to bring vengeance and to vindicate. Don't compete with His expertise.

The list on what grieves the Holy Spirit continues into Ephesians 5. Don't overlook the obvious in Ephesians 5:1–7.

Sexual immorality

Paul asks that there not be "even a hint" of sexual immorality. This means that you cannot be too careful when it comes to sexual behavior and temptation. This includes flirting—saying something that you hope will ignite a person to have lustful thoughts toward you. When James talks about a "small spark" setting a forest on fire (James 3:5), this can happen either by venting your anger, by an unguarded comment, or by making an intentional remark that would tempt another.

Let's face it; sexual promiscuity has been a salient problem among both charismatic *and* conservative evangelical leaders. What is astonishing is that it is so often swept under the carpet. Nothing brings disgrace upon the name of Christ and the church like sexual scandal. The world loves it. The press loves it. The glossy magazines love it!

What is saddest of all is the blatant lack of outrage among some Christian leaders who have been sexually immoral and some of their followers. Talk about strange fire. Talk about grieving the Holy Spirit.

SPIRITUAL GIFTS AND SPIRITUAL FRUIT

Many people who follow high-profile leaders can be duped by their leader's apparent continued success—people falling down when prayed for or seemingly healed. Or the big crowds. When there are spectacular words of knowledge—even healing—many sincere Christians take this as a sign God is still with that person and that we should support him or her as much as ever. I'm sorry, but this is a fatal mistake. "But how could these preachers have such power?" I answer: the gifts and calling of God are "without repentance" (KJV)—irrevocable (Rom. 11:29). This partly means that one's gift can flourish regardless of his or her personal life. King Saul continued to prophesy on his way to kill young David (1 Sam. 19:23–24).

One's gift may therefore sometimes flourish regardless of that person's personal morality. But when the Spirit is grieved, it means that one's ability to hear from God is closed down. You will ask, "How do they get these words of knowledge? Does that not mean they are hearing from God?" No. This does not mean the Dove remains on such a person. It means that an irrevocable gift of healing, prophecy, or word of knowledge still works.

On the other hand, take Peter and John approaching the Beautiful

Gate at the temple when they suddenly stopped to heal the lame man. They walked by this man several times before. How did they know spontaneously to say to the crippled man, "Look on us"? (Acts 3:4, KJV). Answer: they heard the Holy Spirit speak directly to them; they were walking together in the power of the ungrieved Spirit. There was no rival spirit between them. They did not know this would happen until the last moment. The Dove had remained on them.

A spiritual *gift*—but not fruit of the Spirit—may flourish whether or not a person has grieved the Holy Spirit. But the immediate and direct guidance only follows when the Spirit is not grieved in a person. The gifts of the Spirit are constant—you get to keep them. But the fruit of the Spirit is not necessarily constant. The Dove may remain or lift; this depends on our personal relationship to God. A close walk with God is determined by our careful obedience to His word.

The gifts may flourish, and you can still get into all kinds of trouble. The ungrieved Spirit indwelling you will keep you from trouble—and keep you from bringing disgrace upon God's name.

Mind you, I must repeat that neither charismatics nor conservative evangelicals are exempt from sexual scandals. My own background is with the "Word" people. I blush to think of those in the Reformed camp who judge charismatics so loudly and harshly.

We should pray for one another. And yet when there is sexual immorality without repentance, such a person should stay out of ministry until there is clear evidence of both remorse and change of life. I have written a book *God Gives Second Chances* and show that a person can be restored to ministry.[3] But one important evidence of someone being qualified to minister again is unfeigned repentance. After all, Peter—who sobbed his heart out when he realized what he had done by denying the Lord (Matt. 26:75)—was restored.

Greed
This is an excessive and selfish desire for wealth or material things. It is called *coveting*. Greed is an internal condition, so there is no way to know if another person is greedy or covetous. We must avoid judging.

But we should know whether *we ourselves* are greedy. We should want to know it when we are covetous.

Like every single one of previously mentioned sins that grieve the Holy Spirit, we are all vulnerable. We have all failed. We have all sinned. Paul said he felt he was without sin until the Tenth Commandment—"You shall not covet" (Exod. 20:17; Rom. 7:7–25)—sank in. We have all broken the Tenth Commandment.

The common denominator that holds Pentecostals and charismatics together is no longer the gifts of the Holy Spirit; it is prosperity teaching.

Appealing to people's need or greed to support one's ministry is strange fire. One cannot help but feel that the reason for the preponderance of prosperity teaching in the last twenty years is to raise money. The *prosperity gospel* seems to be in your face much of the time if you watch Christian television channels.

I wrote a book called *Tithing*.[4] It is still in print after thirty years. Churches that have given it to all their members have testified to an increase of 30 percent in income. It is endorsed by Billy Graham, John Stott, and the Archbishop of Canterbury. There is no doubt that Malachi appeals to Israel's self-interest when he says that if we tithe, we will receive so much blessing that one will "not have room enough for it" (Mal. 3:10). But as I said in the previous chapter, something very wrong has emerged in recent years. Some preachers look for and find *prosperity teaching* in too many passages in the Bible and give the undoubted impression that Jesus died on the cross mainly so we can be prosperous. This is wrong. As the lottery often appeals to poor people, so do many poor Christians support ministries that are built almost entirely on the promise of financial blessing if you give to them. If Jesus came to many churches today, the first thing He would do is to make a whip out of cords and drive money changers out and overturn their tables, as described in John 2:14–15.

Greed grieves the Holy Spirit, and appealing to people's need or greed to raise money for God is a reproach to His name.

Jesus said, "Seek first his [God's] kingdom and his righteousness, and all these things [food, shelter, clothing] will be given to you as well" (Matt. 6:33). This means that we must focus on God and His righteousness and *not* focus on what comes as a by-product of putting Him first. God promised to supply all our needs (Phil. 4:19). Indeed, when we sow generously, we will reap generously—and will be "rich in every way" (2 Cor. 9:6, 11). But if we focus on what we will *get* and not upon God Himself, we put ourselves in a no-win situation. As C. S. Lewis put it, "Aim at heaven and you will get the earth thrown in. Aim at earth and you get neither." We first look to Christ—and stay focused on Him—and God will look after us. But when we are consumed with "what's in it for me" we lose all the way around. Or once again we remember the words of Charles Spurgeon: "I looked to Christ and the Dove flew in; I looked to the Dove and He disappeared."

Chapter Seven

MY PERSONAL TESTIMONY

Continue in what you have learned and have become convinced of, because you know those from whom you learned it, and how from infancy you have known the holy Scriptures, which are able to make you wise for salvation through faith in Christ Jesus. All Scripture is God-breathed and is useful for teaching, rebuking, correcting and training in righteousness, so that the man of God may be thoroughly equipped for every good work.

—2 Timothy 3:14–17

He who hears not the music thinks the dancer mad.

—Anonymous

I WAS CONVERTED AT THE AGE OF SIX, ON EASTER MORNING APRIL 5, 1942. As we were getting ready to go to church, I told my parents I wanted to be a Christian. Whether the fact that it was Easter had anything to do with my prompting, I don't know. I remember that my father turned to my mother and said, "We don't need to wait until we get to church. We can pray right here." I knelt at my parents' bedside, confessed my sins, and asked the Lord to save me. As for sins in my life, I only remember feeling ashamed at the way I talked back to my parents. I wept as I prayed and felt that God forgave me. I believe I was saved that morning. Several years later as a teenager I felt I was sanctified—this being a second work of grace as my church taught me.

I was brought up in the Church of the Nazarene, a denomination for which I maintain deep respect. My parents were godly. My earliest memory of my dad was seeing him on his knees for about a half hour every morning before he went to work. He was a layman, not a minister, but a preacher's dream; he was very faithful to our church in Ashland, Kentucky. My mother was the church organist. My earliest memory of her was seeing her on her knees every day after Dad went to work. As she finished praying, she would lift her hands into the air, sometimes with tears running down her cheeks. She always prayed for me before I left for school. Sometimes the kids who came along were invited in to hear her pray for me—which I found embarrassing. She died at the age of forty-three on April 8, 1953, when I was seventeen years old.

I entered Trevecca Nazarene College (now University) in the autumn of 1953. A year later I felt the call to preach the gospel. My church in Ashland immediately issued a preacher's license while I was a student at Trevecca. I preached my first sermon on the first Wednesday evening of December at Calvary Church of the Nazarene in Nashville—on the "Faithfulness of God"—taking my text from Lamentations 3:23. I was offered the pastorate of a little church in the mountains of east Tennessee three months later—in Palmer, Tennessee. My grandmother bought me a brand-new 1955 Chevrolet for me to use in order to travel to Palmer from Nashville (about 115 miles one way) on weekends. I would normally drive there on Friday afternoon, usually returning on Sunday evening.

After I had been there for approximately six months, maintaining all my college courses, I went through a period of great anxiety. I don't know any other way to describe it. It was a feeling of loneliness, feeling cut off. I felt I was traveling in unprecedented waters. I remember going to my dormitory room to pray when I had an hour between classes. I will never forget the weekend of October 29–30, spending time alone kneeling at the altar of my little church—just praying. I didn't know what I was praying for. I only felt that spending a lot of time in prayer could not be wrong. I wanted a breakthrough in my relationship with God. I felt something was wrong. I wanted to get over this anxiety. I wanted to be as close to God as I could possibly be. The uncertainty drove me to my knees.

What I Now Relate Is What Happened to Me

At six thirty on Monday morning—October 31, 1955—while driving back to Nashville, I decided to spend the journey in prayer rather than play my car radio. I had no idea that the greatest experience of my life up to then was about to take place. I can take you very near the spot on old US 41—at the bottom of Monteagle Mountain—when a heavy burden came on me as I prayed. The anxiety again returned—with a vengeance. I found myself in agony. I cried to the Lord, "Am I not sanctified? Am I not even saved?" I did not feel God at all. Two scriptures, however, came to me. First Peter 5:7: "Casting all your care upon him; for he careth for you" (KJV); and Matthew 11:30: "My yoke is easy, and my burden is light" (KJV). But my burden that morning was heavy. So heavy. I reasoned that if I could somehow cast my care upon the Lord, I would be able to say my burden is light.

All of a sudden as I drove, there to my right was Jesus Christ interceding for me at the right hand of God. It was as real as anything I had ever seen. I felt He was my elder brother, loving me more than I love myself, caring more about me than I cared for myself. But I could not tell what He was saying. It was clear to me that He was at the Father's right hand and putting His entire relationship with the Father on the line—as if He said, "Come to his rescue, or I resign." I did not hear those words, but that was the impression I got as the Lord Jesus interceded for me. I burst into tears. I stopped praying and became a spectator. He took over. The next thing I remember— about an hour later—driving through Smyrna, Tennessee, I heard

Jesus say to the Father, "He wants it." The Father replied, "He can have it." At that moment a surge of *holy fire* entered into my chest. I was cleansed. I literally felt warmth, also remembering how John Wesley testified to his heart being "strangely warmed" at a Bible study in Aldersgate Street, London. I never felt such peace in my life. This peace was not merely the absence of fear—the anxiety was gone—but the presence of a most blissful rest of soul. I continued to drive on US 41 toward Trevecca, by then only a few minutes away. As I drove, there was Jesus looking at me. I saw His face. It lasted for less than a minute. I parked my car near my dorm in Tidwell Hall, shaved quickly, and went to my first class at 8:00 a.m., wondering whatever had just happened to me.

The major thing in those early moments was how real God is and how true the Bible is. The elementary doctrines of the faith were vindicated as if before my eyes. For example, I knew without any doubt that Jesus was literally raised from the dead. I could see how the early church was convinced that Jesus was alive by the Holy Spirit. I could see that Jesus really was seated at God's right hand—and interceding for us. I knew indeed that Jesus Christ had come in the flesh, that He still has a *body*, and that He was a *man* in glory. I had never had a problem with Jesus's deity, but what was stunningly true to me was that He is truly human! The Second Coming was equally real to me—not that any particular eschatological perspective emerged, but that He was truly and literally coming again! I was given an infallible assurance of these things—truths I had been taught all my life but was now seeing for myself that they were *so* true!

On the same day this happened, my friend Bill Kerns, who lived in the room next to mine, said he noticed something different about me. He asked, "What has happened to you?"

I replied, "I don't honestly know. But something has happened to me." I queried whether I had received a third work of grace. Nazarenes taught two works of grace—being saved and sanctified. I professed to both. But what happened that morning was totally different. I said to Bill, "Whether it is a third work of grace, I do not know; I only know I am *saved*."

And that was the main thing I realized during those early hours: I was truly saved. Eternally saved. Rightly or wrongly I told this to my roommate and friends in my dormitory. I said I knew I was saved. They replied, "Of course you are saved. Why say that?"

I said, "Because I know I am eternally saved, that I cannot be lost." I knew that absolutely and infallibly on the very day this happened to me. My mistake (perhaps) was telling this to my Nazarene friends, who had no idea of assurance of salvation. I even said (perhaps unwisely), "I will go to heaven when I die, no matter what I do between now and then."

They said, "John Wesley once thought that. He changed his mind. So will you." I can only say that I knew then that I would never change my mind. It was so real to me. The truth is, I have never doubted my eternal salvation from that day to now. I knew I would not change my mind, and I never have.

However, I seriously wondered about one thing, "Where in the Bible could I find a scriptural basis for what has happened to me? Had I received something new? Is this truly a third work of grace? Did this happen to John Wesley?"

I was bubbling over with joy and peace. I enjoyed a sense of God I did not know a person could have in this life.

Before sundown that day I began to see that what happened to me was a work of the Holy Spirit. I could not make this happen. I only know how I yearned for a closer walk with God in those days. God had imparted to me a desire for more of Him. And He answered me. Simple as that. The embryonic seed of Reformed theology had been firmly implanted and began to grow rather quickly. I was assistant to the dean of theology—Dr. William Greathouse (who later became president of Trevecca and a general superintendent in the Church of the Nazarene). He warned me that I was beginning to imbibe teaching that "our church doesn't believe."

I replied, "Then our church is wrong." I had not read a single line of St. Augustine (354–430), Martin Luther (1483–1546), John Calvin, or Jonathan Edwards except excerpts of his sermon "Sinners in the

Hands of an Angry God." I wondered if I had discovered something new—which worried me.

Over the next several months I began to have visions. Never before had this happened to me. I could see clearly that my future would not be in my old denomination. Not only that, but I also saw I would one day have a worldwide ministry, something that seemed extraordinary for a provincial Nazarene.

But there is more. About four months later—in February 1956—again while driving in my car—I felt a stirring in my inner being. It seemed to be in my stomach—like a well that wanted to spring forth. The only way I could let it out was to utter what I can only call unintelligible sounds. This time others were in the car. I'm sure they heard me. I was embarrassed. I remember (for some reason) rolling down the window. I said nothing, because I knew I had spoken in tongues—something Nazarenes didn't do. Ever. They were vehemently against tongues, possibly more against tongues than they were Calvinism. I did not discuss this with anybody. *Anyone.* I kept it largely to myself for years. One of the first persons I told was Dr. Martyn Lloyd-Jones some twenty-one years later.

At the same time I spoke in tongues, something else happened. I was given a clear mandate to offer my resignation to my church in Palmer on the following May 6—letting May 20 be my final Sunday. When I got back to my room at Trevecca, I checked the calendar to be sure both dates were Sundays.

A few weeks later after my resignation—driving in the same car—I looked at my dashboard. It was totally different. I was given a vision of a *1953* Chevrolet dashboard. The reason I knew the year is because my roommate Ralph Lee had a 1953 Chevrolet. This was in June 1956. I felt by that vision I would somehow be losing my car. After returning to Ashland, Kentucky, two weeks later, my grandmother took the car back, sensing that I was not going to be a Nazarene for much longer. She gave it to my dad, who traded it in on a new Chrysler. My father felt I had disgraced him and my old church. He accused me of "breaking with God." He then required that I pay rent if I was to remain at home. I was offered a job the same day by Creamens

Quality Cleaners on 29th Street in Ashland, and also given a Chevrolet truck to drive and pick up people's dry cleaning. It was a 1953 Chevrolet. The moment I sat behind the wheel, there was the dashboard of a 1953 Chevrolet—exactly as in the vision. I knew for certain that I was firmly in God's will.

I had listened to Rev. Henry Mahan a number of times on the radio. He was the pastor of the 13th Street Baptist Church in Ashland. I was fascinated with what I heard him preach over the radio. I found the address of his home and went to meet him. I became nervous when he answered the door. I asked if he had any clothes he wanted cleaned. Yes. He brought me a suit. I then said, "I really didn't come here to see if you needed any dry cleaning. I have been listening to you on the radio. I think I believe what you preach." When I told him I was a Nazarene, he was surprised. After questioning me and stating what he believed, he was shocked to find that I believed those same truths but actually got them from the Bible and from no other book. A friendship began that day. His church ordained me to the ministry years later. Both my father and grandmother graciously came to my ordination service. It must have been very difficult for these loyal Nazarenes to come into a Calvinistic Baptist church to see their son/grandson ordained.

In 1956 I tried my best to convince my godly father that I was not out of God's will, but very much *in* His will. I told him some of my visions—which was probably a mistake—hoping that they would impress him. They didn't. I knew I would one day have an international ministry. He had one question: "When?"

I replied, "In one year." He asked me to write it down on a sheet of paper. I did. That was another mistake, trying so hard to win over my dad. One year later I wasn't even in the ministry at all. Five years later I was working as a door-to-door vacuum cleaner salesman.

In June 1958 I married Louise Wallis of Sterling, Illinois. The greatest single objective evidence that I had the favor of God in those difficult years was Louise. How kind and merciful God was to me to give me this beautiful, intelligent, and faithful wife. My dad seemed to accept her more than he did me! Our first home was in Springfield, Illinois.

101

We moved to Fort Lauderdale, Florida, in November 1958. I worked as an insurance salesman for Life and Casualty Insurance Company for more than two years, then began selling vacuum cleaners.

In July 1962 I accepted a call to be the pastor of Fairview Church of God, a small church in Carlisle, Ohio. My dad phoned to say he would come and hear me preach the following Sunday. I said to Louise, "Dad will be wearing a light mint-colored green suit. At some time during the service he will walk down the center aisle, turn to the right, then go back." In 1956 I had a vision of my dad wearing that mint-colored green suit. When he and his wife, Abbie, my stepmother, came to hear me, sure enough he was wearing that suit. After the morning service there he came walking down the aisle, turning to the right and then going back. It was exactly as I had seen earlier. You may ask, "What's the point?"

I answer: "I knew I was firmly in the will of God." It was also absolute proof to me that God knows the future perfectly since that vision had come to me in 1956.

The pastorate in Ohio lasted eighteen months, ending in failure. My rather intellectual approach to Scripture (and Calvinistic interpretation of it) was more than they could take in. The people of the small church got up a petition to vote me out. They were short one vote, but we left, returning to Fort Lauderdale in January 1964. I turned again to selling vacuum cleaners. During my vacuum cleaner days our son, Robert Tillman II, was born (we call him TR). I also was given invitations to preach in Presbyterian churches around Fort Lauderdale. Dr. D. James Kennedy of the Coral Ridge Presbyterian Church asked me to join his staff and head an evangelism program he was beginning. It later became known as "Evangelism Explosion." I did not have peace to do this, but Jim and I remained good friends. In early 1968 I became the pastor of the Lauderdale Manors Baptist Church. Our daughter, Melissa Louise, was born in August 1970. In the autumn of 1970 I returned to Trevecca and graduated the following December. In January 1971 I entered Southern Baptist Theological Seminary in Louisville. I also became the pastor of the Blue River Baptist Church in Salem, Indiana, commuting every day (a thirty-five-minute drive). In

December 1972 I became the first student ever to complete the MDiv in two years (a three-year course) while also achieving the highest academic record in their history. They recommended me for Oxford.

On September 1, 1973, our family landed at London Heathrow Airport, taking up residence in Headington, Oxford. My supervisor, Dr. B. R. White of Regent's Park College, Oxford, accepted me to do research on English Puritanism. He also recommended me to be the pastor of the Calvary Southern Baptist Church in Lower Heyford, Oxfordshire, which was made up largely of US military and their families. During those three years Dr. and Mrs. Martyn Lloyd-Jones became like family to Louise and me, although none of us remotely envisaged my coming to Westminster Chapel later on. While waiting for my *viva voce* (oral exam) for the DPhil, I was invited to speak at Westminster Chapel for the second time. The deacons asked me to stay for six months with no obligation to remain after that time. Dr. and Mrs. Lloyd-Jones came to see us a few days later, telling Louise and me why we should stay. "You have nothing to lose. You need to come down from being at Oxford. It will be good for you; it will be good for them." We moved into London and began our ministry on February 1, 1977, retiring February 1, 2002.

As for those twenty-five years at Westminster Chapel, they were "the best of times; they were the worst of times." Our greatest joys, friendships, and successes were in London. Our greatest trials, hurts, and disappointments were in London.

In 1978 on a train from Edinburgh, Scotland, to King's Cross, London, my dad—who had come to visit us now that I was the minister of Westminster Chapel—said to me as we were entering the station: "Son, I'm proud of you. You were right; I was wrong." This of course was deeply reassuring to hear, but it took twenty-two years from the time I told him of those visions back in 1956.

Between the years from 1956 to 1977 I was sometimes in an ecclesiastical wilderness. I knew where I stood theologically. But I had no idea where I was going when it came to ministry. I began preaching for Baptists, Orthodox Presbyterians, Southern Presbyterians, Christian Reformed, Reformed Church of America, and others. I developed an understanding of several church cultures, wondering in those days where I would end up. But all this shaped me for what would be coming down the road. To this day I am frequently introduced as one who speaks for different theological streams; that is, Baptists, Reformed, conservative evangelicals, Pentecostals, and charismatics.

The *only* reason I have told how the Holy Spirit taught me Reformed theology is that, should you be of a Reformed persuasion, you might feel I am a true friend and that you will not be threatened by what I am teaching regarding the Holy Spirit. I realize that many Reformed people are *cessationists*, and you may think that the doctrines of grace and the immediate witness of the Spirit are incompatible. Believe me, there is no incongruity in holding these views. They are not polar opposites but totally complementary. Indeed, they not only perfectly cohere but also mutually vindicate and elucidate each other.

In the spring of 1994—during a time when Louise was very ill—I found myself crying out in desperation to God. Sitting alone in the apartment of one of my closest friends, I began speaking in tongues. It was the first time I had done that since 1956. I have done this ever since. I am personally convinced that it is what Paul was describing in Romans 8:26–27—when the Spirit intercedes for us according to the will of God "with groans that words cannot express." It connects perfectly to 1 Corinthians 14:2 (ESV); when one prays in a language no one understands, "he utters mysteries in the Spirit." When I pray in this manner, I know one thing for sure: I am praying in the will of God.

We had a good ministry at Westminster Chapel. But the revival I hoped for never came. It would be a mistake to underestimate the times of refreshing that came, the number of people who were saved, healed, or blessed in different ways. But I do not write this book as an example of great success. If you are in the ministry, I write it hoping you might see in your lifetime what I didn't. Toward the end of my time I decided twenty-five years was enough. It was sweet, of course, when the deacons asked me to stay another five years. But I recalled my hero—Joe DiMaggio, the great New York Yankees baseball player. He quit while he was still going strong, and I thought I should retire because they wanted me to stay! But then I wondered, "What will I do? Nobody in America knows about me." In that moment I felt a definite impression, "Your ministry in America will be to charismatics." "Oh no," I thought. "If I am going to have a ministry in my own country, let it be to Reformed churches or to conservative evangelicals. I have the credentials. I am one of them. I know how they think. Why can't I have a ministry to them?" But no, it would be to charismatics. It has largely turned out that way. Most of my invitations have been to charismatic and Pentecostal churches.

Our retirement from Westminster Chapel began on February 1, 2002, exactly twenty-five years from the day we began. We moved to Key Largo, Florida. I took up a ministry with Jack Taylor and Charles Carrin, holding Word, Spirit and Power conferences all over the United States. In July 2002 I was invited by Canon Andrew White to meet the late Yasser Arafat. Surprisingly, a friendship with President Arafat was begun. I visited him five times, dined with him, and laughed with him, always praying for him and often anointing him with oil. I wept when he died. Andrew White also took me to Iraq, where I preached in the late Saddam Hussein's palace area and also in St. George's Anglican church in Baghdad. During this time I was part of the Alexandria Peace Process, led by Lord Carey, Archbishop of Canterbury. Through this I became friends with Rabbi David Rosen. David and I wrote a book together—*The Christian and the Pharisee*—which was launched at Westminster Abbey.[1] My writing ministry has widened, and I have had open doors all over America and many places in the world.

I have been in the ministry for almost sixty years. Louise and I have been married fifty-five years. We have two lovely children and two grandsons. Louise has traveled with me to most places, and our son, TR, has also traveled extensively with me. I continue to travel, preach, and write books. God has been extremely kind to me.

I have written this chapter at the request of my publisher, who asked that I share my testimony. It is my most ardent desire that this book has been a blessing to you so far. I pray it will put a burning in your heart, a fervent craving for an ever-increasing closer walk with

God. When the two men on the road to Emmaus saw the risen Lord but did not know at first who He was, they reflected how their hearts *burned* as He spoke. Holy fire burns. My aim in this book is lead you to experience Him immediately and directly for yourself. With my background put to you, let us turn to the important topic coming up in the next chapter—cessationism.

Chapter Eight

CESSATIONISM

Jesus Christ is the same yesterday and today and forever.
—HEBREWS 13:8

There are many streams of cleansing—beginning with the blood of Jesus Christ! I want to study and experience them all, as God works among us to free, heal, and mature His people.

—JACK HAYFORD

WHEN MY FRIEND CHARLES CARRIN WAS PASTOR OF A CHURCH (before being an itinerant minister), he received a phone call from a stranger:

"Is your church a Bible-believing church?"

"Yes."

"Do you believe in the inerrancy of Scripture?"

"Yes, and we also believe in the inerrancy of 1 Corinthians 12 and 14. We believe those passages are just as inerrant as the rest of the New Testament."

"Do you mean tongues?"

"We believe that all the gifts of the Spirit, including tongues, are included in the Scripture's inerrancy and are to be believed."

"Well, I don't."

The above conversation is taken from Charles Carrin's booklet *On Whose Authority?: The Removal of Unwanted Scriptures.*[1] Charles, who had been an ardent cessationist and entrenched five-point Calvinist for many years, was the pastor of a Primitive Baptist Church in Atlanta, Georgia. But one day he prayed something like this: "Lord, I want to be filled with Your Holy Spirit. But I have three conditions: I don't want to shout, I don't want to be spectacular, and I don't want to speak in tongues. Now with that in mind, You may proceed." Nothing happened. But as it turns out, he was also a chaplain at the federal prison in Atlanta, Georgia. He was assigned to a man who had been converted and filled with the Holy Spirit after being imprisoned.

Whereas Charles went weekly to minister to this man, the prisoner began to minister to Charles. It is one of the most amazing reversals of role I have come across. Little by little Charles became hungry for God in a fresh way. His story is written up elsewhere. The bottom line: after a long while Charles became willing to ask this prisoner to lay hands on him—with the prison guards watching. He invited the Holy Spirit to fall on him without any preconditions. He was filled with the Holy Spirit that day and was never to be the same again. He was eventually forced to resign his church.

I am not sure exactly when I first heard the word *cessationist.* It was certainly after I met some Reformed ministers back in 1956. The funny thing was this. They all welcomed me warmly as a Nazarene who now embraced sovereign grace. They thought this was amazing! But I was also an enigma to them. Given the supernatural manner by which I came to embrace the doctrines of sovereign grace, they struggled with me. My experience went against their own assumption about God doing supernatural things today.

They were cessationists; they subscribed to what I believe to be an unbiblical view—that God by His own will "ceased" long ago to deal with His people in a direct manner supernaturally. No more supernatural healings. No visions, no direct revelation. None of the gifts of the Holy Spirit in operation. When did God first withhold His power? Some say around AD 70. This meant that the Holy Spirit worked powerfully for the first generation of the church alone. Some, however, think the year 100 was when the power diminished (when the apostle John died). Some stretch the period of supernatural power to the era of Constantine (d. 337). In any case, with the choice of the canon of Scripture led by Athanasius (296–373) finally agreed upon, there was no need for supernatural power. That kind of power was a launching pad for the earliest church, giving the Christian faith credibility and encouragement. But at any rate, the gifts of the Spirit, including speaking in tongues, healing, prophecy, and receiving direct revelation by the Holy Spirit, eventually ceased.

There were a good number of Reformed ministers who came to our services at Westminster Chapel who were cessationists. Some of them became my friends. But you might be forgiven for thinking there could be a strong similarity to cessationism and the teaching of deism. Deism is a belief in God that seems harmless if not respectable at first. Many of the Founding Fathers of the American Constitution were deists. But they deny supernatural revelation. Some refer to the deist God as an "absentee watchmaker"—He made the world but then left it to run on its own. Deists believe in one God but could not accept the supernatural. Cessationists do believe in the supernatural in Scripture of course, but have no expectation that God will intervene supernaturally today except, perhaps, through providence. But the notion of the gifts of the Spirit being in operation today, as in 1 Corinthians 12:10–12, is out of the question.

THE ORIGIN OF CESSATIONISM

As every Christian is worth understanding, so is nearly every movement in the history of the Christian church. Sometimes movements are reactions to extremes. Agree or disagree, Rolfe Barnard—who was no charismatic—used to say, "If we Baptists had been what we should have been, there never would have been a Salvation Army, and there never would have been a Pentecostal movement." Dr. Michael Eaton suggests that there are two things worth noting about the origin of cessationism.

1. The intellectualism of the Reformers

This is no doubt part of the explanation. As far as I can tell, cessationism sprang up in the sixteenth century, led by the Martin Luthers and John Calvins of this world. The last thing on their minds, however, was to cause a teaching to spring forth that could be unhelpful. In Luther's immortal hymn "A Mighty Fortress Is Our God," you will come across the line "the Spirit and the gifts are ours."[2] But don't hastily assume he believed we should expect to receive the gifts of the Spirit. There are of course exceptions, but intellectuals are often suspicious of anything emotional. Christian intellectuals sometimes tend to fear any emphasis on experiencing God directly. Calvin's doctrine of the inner testimony of the Spirit was not what Dr. Martyn Lloyd-Jones meant by the immediate and direct witness of the Spirit. To Calvin, the inner testimony of the Spirit meant the "analogy of faith," based upon Romans 12:6 (ESV): prophesying, that is, preaching, should be done according to one's "proportion" (Greek *analogia*) of faith. This means comparing Scripture with Scripture. Few if any have exceeded Calvin since in the ability to expound Holy Scripture. And yet Calvin himself, referring to the anointing of oil for healing in James 5:14, said that this refers to "miraculous powers which the Lord was pleased to give for a time."[3] It was relevant only to the apostles and "pertains not to us, to whom no such powers have been committed."[4]

2. The charistmatics of the sixteenth century

They are also called mystics. Luther tried to find help from them and embraced them for a while. But they severely let him down. Their way of reading the Scripture was allegorical and not likely to convince anyone such as Calvin, who was trained in reading texts in their historical context and with linguistic accuracy. The charismatics and mystics of the sixteenth century were famous for their instability and eccentricity. You could therefore say that the Reformed tradition inherited a fear of the charismatic.

B. B. Warfield (1851–1921) was a great opponent of mysticism. He disliked the tendency in his day to move away from apologetics and put more trust in the witness of the Spirit. There are Christians who are no doubt too intellectualist; there are those who are also too anti-intellectualist. There are those who are too emotional—today we might call them *flakes*; there are those who are too anti-emotional. Dr. Lloyd-Jones would say that man is made up of heart, mind, and will. The mind is given to think, the heart to feel, and a will whereby he can act. It is not always easy to maintain the balance, but we should try.

One should never underestimate our cessationist friends' love for God, Scripture, sound teaching, and holy living. They are the salt of the earth. Some of them are among the greatest vanguards of Christian orthodoxy. I repeat: they certainly *do* accept the miraculous in the Bible. They simply do not believe that God reveals Himself immediately and directly by revelation any more. God of course *could* do it; He has sovereignly chosen not to show His power as He did in the earliest church. The absence of power therefore is not owing to our unbelief, lack of faith, or expectancy. God Himself decided that kind of power was for the earliest church. Any amount of praying, fasting, intercession, and waiting on God will not bring about His power. You cannot twist God's arm to do what He decreed *isn't going to happen.*

And yet that was indeed what happened to me. I don't think the Nazarenes in my day had a clue what cessationism is. I'm glad I didn't know about it; otherwise I might never have cried out to God for help that Monday morning. Cessationism is pretty much a Reformed point of view. I found out later just how much the very experience of October 31, 1955, annoyed many high Calvinists and went right against the Reformed theology of these men whose theology I embraced! I realize now it was silly of me that I wondered for a while, in the days immediately following my experience, if I discovered something new, or if I was the first since Paul to see these things. It was certainly not new revelation—except that the things I saw were *new to me.* Hardly any of my old Nazarene friends truly understood what happened to me or the theology I was beginning to embrace. Many Reformed ministers accepted me warmly but remained perplexed at how I could see the teaching of predestination, election, and the eternal security of the believer without reading John Calvin or his followers. They had been spoon-fed the "five points of Calvinism" (following the acrostic TULIP = total depravity, unconditional election, limited atonement, irresistible grace, and perseverance of the saints). They knew I would not have gotten this from Nazarenes. When I relayed to them the aforementioned experience—including the vision of Jesus—they would respond with a polite silence.

Be Fair With Cessationists

I can truly sympathize with cessationism. The people who adhere to cessationism would by and large change their stance if they saw hard evidence of undoubted miracles today. Cessationists do not want to appear smug or unreachable; they simply *do not believe* the claims of charismatics and Pentecostals who have reportedly seen the miraculous. They are not questioning our honesty; they feel we have been either too optimistic, perhaps gullible, if not actually deceived. Furthermore, cessationists understandably get turned off by flamboyant healing evangelists who make their extravagant claims. Those people who are said to be *slain in the Spirit* and fall backward are also supposedly healed. That is certainly the impression that is given. But when honest skeptics—who want to get to the bottom of the claims—go back to these same people to interview them, the results are often rather sobering. It often turns out that very few, if any, were actually healed. This scenario has been repeated again and again. It is a bit like the claim I mentioned earlier when people say, "The Holy Ghost fell on us," only to find out it wasn't the presence of the Dove but pigeon religion.

I find it disquieting too when prominent healing evangelists absolutely forbid people in wheelchairs from being pushed to the front of the auditorium before the services. Ushers are positively told *not* to let people in wheelchairs be positioned near the stage; it draws attention to them, especially when the handicapped people are not called out to be prayed for. But in the years between 1949 to 1951 it was very different. I have good reason to believe that healings of crippled people actually took place. People in wheelchairs were welcomed—and often healed. They often carried their own wheelchairs back to their cars. And they stayed healed. I will tell you why I believe this. I have personally talked with three men (and others who knew them well) who were very prominent in the healing ministry in the 1950s. They have shown me photographs, letters, and testimonies of people who wrote to them. I got close enough to some of these men to know they were not making things up. What convinced me further is when they also admitted that the healings came to a halt. They were vulnerable to admit to this. It made me feel that the photographs and letters were genuine. But for some reason the miraculous healings diminished in the 1950s, although some of the evangelists did their best to keep praying for people as they had previously done—but with fewer results.

MY OWN HYPOTHESIS

Cessationism is a hypothesis. It is not a teaching grounded in Holy Scripture—like the virgin birth, the deity of Christ, the resurrection of Jesus, and salvation by the blood of God's Son. Cessationists have *chosen* to believe that God does not reveal Himself directly and immediately today. I also think many cessationists would sincerely welcome supernatural healing if they actually saw a person healed or if they themselves were healed (should they become willing to be prayed for)—and remained healed. Most cessationists would be thrilled with a miracle—if indeed it was genuine and had the undisputed facts *before* the healing and *after* the healing. Sometimes this actually happens—when a cessationist is convinced of a miracle and changes his or her views. But not often. Why? I cannot be sure.

But I have my own hypothesis: it is to test the faith of those who actually see the miraculous but have to enjoy it in relative solitude, without their friends being convinced. That solitude can in a sense become downright painful—when one's integrity is questioned and yet they know for a fact what God did. It is like the earliest church being convinced of Jesus's resurrection—whether they saw the resurrected Christ or because of the immediate and direct witness of the

Spirit—so real to them and so foreign to others. I will return to my hypothesis shortly.

I do know that some cessationists understandably become open to the miraculous when one of their own loved ones becomes seriously ill. God sometimes uses a critical illness to get our attention. I don't mean to be unfair, but there is nothing that changes the mind-set of a cessationist like one's own fatal illness or the serious sickness of a loved one. That often makes them open in way they would not have been before. General Douglas MacArthur used to say, "There are no atheists in foxholes." So too desperation is something God may use to give us a wake-up call.

What causes some cessationists to dig in their heels is not only the lack of hard evidence but also that the claims to healing miracles are so often surrounded with Hollywood-style showmanship and questionable teaching. These television evangelists sometimes appear like movie stars who love the attention. It seems to me that this is far removed from the humility of the early apostles.

But what would also worry me is this: if cessationists would be *disappointed* if the irrefutable evidence of genuine healings came forth. It is surely not good if they turned the hypothesis of cessationism into a dogma—and then would resent it if a person were miraculously healed. If only such people would uphold cessationism as plan B in the event God might intervene and show His undoubted power.

But now to return to my own hypothesis. What if God in some cases *keeps* some skeptics from seeing the miraculous even though it actually takes place? What if miracles are largely for those believers in God's family who have accepted the stigma of being "outside the camp" (Heb. 13:13)? After all, why didn't the resurrected Christ appear to everybody on Easter Sunday? One might choose to argue that this would have been a reasonable thing to do if God truly wanted everybody to believe on His Son. Why did Jesus reveal Himself only to a few? Why didn't Jesus knock on Pontius Pilate's door on Easter morning and say, "Surprise!"? Why didn't Jesus go straight from the empty tomb to Herod's palace and say, "Bet you weren't expecting Me!" He appeared only to a few—those who were His faithful followers.

I also suspect that God sometimes allows just a *little bit of doubt* when it comes to the objective proof of the miraculous. This keeps us humbled. And sobered. Pastor Colin Dye of London's Kensington Temple has put it like this:

> Miracles always leave room for doubt as they were not intended to replace faith, only to reveal the heart. Also, the fact that Jesus' miracles in Galilee were not believed shows that the very best of them were not knock down proofs for those who are hard of heart and unbelieving, and to reject their testimony is to bring greater judgment on those who witness them. Perhaps it is out of God's mercy that God is pleased sometimes to withhold them, at least until the time is right to bring to light the true state of people's hearts—to bring in the elect and to reveal the apostates.[5]

Perhaps you and I need patience while our friends or loved ones are totally convinced that "there's nothing to it" when it comes to the miraculous. After all, how could Peter prove that Jesus had ascended to the right hand of God on the Day of Pentecost? He couldn't. But he believed it. And all the rest could do was to believe his word—or reject it.

Jesus was "vindicated by the Spirit" (1 Tim. 3:16) in the days of His earthly ministry. This meant He got His approval through the Holy Spirit from the Father alone—not from people's approval. It also referred to His followers who were drawn to Him in faith by the Holy Spirit. Faith is a gift of God (Acts 13:48; Eph. 2:8–9). This means that those who believed in Jesus had been drawn to Him by the Spirit (John 6:44). Jesus's vindication by the Holy Spirit continues to this day. Even though He is at the right hand of God and is highly exalted in heaven, the only ones who *believe* this are those whose hearts have been drawn to Him by the Holy Spirit.

My hypothesis then is that the principle of vindication by the Spirit is at stake when it comes to the miraculous. Vindication by the Spirit is an *internal* vindication. The Holy Spirit witnesses in our hearts. Furthermore, those who are faithful believers in Jesus's power today are more likely to see His healing miracles than those who say, "I will believe it when I see it." In other words, as Jesus appeared to those who were previously drawn to Him, it may be that God shows His manifest power to those who have previously *believed* He is willing to show His glory.

So could it be that God withholds the lack of hard evidence to skeptical people for *our* sakes? If so, it becomes a rather huge testing for us. The issue is this: Will you and I still be faithful without our cessationist friends seeing God's manifest power for themselves? Many of us would so *love* to be openly vindicated. But what if God is behind the withholding of His manifest power to our critics in order that we get our vindication not from people's approval but from the Father alone? This would mean that we too are vindicated by the Spirit—His internal witness—and not by the external, visible, and tangible proofs of His power.

God could show His healing power at any moment. A few years ago I received a curt letter from a very close friend. He lovingly chided me for my associations with Pentecostals and charismatics. But since he wrote me that letter, his own daughter became critically ill and was expected to die. The very charismatics he would not normally turn to prayed for his beloved daughter. She was gloriously healed. And stayed healed. My friend made a 180-degree turn. He announced to his friends, "I am a Baptist charismatic."

But why doesn't God do that all the time? You tell me.

My point is simply this. Let us not live for the vindication of our theological views. God wants us to receive the praise that comes from Him alone (John 5:44). If we became openly vindicated of our position that God manifests His power and glory today through the gifts of the Spirit, we might succumb to the praise of people. We could. We all have fragile egos. God forbid that this should happen to us—that we would start saying, "I told you so."

Chapter Nine

THE CONSEQUENCES
OF CESSATIONISM

Wisdom is proved right by her actions.

—MATTHEW 11:19

One of these days someone is going to come along and pick up a Bible and believe it—and put the rest of us to shame.[1]

—ROLFE BARNARD
(1901–1968)

I**T IS MY VIEW THAT CESSATIONISM QUENCHES THE HOLY SPIRIT.** As we have seen, it is easy to grieve the Holy Spirit—by bitterness, anger, and not totally forgiving those who have hurt us. God won't bend the rules for any of us, and if we do not overcome bitterness, the Dove will not come down on us and remain. You and I will see fresh things in Scripture to the degree that the Holy Spirit is ungrieved in us. Such insights will not come owing to our education or intellect; it is the Holy Spirit Himself who will give us full assurance of understanding (Col. 2:2). It is also easy to quench the Holy Spirit. We quench the Spirit largely by unbelief or fear—being too cautious lest we allow the counterfeit to take over. But this, sadly, could lead to spending all our lives being governed by caution and never seeing the glory of God openly displayed.

The Holy Spirit can therefore be quenched by a doctrine that does not allow for Him to show up.

It seems to me that cessationists have uncritically imbibed the otherwise outstanding teaching of B. B. Warfield and J. Gresham Machen (1881–1937) and, like so many, turned cessationism into a *dogma*. It is one thing to hold cessationism as a possible theory, quite another when cessationism becomes normative teaching to which a person must subscribe in order to become a minister—or hold on to their position in the church.

If you are a cessationist, would you be willing to go to the stake for your cessationist belief?

It also seems to me that one of the more serious fallouts of being a cessationist is that it can eliminate any expectancy for God to work powerfully in our hearts and lives. One may become too content with his or her sheer intellectual grasp of the gospel. The consequence is that we don't even consider—much less expect—that God will manifest His power in our lives. As we will see in chapter 10—"The Baptism With the Holy Spirit"—cessationism is consistent with the view that all Christians are baptized with the Holy Spirit at conversion. If you take that position, such a Christian never expects *more* after being saved.

Dr. Michael Eaton also points out that there are other matters that cessationist teaching has affected, one of which is *mission*. Until the time of William Carey (1761–1834), many Christians believed that the Great Commission—"Go and make disciples of all nations" (Matt. 28:19)—was for the first generation of the apostles only. This was a kind of cessationism that delayed the missionary movement. Carey put his case for reaching the heathen all over the world to a ministerial meeting in Northampton, England, in 1786. The moderator's famous words to Carey were: "Sit down, young man! When God is pleased to convert the heathen, He will do it without your aid, or mine."[2] Whereas the moderator was chiefly governed by his own doctrine of election, there was equally a tradition in those days that the Great Commission was no longer relevant. Carey therefore had to overcome a rather different kind of cessationism. But he wonderfully succeeded in the end. That said, Reformed cessationists today generally no longer believe that the Great Commission was limited to the first century. This shows they can change.

Although there is more than one kind of cessationism, as we will see further below, some cessationists take the view that Paul actually forecast cessationism when he said prophecies would pass away, tongues would cease, and that the "perfect" would come (1 Cor. 13:8–10). Some take the "perfect" to be the Bible—when the church finally agreed upon the exact canon of Scripture. Whereas I too agree that the Bible is perfect, that is not what Paul means in 1 Corinthians 13. While it could be argued that the "perfect" refers to when we are in heaven, Paul surely meant "perfect love," which my book *Just Love* (a verse-by-verse exposition of 1 Corinthians 13) shows.[3]

Some cessationists build their case on what John declared at the end of the Book of Revelation—the last book of the Bible. He gave a solemn warning: "If anyone takes away from the words of the book of this prophecy, God will take away his share in the tree of life and in the holy city, which are described in this book" (Rev. 22:19, ESV). Because it is the last book in the formation of the canon, they take "this book" to refer to the entire Bible, whereas John surely meant that we should not add or take away from the Book of Revelation itself. Some cessationists also quote Hebrews 2:4, that God "testified" to our great salvation by signs, wonders, and various miracles—as if miracles were only a thing of the past. This could hardly be the position of the writer of the Epistle to the Hebrews who urges people to come into full assurance and experience God directly swearing an oath to them (Heb. 4:1; 6:9–20).

Dr. Martyn Lloyd-Jones used to say again and again: "The Bible was not given to replace the miraculous but to correct abuses."

Such abuses sometimes arise in the context of visions, dreams, and perceiving a direct word from the Holy Spirit. I myself have experienced visions, dreams, and direct words that I believe were from the

Lord. As for dreams, it is a vast subject that deserves separate treatment, but covering this is beyond the level of my competence. As for direct words from God, this has happened to me probably five or six times. Dr. Lloyd-Jones told me how he came to write his book *Spiritual Depression*. On the Sunday morning he had planned to begin his sermons on Ephesians, the Holy Spirit spoke directly to him as he was getting dressed for church. "As I lifted my braces [suspenders] over my shoulders, I was suddenly told, 'You are not to begin your sermons on Ephesians. You are to speak for the next several weeks on the subject of spiritual depression.'" He said he hurried to his dresser to reach for a pen and paper and wrote down the titles of each sermon as fast as he could write as he was given them in chronological order. His book *Spiritual Depression*—possibly my favorite of all his books— came out years before his series on Ephesians and has been a blessing to thousands.

In a word: the cessationist view is not only weak, but it also has no biblical warrant to uphold this teaching. There is no mandate in Scripture to take a stand for what is speculative teaching at best. These people are putting all their eggs into one basket, assuming they are right about the miraculous today. I sometimes fear they are gambling that their view about God not performing miracles any more is true. This to me is serious—and a very precarious position to take, namely, ruling out categorically the possibility of God manifesting His glory in signs and wonders today and deleting a great portion of the Bible for today. Consider how much the Bible has to say about God's power. Healing. Signs and wonders. Revelation of truth by the Holy Spirit. Consider what is left in Holy Scripture when you rule out the miraculous or the gifts of the Holy Spirit. Try this: take scissors; work your way through the New Testament and cut out every reference to healing, miraculous power, or spiritual gifts. See what you have left—a Bible in shreds.

Take, for example, a new convert. He or she assumes the Bible is true or that person would not have received Christ as Lord and Savior. This person assumes that one can believe all of the Bible. When a person is converted and is given a Bible to start reading, he or she assumes that the God of the Bible is the same God as ours; that Jesus Christ truly is the same yesterday and today and forever (Heb. 13:8). Unless the minister steps in quickly to say, "Oh by the way, when you read the New Testament—especially the four Gospels and the Book of Acts and a lot of 1 Corinthians—don't start thinking these things can happen today," the new child of God will assume the Bible is to be believed—and practiced. What a disappointment—possibly disillusionment—when the new Christian is told, "Don't expect to see anybody healed. Ignore that part of 1 Corinthians that talks about the gifts of the Spirit. That part of the Bible was only relevant two thousand years ago. And don't go around anointing people with oil. All that is finished."

Fortunately the cessationist perspective did not hit the third world before the gospel spread into Latin America, South America, Africa, or Indonesia. Or Singapore. Malaysia. China. Christianity has invaded these countries with a tremendous surge of power in recent decades. Virtually all of them are charismatic or Pentecostal and practice the gifts of the Holy Spirit unhindered. Are we to think it is strange fire that has broken out in these nations? Or is it not holy fire?

THE GOD WHO HIDES HIS FACE

The cessationist point of view has basically one purpose: to explain why miracles do not happen. By the way, it is granted that miracles do not always happen. They didn't always happen even during the apostolic era. Paul told Timothy not to drink water but take a little wine for his stomach and frequent illnesses (1 Tim. 5:23). Why didn't Paul pray for him to get well or ask Timothy to pray for himself to get well? Paul said that he left Trophimus "sick" in Miletus (2 Tim. 4:20). Why? That was during the time when miracles had not *ceased*. It is granted that there was an apparent diminishing of power and miracles before the age of St. Augustine and St. Athanasius. Why?

I can attempt an answer as to why God does not always heal and why He can manifest His power in one generation and bypass the next. It is because it is one of God's sovereign prerogatives to hide His face. "Truly you are a God who hides himself, O God of Israel, the Savior"

(Isa. 45:15, ESV). He said He would have mercy on whom He will have mercy (Rom. 9:15). Jesus almost certainly walked through the temple gate Beautiful many times where a forty-year-old lame man lay. And Jesus walked on by—possibly dozens of times. So did the disciples after Pentecost. Then one day, suddenly Peter and John said to the same crippled man, "Look at us!," and he was instantly healed (Acts 3:1–8).

What if there had been no great thinkers such as Augustine or Athanasius for hundreds of years? Would we be compelled to say, "God doesn't use great intellects any more"? That is the principle that cessationism is based on: since there were so few miracles after the canon of Scripture was complete, some concluded we don't need them since we have the Bible. Likewise we should not need great minds either! But we do need them, and thank God when He does raise up an Athanasius or a Jonathan Edwards. Cessationists erected a doctrine to justify the absence of miracles, even implying that God never intended signs and wonders and miracles to extend beyond a certain period. As a consequence of this teaching, cessationists sometimes feel forced to deny anything that smacks of the supernatural. I know some are so defensive for their cessationism that they choose to call anything supernatural demonic! I have had them actually admit this to me. Some are ready to affirm the demonic, but not the Holy Spirit! And if it is miraculous or supernatural, *it must be of Satan* because God doesn't perform miracles today! I am sure there must be exceptions, but the cessationists I know do not even believe that the church can cast out demons, for that would be a miracle. In a word: the devil has power and has freedom to show it. But not the church. God has purposefully and strategically handcuffed His servants from praying for the sick, casting out demons, or hearing a word directly from the Holy Spirit.

I will never forget Dr. Martyn Lloyd-Jones addressing the Westminster Fellowship on this. It was the practice of the Westminster Fellowship, which met the first Monday of each month at Westminster Chapel, to deal with a question that one of the ministers put. One day the subject was cessationism. There were those present who held to this. Some had been influenced by B. B. Warfield, the famous theologian of Princeton University, and J. Gresham Machen, the main founder of the Orthodox Presbyterian Church. These were great men. I thank God for them. They were called to be staunch believers of Holy Scripture and fight error in their day. Warfield had observed the extremism and superficiality in the latter part of ministry of Charles Finney (1792–1875), and Warfield felt obliged to produce a teaching to fight the spreading of fanaticism. But Dr. Lloyd-Jones did not agree with these great men when it came to the issue of cessationism. "Am I to believe," Dr. Lloyd-Jones said that morning, "that demon possession still exists, but that we are necessarily helpless to deal with such?"

MORE THAN ONE KIND OF CESSATIONIST

Some cessationists believe that God ordained the miraculous only for one generation (the strongest form), while some say the miraculous era extended to the days of Constantine. Some cessationists believe that the miraculous ceased with the established church (as in the West), but that God may bring about the miraculous in unevangelized areas (as in the third world) in order to authenticate the gospel. There are hints of this point of view in Martin Luther and John Calvin. There are other cessationists who believe that God may work through supernatural Providence and provide miraculous guidance. Some might even allow for the occasional healing as long as it does not suggest new revelation.

Dr. Lloyd-Jones was fond of telling of the well-documented account of the son-in-law of John Knox (1514–1572), who was raised from the dead! No one appeared to dispute this at the time. For further reading, see Jack Deere's *Surprised by the Power of the Spirit*.[4]

There are many church leaders who are open to the Spirit and who have had a taste of the gifts of the Spirit. There are a growing number of pastors like this. They want to see the Word and Spirit come together. There are leaders who are so cautious that nearly any move of the Spirit that comes along tends to be rejected by them. They truly are open to the supernatural and the miraculous in theory—but with their seatbelts firmly fastened! I understand that. I do not criticize them. My fear is that in their caution they—just maybe—unwittingly quench the Holy Spirit and could therefore miss out on what God may be doing today. My old friend Rolfe Barnard often referred to Jonathan Edwards, who taught us that the task of every generation is to discover in which direction the Sovereign Redeemer is going, then move in that direction. How do we discover in which direction the Sovereign Redeemer is moving? I think it requires our being vulnerable and to stop worrying what people will think of us. I would encourage you to throw caution to the wind and become more vulnerable.

There is no need to miss the blessing of the Holy Spirit because of our fears. Reformed people today tend to applaud the ministry and success of someone like George Whitefield (1714–1770)—whom God used mightily in England and New England. But I wonder what they would have thought had they been alive then and seen some of the fallout of his preaching—when people laughed, cried, shouted, and barked like dogs! Many cessationists today would have called George Whitefield's ministry *strange fire*.

John Wesley (1703–1791) fiercely criticized Whitefield for allowing fanaticism to exist under his preaching. Whitefield acknowledged that not all that took place under his ministry was of God. Some of it was of the flesh indeed. "Then stamp out the flesh and what is false," countered Wesley.

"But," said Whitefield, "if you stamp out what is of the flesh you will stamp out what is real as well." You have to let what happens flow. It is part of the stigma of true revival. Nothing is perfect in this life. In other words, when God comes in power, you should *expect* to see things that make you cringe. But we should not let this stop us from welcoming the Holy Spirit with open arms—even if the devil gets involved too. Expect this. Revival simply does not come in a neat and tidy package.

The boldest public decision I ever made was to invite Arthur Blessitt (who carries a cross around the world—he holds the Guinness Book of Records for the longest walk) to Westminster Chapel in April and May 1982. It was the best decision I made in my twenty-five years there. But my heart sank again and again during those six weeks. Before he agreed to accept my invitation to stay with us for the whole month of May, he had asked, "Are you going to handcuff me or let me be myself?" Oh, dear.

I then replied, "I promise to let you be yourself." I was true to my word, and he was truly himself! I died a thousand deaths as I watched the unusual things that happened, and I was personally confronted with hard lessons of obedience. It was the Wesley-Whitefield scenario described above that got me through those weeks. I nearly lost my job over having him. But I never was sorry; it opened the door for me to remember my reputation as unimportant as it was and go all out for whatever God may want to do.

We eventually became open to the prophetic type of ministry as well. This was totally new to all of us. Even though I later became disappointed with some of the conduct in their personal lives, we as a church were still all the better for inviting people such as this. We also began offering the anointing of oil, inviting people to come forward to be prayed for if they were unwell. (See James 5:14–16.) There was little indication at first whether anyone was healed. Then one day I received a letter from a man in Scotland who said that two years before, when he was in London, he came to Westminster Chapel. He had never been in a church where they had the anointing of oil. So he decided to come forward since nobody knew who he was—what did he have to lose? He had a problem with vertigo for several years, even having to spend three or four hours each day lying in a cot at his place of work. When he returned to Glasgow on the Monday after, he noticed he was not dizzy all day. Or the next. After six weeks he removed the cot. He never needed it again. He waited two years to tell me!

We slowly began to hear of other people who were healed. One Sunday evening a lady from Chile came up to me and said in broken English, "Pray for my husband. Last week you healed me, now heal him."

I said, "What? I healed you?"

"Yes. I had a snake bite in Chile many years ago. My right leg has been swollen—huge. Big. You prayed for me last Sunday night. On Monday morning the leg was the same size as the other. No doctor. No medicine. Now heal my husband."

I then asked him, "What's your problem?"

"I don't sleep," he replied. "I haven't had a full night's sleep in twenty-five years. The spirits keep kicking me out of bed." (We found out later his mother was a witch.)

I asked a deacon to join me in anointing him with oil. I suppose some would advise me to cast the demon out. But we anointed him with oil. The following Sunday he returned to say, "I slept three nights this week, first time in twenty-five years. Would you have another go?" We prayed for him again. The following week he said he slept "like a baby" all week. He was still sleeping like a baby when we retired.

Had I not taken a few risks in 1982, I would have probably continued to wait indefinitely for God to move in with power that would knock everybody down. I am so glad we did not wait that long. Jesus said whoever is faithful in that which is least will be faithful in much (Luke 16:10).

The members of Westminster Chapel well recall a serious cough that my wife, Louise, had. It went on for about three years. It was horrible. Five nights out of seven she would sleep in a different room to keep from waking me up. We had hoped the clear air in Florida during our summer holidays would solve the problem. It didn't. Our local physician finally sent her to the Brompton Hospital (heart and lung specialists) in London. It did no good. On one occasion Louise went to the emergency room at St. Thomas Hospital in London with an eye problem that was caused by the cough. The ophthalmologist told Louise that if she didn't stop coughing, she would end up with a detached retina. Those were awful days; I worried that I might have to resign my ministry and return to America.

We had prayed for her again and again. But a man I hardly knew offered to pray for her. He and his wife kindly came to Westminster Chapel one Saturday morning to pray for her. Louise had been up most of the night from the cough but said, "I want that man to pray for me." She was barely awake but managed to get to the church. There was no hype, no worship, no warning her, "You must believe." None of that. They just prayed for her for some five minutes, laying hands on her (and praying in tongues). That's all.

She was instantly healed. That was in December 1994. It was Louise's healing that made it easy for us to continue in the things of the Holy Spirit at Westminster Chapel. All knew it had to be genuine. The horrible coughing never returned. Her eyesight is fine. More than that, it changed Louise's own prayer life. She wanted more and more quiet time with the Lord and His Word—an hour or more a day whenever she could.

Word of this spread to a lot of places. A physician whose husband was churchwarden of a prominent Anglican church came up to me at a reception to ask about Louise. After I told her, she looked at me and said with tears, "I would give anything in the world if that sort of thing would happen to me." This surprised me, and yet it shouldn't have.

What is regarded as the lunatic fringe in American Christianity is virtually mainstream in Great Britain. There have been two different Archbishops of Canterbury in recent years who are regarded as charismatic. And it is often the upper-class society of England that has been the most open to the immediate work of the Spirit.

And yet we got a letter a few months after Louise's healing from a physician in Yorkshire who wanted us to know that what happened to her was entirely psychosomatic—that it was the power of suggestion that caused her healing! Louise had been in an almost comatose condition that morning she was healed. Barely awake, she just sat as they prayed. "I had no faith at all," Louise has often said. As to why she was not healed through our own weekly ministry of anointing of oil, you tell me. Perhaps to open our chapel people to a wider perspective as opposed to being too insular. But we never looked back, only thanking God for what He did for us.

To quote Rolfe Barnard again, the legendary Reformed evangelist who ministered throughout America, who used to say: "One of these days somebody is going to come along and pick up a Bible and believe it—and put the rest of us to shame."

Chapter Ten

THE BAPTISM WITH
THE HOLY SPIRIT

For John baptized with water, but in a few days you will
be baptized with the Holy Spirit.... You will receive power
when the Holy Spirit comes on you; and you will be my
witnesses in Jerusalem, and in all Judea and Samaria, and
to the ends of the earth.

—ACTS 1:5–8

If we function according to our ability alone, we get the
glory; if we function according to the power of the Spirit
within us, God gets the glory.[1]

—HENRY T. BLACKABY

T HE NEW TESTAMENT TEACHING REGARDING THE BAPTISM
with the Holy Spirit has been immersed in controversy, especially during the last century. For one thing, should it be called baptism *in* the Holy Spirit, *by* the Holy Spirit, or *with* the Holy Spirit? And
should we be talking about the baptism *of* the Holy Spirit? My own
opinion is, it does not matter. Historical controversies often center on
terms that can divide unnecessarily. The first reference in the New

Testament to the baptism with the Holy Spirit is that of John the Baptist, who contrasts his baptism with water and Jesus's with the Spirit: "He will baptize you with the Holy Spirit and with fire" (Matt. 3:11; Luke 3:16). Mark's account (Mark 1:8) omits "with fire." John the Baptist also said, "The man on whom you see the Spirit come down [as a dove] and remain is the one who will baptize with the Holy Spirit" (John 1:33). Although John's Gospel has the most to say about the Holy Spirit, John the Baptist's word is the only explicit reference to being baptized with the Spirit in the fourth Gospel. The next reference to the baptism with the Holy Spirit is Luke quoting Jesus just before His ascension to heaven: "For John baptized with water, but in a few days you will be baptized with the Holy Spirit" (Acts 1:5).

When Jesus asked to be baptized by John the Baptist, John tried to deter him: "'I need to be baptized by you, and do you come to me?' Jesus replied, 'Let it be so now; it is proper for us to do this to fulfill all righteousness'" (Matt. 3:14–15). John consented. As soon as Jesus was baptized, "heaven was opened, and he saw the Spirit of God descending like a dove and lighting on him" (v. 16). This is when Jesus Himself was given the Holy Spirit without limit (John 3:34) and became fully conscious of who He was. "A voice from heaven said, 'This is my Son, whom I love; with him I am well pleased'" (Matt. 3:17).

These references show that the baptism with the Spirit is what Jesus does in heaven where He is seated at God's right hand. The experience of people being baptized with the Holy Spirit is obvious in at least five places in the Book of Acts:

1. "All of them were filled with the Holy Spirit and began to speak in other tongues as the Spirit enabled them" (Acts 2:4).

2. "Then Peter and John placed their hands on them, and they received the Holy Spirit" (Acts 8:17).

3. "Placing his hands on Saul, he [Ananias] said, 'Brother Saul, the Lord—Jesus, who appeared to you on the road as you were coming here—has sent me so that you may see again and be filled with the Holy Spirit.' Immediately,

something like scales fell from Saul's eyes, and he could see again" (Acts 9:17–18).

4. "While Peter was still speaking these words, the Holy Spirit came on all who heard the message" (Acts 10:44). We may infer this to be the baptism with the Holy Spirit because Peter, recalling this event to the other disciples, said: "Then I remembered what the Lord had said: 'John baptized with water, but you will be baptized with the Holy Spirit'" (Acts 11:16).

5. "When Paul placed his hands on them, the Holy Spirit came on them, and they spoke in tongues and prophesied" (Acts 19:6).

While the aforementioned references indicate an *initial* baptism with the Spirit, it could be argued that the same phenomenon could happen to the same people again: "Peter, filled with the Holy Spirit, said to them..." (Acts 4:8). Whereas this verse could well have described Peter generally in those days, some scholars believe Peter had a fresh filling then and there as he addressed the rulers and teachers of the Law. If so, this happened to Paul: "Then Saul, who was also called Paul, filled with the Holy Spirit, looked straight at Elymas..." (Acts 13:9). Furthermore, following a great prayer meeting where the place was "shaken" the disciples were "all filled with the Holy Spirit and spoke the word of God boldly" (Acts 4:31). These were possibly fresh baptisms with the Spirit, even if the Pentecostal phenomena of wind and fire were not repeated.

Jesus also used the term *baptism* in an entirely different way. He asked the disciples, "Can you drink the cup I drink or be baptized with the baptism I am baptized with?" His immature disciples hastily replied, "We can" (Mark 10:38–39). They did not know what they were saying. Jesus was speaking of an ordeal not far away—when He would drink the cup the Father had prepared for Him. He later prayed in Gethsemane, "My Father, if it is possible, may this cup be taken from me" (Matt. 26:39). Jesus was speaking of a baptism of incalculable suffering, one that meant physical pain, rejection, injustice, and the worst imaginable ordeal—that of the cross. "I have a baptism to undergo, and how distressed I am until it is completed" (Luke 12:50).

The word *baptize* technically means, "to be immersed or drenched." And yet the Spirit is said to *fall* or *come* on people (Acts 8:16, KJV; 10:44, KJV). The disciples were to be clothed with power "from on high" (Luke 24:49), which means the Spirit comes down from heaven. Some are adamant that the baptism with the Spirit is an initial once-for-all experience; others (such as Dr. Martyn Lloyd-Jones) believe it can happen again and again. It seems to me there is nothing to prohibit the Holy Spirit falling on a person repeatedly, whether the person had already been baptized, or drenched, with the Spirit.

There were at least two movements that emerged in the early twentieth century that frequently used the term *baptism with the Holy Spirit*. The best known is that which came largely out of the Azusa Street Mission in Los Angeles, California, in 1906. The Holy Spirit fell on this group in great power, and speaking in tongues became prominent. Classic Pentecostalism owes its existence to the Azusa Street meetings. The baptism with the Holy Spirit became synonymous with speaking in tongues. The second movement was the early Holiness movement, which gave rise to the Church of the Nazarene in 1908. Having its roots in Wesleyan perfectionism, the Church of the Nazarene taught that baptism with the Holy Spirit was connected to their doctrine of entire sanctification. Nazarenes taught that sanctification was an experience to be received, but it had nothing to do with tongues. Indeed, the original name Pentecostal Church of the Nazarene became Church of the Nazarene, as they wanted to be sure nobody confused them with the "tongues movement," as it was called.

There are therefore at least three views regarding the baptism with the Holy Spirit. First, the prevailing conservative evangelical view is that the baptism with the Spirit is an unconscious event that comes to every believer at conversion. This would be the Reformed view of the baptism with the Spirit. The biblical support for this view, as held by the late Dr. John R. W. Stott (1921–2011), is based almost entirely on 1 Corinthians 12:13: "For we were all baptized by one Spirit into one body—whether Jews or Greeks, slave or free—and we were all given the one Spirit to drink." For conservative evangelicals, this verse is definitive, clear, and final. The baptism with the Spirit is a part of the package when a person is converted, regenerated, or given saving faith. In Christ "you have been enriched in every way." Therefore "you do not lack any spiritual gift as you eagerly wait for our Lord Jesus Christ to be revealed" (1 Cor. 1:5, 7). Some would say this comes at baptism with water. Others teach that saving faith means that the person was baptized with the Holy Spirit. In any case, according to most conservative evangelicals, all Christians have been baptized with the Holy Spirit. Any word to them that they should *also* receive the baptism of the Holy Spirit is seen as redundant. These people are taught and teach that they "got it all" at conversion. Not all who teach that all Christians are baptized with the Spirit at conversion are cessationists, but all cessationists certainly believe that the baptism with the Spirit is given at conversion.

I have referred to the other two views, namely, the Pentecostal view that the baptism with the Holy Spirit is characterized by speaking in tongues, and the Holiness view (Wesleyan), which would include The Salvation Army, that the baptism with the Holy Spirit is entire sanctification but has nothing to do with tongues. As for the Nazarenes, the baptism with the Holy Spirit became normative from 1928 until the 1970s, when it was argued by a number of scholars that John Wesley himself did not believe this. It would seem therefore that Nazarenes are moving away from their traditional view that sanctification was an experience of the baptism with the Spirit. In any case, both the Pentecostal and the traditional Nazarene view have in common that the baptism with the Spirit is (1) conscious and (2) subsequent to being born again.

THE MEANING OF 1 CORINTHIANS 12:13

What then does 1 Corinthians 12:13 mean—that "we were all baptized by one Spirit"? I reply: Being baptized by the Spirit in 1 Corinthians 12:13 certainly (1) refers to one's initial conversion; (2) describes every believer; (3) is what happens objectively to all Christians; (4) is unconscious; (5) is an event, not an experience. There are many references to baptism with water, showing it to be one's first act of obedience after having believed (Acts 2:41; 8:12–13; 16:33; 9:18; 19:3–4, 5; 22:16; 1 Cor. 1:13–16). Paul therefore may be referring obliquely to their baptism by water and shows that the Spirit *also* immerses or drenches all who believe. Paul, in any case, is saying that all Christians have the Holy Spirit, as in Romans 8:9: "And if anyone does not have the Spirit of Christ, he does not belong to Christ." Indeed, all who have been baptized with water have the Holy Spirit, because they believed and repented first.

However, to superimpose Luke's usage of the baptism with the Holy Spirit upon 1 Corinthians 12:13—and to claim that all Christians automatically experience what the earliest church experienced—is incongruous. Paul is not saying all Christians receive the baptism with the Holy Spirit (as described by Luke in the Book of Acts) at conversion. Certainly not. First Corinthians 12:13 is not describing an experience; it refers to an objective, unconscious event. It is therefore not a reference to the baptism with the Holy Spirit as described in the Book of Acts. Neither is it a verse that says you *get it all* at conversion. And to those who would say that 1 Corinthians 12:13 shows you *get it all* at conversion and is supported by 1 Corinthians 1:7 ("You do not lack any spiritual gift"), I ask: Why does Paul urge the Corinthians in the same letter to covet the best spiritual gifts (1 Cor. 12:31)?

It is surely a *given* that the disciples were regenerate prior to the coming of the Spirit at Pentecost. Jesus said they were made "clean." "You are clean, though not every one of you" (John 13:10), the latter part referring to Judas Iscariot who would betray Him. Again, "You are already clean because of the word I have spoken to you" (John 15:3). In the Upper Room on the day of His resurrection, Jesus breathed on the disciples and said, "Receive the Holy Spirit" (John 20:22–23). I am satisfied something happened to them, although I am not sure what. Perhaps it was a further measure of the Spirit and higher level of preparation for what was coming in a few days. We need not be sidetracked on this verse and debate what all happened to them right then, but in any case it may be assumed that the disciples were saved prior to Pentecost despite their lack of acute understanding. It was the baptism with the Holy Spirit that cleared everything up for them.

My point is this. The disciples' experience of the baptism with the Spirit on the Day of Pentecost therefore shows that it was conscious and came to them having believed already.

THE FIRE

What is the meaning of the fire—that Jesus would baptize with the Holy Spirit and with fire? The properties of fire include at least three things: power, illumination, and cleansing. (See Appendix: Fire.) The first thing Jesus mentioned in promising the Spirit was "power" (Luke 24:49; Acts 1:8). This is what enabled the disciples to evangelize with effectiveness and without fear. Second, fire also provided illumination; it is what enabled the disciples to *see* why Jesus died and rose from the dead. The baptism with the Spirit provides great clarification with regard to assurance of salvation and sound teaching. Third, fire cleanses; the baptism with the Holy Spirit cleanses the heart— purifying the heart (Acts 15:9). It does not eradicate the sinful nature, but it enables the heart to focus clearly on what brings honor and glory to God.

Why is it that some Christians are uneasy at the thought that there may be *more* for them after their conversion? Is it something they don't want to think about? Is it something that would challenge their theology? Or pride? Does the idea of a baptism, or sealing, of the Spirit beyond conversion suggest they would have to move out of their comfort zones? Or is it not a thrilling possibility—that of experiencing the power, the peace, and joy from the immediate witness of the Holy Spirit?

When the Samaritans had accepted the Word of God, Peter and John went to see them. The new disciples there wanted more. Peter and John "prayed for them that they might receive the Holy Spirit, because the Holy Spirit had not yet come on any of them; they had simply been baptized in the name of the Lord Jesus. Then Peter and John placed their hands on them, and they received the Holy Spirit" (Acts 8:14–17).

The context shows unmistakably that these people in Samaria—some of whom were healed, some of whom were delivered of evil spirits (Acts 8:7)—had truly believed Philip's word and were already converted. Then did they not already have the Holy Spirit? Of course they did. If they did not have the Spirit, they did not have Christ (Rom. 8:9). No one can say "Jesus is Lord" but by the Holy Spirit (1 Cor. 12:3). They all were baptized by the same Spirit (1 Cor. 12:13). But they wanted more. What was lacking? The conscious baptism with the Spirit. That is what is meant by the words, "The Holy Spirit had not yet come on any of them," although they were baptized (by water). All this goes to show that the baptism with the Holy Spirit is a conscious experience and generally follows one's having believed.

Saul of Tarsus was converted on the road to Damascus, and yet Ananias was sent to him that he might "see again and be filled with the Holy Spirit" (Acts 9:17–19). This is the usual pattern with believers: first, regeneration or saving faith; second, the receiving or baptism with the Holy Spirit. In a word: Paul's filling was (1) subsequent to his conversion, and (2) a conscious experience.

You have a similar pattern later when Paul arrived at Ephesus. He found some disciples there and asked them, "Did you receive the Holy Spirit when you believed?" (Acts 19:2). Why did Paul ask this question? First, he was talking about the baptism with the Spirit when he mentioned the receiving of the Spirit. After all, if they had believed, they would already have the Holy Spirit. We cannot believe apart from the Holy Spirit (John 6:44). Paul could see that a genuine work of regeneration had begun in them. Second, had they "received" the Spirit, they would know it; they would remember it. Receiving the Spirit is a conscious experience. Passive though it is, it is conscious. Third, Paul accepts the obvious fact that they were true believers. He was not questioning whether they were believers; he was questioning whether they had received the baptism with the Holy Spirit. Paul accepts it as a *given* that they had believed. They were regenerate. It was what John Calvin called "implicit" faith—when their understanding was limited but their hearts fully open to what they had heard. Calvin called implicit faith true faith. This is the way he described the woman of Samaria who had fully embraced Jesus but was lacking in understanding (John 4). This was exactly the state of these people at Ephesus. They were believers. They were regenerate. They had a lot to learn. They had not received the baptism with the Spirit. They were hungry. Open. Eager. The proof of this: as soon as Paul told them the next step forward, they accepted his word with both hands. "When Paul placed his hands on them, the Holy Spirit came on them, and they spoke in tongues and prophesied" (Acts 19:6).

Is "Tongues" a Sign of the Holy Spirit?

This brings up the issue whether speaking in tongues is a necessary sign that one has been baptized with the Holy Spirit. Speaking in tongues characterized the disciples at Pentecost (Acts 2:4), Cornelius (Acts 10:46), and the twelve men at Ephesus (Acts 19:6). Nothing is said of speaking in tongues when Peter and John prayed for the people of Samaria (Acts 8:17) or when Paul received the Spirit (Acts 9:18). This does not mean that the Samaritans didn't speak in tongues. Most Pentecostals or charismatics would say they did even though the Word does not say it explicitly. Nor does it mean that Paul did not speak in tongues when Ananias prayed for him. He may have. We certainly know he did later (1 Cor. 14:18). Most Pentecostals and charismatics believe that the baptism with the Spirit is always accompanied with speaking in tongues. According to them, if you don't speak in tongues, you have not been Spirit-filled. The term *Spirit-filled* is often an expression charismatics and Pentecostals use for people who speak in tongues.

But I have to say in all honesty and candor that when I was baptized with the Holy Spirit on October 31, 1955, I did not speak in tongues. This came several months later. Charles Carrin testifies that on the day the prisoner prayed for him and the Holy Spirit came down in power and delivered him of all sorts of rubbish, he still did not speak in tongues; it came several months later. I say this because I think it is a mistake to make *tongues* the proof of having received the Spirit. There are sincere Christian people who may not speak in tongues. For one thing, if one is truly pushed to speak in tongues, they probably will. But is it the *real thing*? There may always be a doubt. Sometimes it is real, but not always. I happen to believe that my Pentecostal and charismatic friends would have greater influence, have more success with non-charismatics, and be more respected if they would cut some slack for those who do not speak in tongues. I also know of sincere people who have tried hard to speak in tongues—but can't.

Dr. Martyn Lloyd-Jones says this about the baptism with the Holy Spirit:

1. It is conscious.

2. It is usually subsequent to a person having believed

3. It is the highest form of assurance.

He loved to quote D. L. Moody's experience. Moody was walking down the streets of Brooklyn, New York, when one day unexpectedly the Spirit of God came down on him. The experience was so powerful that Moody actually thought he would die. He said, "I asked God to stay His hand," lest he die right on the spot. It was that powerful. God can certainly do that for you.

WHAT TO DO NOW?

Can one hasten the coming of the Spirit? Some would say *yes*—just go for it. Some would even encourage you to work it up. One might succeed, but down the road in times of testing the enemy could make a person like that doubt and come to despair. You surely don't want strange fire. What happened to me was passive, out of the blue. Perhaps not so with others. You may have to seek it. You may have to wait. But personally I would be loathe to do anything that might encourage an imitation or counterfeit to come along. The baptism with the Holy Spirit is real. You don't need to work it up. When you seek God with all your heart, you will find Him. "You will seek me and find me when you seek me with all your heart. I will be found by you" (Jer. 29:13–14).

"Let us not become weary in doing good, for at the proper time we will reap a harvest if we do not give up" (Gal. 6:9).

God is never too late, never too early, but always just on time.

Two things often precede the coming of the Spirit. First, a deep hunger. A yearning. A longing for the Holy Spirit to come. It is God's way of testing you to see how important He is to you. Second, although I would not want to push this too far, do not be surprised if there is a bit of suffering—just enough that may drive you to your knees. It is often God's way of getting your attention. Here is a verse that has meant a lot to me in this connection: "And the God of all grace, who called you to his eternal glory in Christ, *after you have suffered a little while*, will himself restore you and make you strong, firm and steadfast. To him be the power for ever and ever. Amen" (1 Pet. 5:10, emphasis added).

Chapter Eleven

GIFTS OF THE SPIRIT

There are different kinds of gifts, but the same Spirit.... Now to each one the manifestation of the Spirit is given for the common good.

—1 Corinthians 12:4, 7

Do not be satisfied with God's calling or his gifts in your life. Be satisfied with Jesus Christ himself.[1]

—Liu Zhenying
(known as Brother Yun)

M ANY YEARS AGO WHEN I WAS PASTOR OF A SMALL CHURCH in Carlisle, Ohio, a man who had been featured in *Time* magazine as being the leader of the glossolalia movement was in the area. (What is now called the charismatic movement was then called glossolalia—taken from the Greek word *glossa*—meaning tongue.) He was there to talk about the baptism of the Holy Spirit. As it happened, I sat across the table from him. He told me that the three most important things to happen to him were becoming a Christian, being baptized with the Holy Spirit, and becoming a Calvinist. He was then a minister in the Reformed Church of America. This got my attention.

He prayed for me to receive the gift of tongues. Since he claimed to be Reformed, I felt safe in letting him pray for me. I remember saying to the Lord, "If this is from You, let it come; if not, stop it." I was as open as I knew how to be. When he prayed, nothing happened. He then said, "Take the verse literally; 'Make a joyful noise unto the Lord.'"

I said, "What do you mean?"

He replied, "Just make a joyful noise." I said that I still didn't understand. He then said, "Just make a noise. Say 'Ah.'"

I said, "Ah." Nothing happened. He told me this had always worked for him.

There are at least two movements to spring up over recent years that have caused great church splits. One is being too zealous about tongues; the other is being too zealous about Calvinism. People who are so zealous for these sometimes make it a priority and become more excited about tongues or Calvinism than they are the gospel and leading people to a saving knowledge of Jesus Christ. Both of these movements sometimes do more harm than good.

That said, there are many sincere believers who have been put off of the gifts of the Spirit by those who may well have had the gift of tongues but not the gift of wisdom. I have not come across many who are zealous to pray for people to receive the gift of wisdom, but there are a lot who are eager to get people to pray in tongues.

However, in this chapter I must also defend some people like this. If you are a conservative evangelical, I understand pretty much how you feel. But try to bear with me. There is no doubt that some of these Christians have been amazingly blessed with a gift of tongues. It is sometimes called a *prayer language*. They pray to God but don't know what they are saying. You may say, "That's silly." But Paul says that is the way it is. What is more, such a person "builds up himself" (1 Cor. 14:4, ESV). Indeed some people are so edified by praying in tongues that they want their friends to enjoy this too. Not only that, strange as this may seem, sometimes God honors this. Yes, I am acknowledging that some people receive the gift of tongues in the very manner I myself rejected, as I said earlier. Suggesting that people speak unintelligible words—gibberish—in order to initiate speaking in tongues sometimes leads to a true gift of tongues. And yet I realize by allowing this possibility I play right into the hands of cynics who look for a good reason to dismiss speaking in tongues categorically.

I concede that some learn to speak in tongues with another person helping them along. It is not always the power of auto suggestion, although this must not be entirely ruled out in some cases. The real reason it sometimes works is because a person is so utterly longing to speak in tongues; I am sure God may well honor such a desire. But also it is because God honors vulnerability and the willingness to be childlike. Or to look foolish. It is not a bad thing when the most sophisticated, cultured, learned, and theologically sound person is willing to do this. Jackie Pullinger is a good example. She is a well-bred upper-class English woman who was in a house prayer meeting in Croydon, Surrey, and heard someone say something about speaking in tongues—the last thing on earth that polished Brits might be interested in. "When I first heard this, I knew this was for me," she said to me.

I met Jackie Pullinger in Hong Kong in the late 1980s. I had been extremely prejudiced against her. I heard tapes of her speaking. She seemed to want to talk about tongues all the time. And yet I wanted to meet her. I was told that she was coming to hear me preach at the Hong Kong Keswick Convention. She invited me to come to her place in Kowloon the next day. I was not prepared for what I saw. There were dozens and dozens of newly converted Chinese ex-drug addicts who were singing choruses and praying in tongues hour after hour. That was virtually all they did. I watched and listened with amazement. I remember watching and hearing them singing, "Give thanks to the risen Lord" (I knew the chorus well, though they were singing in Cantonese). They were doing something for which they had no background or dreamed of doing before.

I asked, "Whatever is going on?" Jackie explained that her ministry was almost totally aimed at heroin addicts in the streets of Hong Kong. Their method was to tell them about Jesus who died for their sins and rose from the dead, and that He is the Son of God and they need to receive Him. Some of them, she said, were so near death that they could barely speak. That did not stop her. She would give them the gospel and ask them to believe in Jesus Christ—that He is the Son of God. As soon as they prayed the sinner's prayer she then told them, "Now start speaking in a language not your own." They had no biases of any kind and dutifully did just that—speaking in an unknown language. They spoke in tongues to come down off heroin. Day after day.

Louise and I went to the old walled city in Hong Kong the next day to watch Jackie minister to drug addicts. While in the walled city some of these new converts asked to pray for Louise—and in minutes Louise began speaking in tongues. These were former drug addicts who now prayed for Christians who come from all over the world to see Jackie's ministry. Louise couldn't believe this had really happened to her. But she was thrilled. She was afraid she would lose it by the next morning. She got up in the middle of the night, fearing it had all been unreal. As she prayed, her prayer language took over! She hadn't lost it! She has been praying in tongues privately every day since.

I preached for Jackie the following Sunday afternoon. I met people who had been converted for a short while and also those who were saved years before. I remember how I could not hold back the tears, just sitting in the service. I had never experienced anything like this before.

The city of Hong Kong eventually gave Jackie acres of property to do her missionary work. They recognized that she was the only person successfully taking drug addicts off the streets. She did what hospitals, psychiatrists, and psychologists failed to do. The hospital successes were abysmal by comparison. Her success was phenomenal. A few of these people who made professions of faith lapsed, yes, but a high number of them persevered and came off heroin entirely and totally. They gained weight, got jobs, and became a part of society doing good. Jackie, by the grace of God, achieved all this by literally getting her converts off drugs through speaking in tongues.

This is why I said above that I must sometimes defend what I had previously criticized.

Strange fire? I don't think so. I met a good number of these converts. They were so impressive. There was no doubt in my mind they were truly converted people. You should also know that Jackie has been in this ministry for more than thirty years. She has become a legend. The skeptical BBC did a documentary about her and found her work to be genuine and the results unexaggerated. She was also awarded the coveted OBE (Order of the British Empire) by Her Majesty the Queen.

It seems to me that there are two levels of openness to the Holy Spirit when it comes to the gift of tongues. First, when one says, "I am willing to speak in tongues if God gives it to me. If He wants me to speak in tongues, let Him do it." I think that was partly my attitude when the previously mentioned Reformed minister prayed for me. After all, spontaneous praying in tongues *did* happen to me in early 1956, except that I was not praying for this. It came to me passively and unexpectedly as I drove in my car. So I know for a fact this sort of thing can happen. But it may not ever happen to those who say, "I am willing to speak in tongues, but I am not going to spell *banana* backward to do so." I sympathize. I would not for a moment suggest that a person start repeating the makes of Japanese cars in rapid succession—"Mitsubishi Mazda Isuzu Honda"—to prime the pump! This manner of getting a person to speak in tongues smacks of strange fire. And yet I believe it is also true that the gift of tongues is likely to come to those who are willing to appear foolish and be not a little bit embarrassed. Although it came to me spontaneously without even dreaming of it, I have had to admit since that it often comes to those who eagerly want it. I always say that the gift of tongues may be at the bottom of Paul's list in 1 Corinthians 12:7–12, but one must be humbly willing to start at the bottom. Take the lowest seat, and you might get upgraded to the gifts that seem more desirable.

SPEAKING IN TONGUES IN
ANY CASE IS LIKELY TO COST YOU

So there is a second level—an eagerness of openness. This level of motivation may seem foreign to some. But not to all. It is when a person is so hungry for more of God that he or she is willing to do almost anything to have a closer relationship with Him. That was Margaret—one of our deacons' wives at Westminster Chapel. She was one of the most respected members of the Chapel in those days and possibly the least likely to speak in tongues. She had never spoken in tongues, but she grew more and more eager to have all of God she could have. When she knew that Jackie Pullinger was going to speak at our annual banquet, Margaret asked to meet her. Jackie prayed with Margaret. Margaret afterward came out of the room with a glow and excitement; she couldn't believe it could happen to her—she spoke in tongues and has done so ever since. But for some reason this did not happen to her husband. "Do all speak with tongues?" Paul asked (1 Cor. 12:30). The obvious answer is *no*. We all need to remember this.

There are those who believe anybody can speak in tongues. I don't believe it. Can anybody have the gift of healing? If the gift of tongues comes by working it up, then, yes, perhaps all could. But who would know for sure if it were the real thing? According to Paul, the gifts of the Spirit are as sovereignly given as salvation is. All the gifts are apportioned "to each one, just as he [the Holy Spirit] determines" (1 Cor. 12:11). He blows where He will.

I come right back to this frequently observed fact that the gift of tongues is at the bottom of the list when it comes to Paul's list of the gifts of the Spirit. Wisdom is at the top. Wisdom is without doubt the most important. So why should I spend so much time in this chapter on tongues? I answer: First, because that is where the stigma is. Second, if you want the gift of wisdom—or other gifts such as healing, I repeat: Are you willing to start at the bottom? Paul said that we should "eagerly desire" the greater gifts (1 Cor. 12:31). I don't think you have to speak in tongues to be a good Christian. My own dad didn't, a man of prayer and the most godly man I ever met. My godly mother didn't. But I think you must be *willing* to do this if indeed you desire all of God you can possibly have. After all, Paul said to the Corinthians (who thought tongues was everything), "I thank God that I speak in tongues more than all of you" (1 Cor. 14:18), having said, "I would like for every one of you to speak in tongues" (v. 5). But he also said that the gift to prophesy was more needed (v. 5). And yet I can never forget that Paul was unashamed to say he spoke in tongues.

Whether tongues was a stigma—offense—in Paul's day, I do not know. But it certainly is today. Tongues is the only gift of the Spirit that challenges your pride, as Charles Carrin notes. I sometimes think some church leaders would be willing to drop their theological view that the gifts have *ceased* if tongues were not included in the list of gifts. The word *stigma* comes down to one word: embarrassment. That is what Jackie Pullinger said. She found it embarrassing. She made one other observation to me. She had been in Hong Kong for two years with no good results or success. She decided one day to start praying in tongues fifteen minutes a day *by the clock* (those were her exact words). Every day for fifteen minutes by the clock. "I felt nothing," she said to me. Absolutely nothing. "But that is when we began to see conversions of the addicts on the streets." She linked the two together. And they kept increasing thereafter. I believe God honors those who will accept such a stigma.

The Gifts of the Spirit

Let us now turn to the gifts of the Spirit as found in 1 Corinthians 12:8–11. One general comment: whereas some might have two or more of the gifts below, another person may have only one of them. Also, a gift may flourish only once—and never again. Sometimes a gift of the Spirit may reside permanently in a person.

Wisdom

This is the greatest gift of the Holy Spirit. It heads the list. Wisdom is the presence of the mind of the Holy Spirit. It is knowing what to do next; it shows the next step forward when we don't know what to do. It is having 20/20 foresight vision. We all seem to have 20/20 hindsight vision, realizing too late what we should have done. But wisdom is 20/20 foresight vision, showing what to say or do *now*. It will keep you from mistakes. It will keep you from regrets. It will keep you from putting your foot in it. It will keep you from making a fool of yourself.

Have you ever wondered why the Book of Proverbs (part of ancient Hebrew literature) says so much in early chapters about sexual purity? Go read the first seven chapters and notice how much attention is given to adultery and sexual infidelity. Why? Because sexual purity is one of the first qualifications to have wisdom. It is the last thing some want to hear. It is listed first but is the least talked about, sometimes the least wanted, and sometimes the least evidenced in the church today. Dr. Lloyd-Jones used to say that we are living in the period like in the Book of Judges—"Everyone did as he saw fit" (Judg. 21:25).

If you should covet earnestly the best gifts—and feel some of them are beyond your reach—do not forget that James said we can always pray for wisdom. "If any of you lacks wisdom [don't we all?], he should ask God" (James 1:5). There are two kinds of wisdom: one is from below. It is recognized by bitter envy and selfish ambition. Its origin: the flesh and the devil. There is the wisdom that comes from above— that is what Paul is talking about in this gift that heads the list. It is "first of all pure; then peace-loving, considerate, submissive, full of mercy and good fruit, impartial and sincere" (James 3:17). The gift of wisdom as James describes it comes the nearest of the gifts of the Spirit to seem to be like the fruit of the Spirit.

Word of knowledge

The phrase "word of knowledge" is the KJV translation. The NIV calls it "message of knowledge." The ESV says "utterance of knowledge." The phrase *word of knowledge* has pretty much become the way this gift of the Spirit is referred to, although it is less clear what it actually means. It *could* refer to someone highly gifted in knowledge—like my friend Dr. Michael Eaton. But that is not the way this is normally accepted.

This gift probably refers to special knowledge as may be needed in a crisis. If so, it borders on the gift of wisdom. It may refer to supernatural knowledge about someone in a particular crisis. If so, it borders on the gift of prophecy. A word of knowledge may disclose a person's illness, concern, or specific need. We had a visiting preacher at Westminster Chapel call out a woman who had been deeply worried about her recently deceased husband's salvation. The preacher said to her— calling her name and giving her address: "Elizabeth, the Lord showed you something recently in your apartment that you feared was not really from the Lord. You should know it *was* from the Lord." That's all he said. She burst into tears. She knew exactly what this meant. The visiting preacher who gave the word didn't know what it actually referred to. Louise knew. Elizabeth had told Louise that a few days before she prayed that God would show her whether her husband, Samuel, was really saved and indeed in heaven. He had made a profession of faith only two days before he died, and Elizabeth feared Samuel didn't know what he was doing as he was so filled with medicine. She opened a Bible that was on her coffee table and her eyes fell on the words, "The Lord was with Samuel." That satisfied her. But then she realized it was a children's Bible, now fearing all over again that what she read wasn't good enough. So she was back to square one, not knowing if her husband, Samuel, was really saved. But when our guest speaker (who had no way of knowing who she was or what she was worried about) said to her that what Elizabeth feared as not being from the Lord really *was* from the Lord, she was gobsmacked (as they say in England). She never doubted her husband's salvation again.

Faith

I have always thought it odd that faith would be listed as a gift of the Spirit since we are justified by faith; we are saved by grace through faith. So it would seem redundant that faith should be listed as a gift of the Spirit to people already saved. But this is obviously not talking about salvation.

This gift also refers to a crisis situation. It is sometimes easier to trust God to take you to heaven than it is to get you through the day! As I said, a gift of the Spirit may come to a person only once; it could reside in someone else indefinitely. The great George Müller (1805–1898) was famous for his extraordinary faith. Yet paradoxically he insisted he did not have the gift of faith! But if he didn't have it, I don't know who does! He trusted God to look after hundreds of orphans, living one day at a time and *never telling anybody what the need was.* Time after time there would be no food on the table. Dozens sitting at the table with plates and utensils. They would thank God for the food that wasn't there. Before he finished praying, a knock on the door came with all the food they needed. That happened over and over again. He was a phenomenon in Bristol, England.

During the Welsh Revival there was a man who had a ministry to tramps. According to Dr. Lloyd-Jones, at the height of the revival the man would be told by the Holy Spirit the night before how many tramps would show up to be fed the next morning. One evening it would be "nineteen." The next evening "four," the next night "twenty-two," and so on. But also the exact amount of food needed for these tramps would be provided—not a little bit extra or too little. However, when the revival subsided, the revelations stopped.

Healing

Who wouldn't want this gift? Who has it? I suppose those who see a lot of people healed when they pray for sick people assume they have this gift. I have seen a few healed, but not a lot. I think the gift of healing comes sovereignly, and that those who have it all the time are exceedingly rare. That is, if anybody has this gift all the time. The late Oral Roberts was the most famous of these. I was privileged to meet him at his home in California three times. On one of the occasions he told me of a moment when the Lord spoke powerfully to him in his hallway a few days before. "It was my old anointing," he said. I deduced from that, that the *old anointing* had been withdrawn from him. Indeed, the years 1952–1954 were when he and others saw extraordinary healings. You can go on YouTube and see some of them. The gift of healing can come and go. Nobody can make God do things.

Miraculous powers

What is the difference between healing and miraculous powers? You tell me. Some say healing is gradual, a miracle is sudden. What happened when the forty-year-old man was instantly and miraculously healed at the Beautiful gate? Was it a miracle? Surely. But it is called a healing too (Acts 3:16). Just as the gift of word of knowledge overlaps with the gift of prophecy, so too with the gift of miracles and healing. Perhaps it is the gift of miracles when a person is delivered from demons. But we only anointed the previously mentioned man from Chile with oil who could not sleep well for some twenty-five years owing to his mother being a witch. We did not say, "Come out of him." We merely anointed him with oil. Was it a healing or a miracle?

However, I ministered to a demon-possessed man only once. But when I did so, I followed the wisdom of Dr. Lloyd-Jones. He shared with me this story. To the best of my memory, here is exactly what he said:

> There was a church in Wales for which I preached every year. After the service I said to the host pastor, "Where was Mr. So-and-So tonight?" "Oh, I forgot to tell you, Doctor. He phoned to explain why he could not be there. His wife is extremely ill. In fact, she has been behaving in a very strange manner." No sooner than the pastor told me this that the phone rang. It was this very man on the line who asked to speak to me. He said to me, "Doctor, my wife is behaving in a very strange manner. I have never seen anything like it. I could not bring her to church." After he hung up, I said to the host pastor: "This is a clear case of demon possession. You are to get one of your elders and go to this house and exorcise the demon." The pastor replied, "Oh please, Doctor, you go. I would not know what to do." I replied: "If I go, they will say her condition is medical, that any healing has something to do with medicine and my medical experience. I will not go, but you can do it. You and the elder pray for your own protection before you enter their house—that the blood of Christ will cover you. As soon as you see her, start repeating these words, 'Jesus Christ is come in the flesh. Jesus Christ is come in the flesh. Jesus Christ is come in the flesh.' Keep saying that and prepare for a violent reaction. Then speak to the demon, 'In the name of Jesus Christ come out of her and go to your place of appointment.'" Then the pastor went to get an elder while I waited for him to return. An hour or so later he returned. He was white as a sheet. The pastor said, "Doctor, it was just as you said. We did as you instructed us. When we repeated, 'Jesus Christ is come in the flesh' several times, she fell on the floor and screamed. When we cast the demon out, she went limp." This lady who I had known for years was at church the next evening, sitting on the front row with a radiant smile on her face.

I led a man called Tony to the Lord in London. He came back the following week to say there was something in his stomach that was cutting as if it were a razor blade. He also said that he had been going to black masses before he prayed to receive Christ. Although he had received the Lord the previous Saturday, I felt he was demon possessed, recalling Dr. Lloyd-Jones's view that a true Christian could have a demon (the lady described above was a Christian, said the Doctor). So I followed Dr. Lloyd-Jones's wisdom. I said to Tony, "Look at me. Jesus Christ is come in the flesh, Jesus Christ is come in the flesh"—repeating this several times. Tony's face became contorted, and he made odd sounds. I said, "In the name of Jesus Christ come out of him." He went limp. I left him alone for several minutes. He then said, "I don't know what you did, but I feel so good inside." There was no cutting in his stomach. He became a faithful member of our congregation.

Prophecy

When Paul urged the Corinthians to desire the spiritual gifts, "especially the gift of prophecy" (1 Cor. 14:1), he was not implying they could become Elijahs or Isaiahs. Neither does prophesying necessarily mean preaching. He was talking about exhortations of encouragement, perhaps cautions too, but not magisterial predictions or pronouncements. I am not sure these Corinthians could become Agabuses either, and yet his predictions about Paul going to Jerusalem did not turn out exactly right. (See Acts 21:10–11, then follow what exactly happened to Paul.) There are levels of prophecy, pointing out that canonical prophets or biblical writers—the highest level—will not be duplicated ever again, just as Scripture is final and complete.

What must be avoided in any case is people saying "Thus saith the Lord" or "The Lord told me." Speaking like this is not only highly presumptuous but is taking the name of the Lord in vain. It is simply unnecessary to bring the Lord's name in when we think we have a word for someone. It is using God's name—the worst possible kind of name-dropping—to elevate our own credibility. You are not thinking of the Lord's credibility but your own when you bring in His name.

The careless practice of prophesying has done a lot of damage to the issue of the gifts of the Spirit. For further reading, see Wayne Grudem, *The Gift of Prophecy in the New Testament and Today* and also his *Systematic Theology*.[2]

Distinguishing between spirits

This is a God-given ability to discern the true from the false—recognizing the Holy Spirit and also the demonic. Too many people think only of the demonic when it comes to this gift. It is more important to discern the presence of the Holy Spirit than the demonic. It is equally important to discern the *absence* of the Holy Spirit when people are making claims about the presence of God.

Speaking in tongues

I have covered this somewhat without entering into the discussion how 1 Corinthians 14:2 (speaking in tongues to God, sometimes called a "prayer language") relates to Acts 2:4 (when the disciples were filled with the Holy Spirit and spoke in tongues). In my opinion, they are not necessarily the same. Speaking in tongues is the gift so many think about when the discussion of the "gifts of the Spirit" comes up. I say again, if it were not for the stigma of this particular gift—given the notoriety it has received, I don't think the gifts of the Spirit would be nearly so controversial.

Interpretation of tongues

This may be the rarest of the gifts. There is a subtle difference between interpretation and translation, but people need to maintain integrity when exercising this gift, especially when a person interprets his or her own "tongue." It would be far more impressive if a different person interprets than the one who spoke it, even more so when the interpretation could be validated by a second person interpreting who had not heard the first. But if the interpretation is absolutely right, it can bring a great witness to God's glory (1 Cor. 14:25).

Twice Paul said we should "eagerly desire" the gifts (1 Cor. 12:31; 1 Cor. 14:1). The onus is on us all to show how closely we wish to adhere to Scripture by coveting the gifts of the Holy Spirit.

Chapter Twelve

THE ULTIMATE PROOF
OF THE HOLY SPIRIT

For God gave us a spirit not of fear but of power and love
and self-control.

—2 Timothy 1:7, esv

I like your Christ; I do not like your Christians. Your
Christians are so unlike your Christ.[1]

—Mahatma Gandhi
(1869–1948)

For some reason I have always been fascinated with New York City. I don't know why, but as a boy from Kentucky I wanted, among other things, to see the Empire State Building with my own eyes and to see my hero Joe DiMaggio play at Yankee Stadium. When I was ten years old, my parents took me to New York. I will never forget the moment I first saw the Empire State Building. It was at night. I had seen pictures of it, but when I saw it with all the lights, it was so different from what I expected. I just wanted to stare at it and not move on to other places. I was actually looking at the tallest building in the world! A day or two later we went in, taking three elevators to reach the 102nd floor. And I knew this was real.

The New York Yankees weren't playing during the time I was there. But some twenty years later we were living in Fort Lauderdale. I attended a spring training game of the New York Yankees. Suddenly there were whispers among the crowds, "There comes Joe DiMaggio." Now retired from baseball, he was being driven to the ball park to help train young players. I made my way to the car and was first to shake his hand. I just gazed at him, and he looked at me and said, "Thank you." Though I was now thirty years old, I was as excited as if I were ten. It was all I could think about for days. I had actually met Joe DiMaggio.

There is no sign in northwest Arizona that assures you are not being deceived by stating, "This truly is the Grand Canyon." There is no sign in Canada that says, "You are looking at Niagara Falls." How does one really know they are not being deceived? How can you be sure you are looking at the Jungfrau when in Interlaken, Switzerland? Or Table Mountain in Cape Town? Or the Sea of Galilee in Israel? I had been fascinated by the Wailing Wall in Jerusalem, recalling stories that a dove would sometimes fly into it. When I first went to the Western Wall, I was keen to find out if I might see a dove. Yes! There it was. I took a photo. But that photo, when enlarged, showed it to be a pigeon!

How do you recognize the Holy Spirit? How do you know you are not being deceived? I know what it is to be deceived, let down, disillusioned, and betrayed by those I adored and trusted. It is enough to make a person a professional cynic. But I have survived.

In America we will sometimes use the phrase "the real deal" when a person really and truly is absolutely genuine. Pure gold. But how do you know a piece of metal is gold? How do you know it when you are holding counterfeit money?

None of us wants to be deceived. What is more, I don't want to deceive anybody, including with the contents of this book. How can you, the reader, be sure that what I have stated is true?

Four Things That Prove
You Have the Holy Spirit

There are four things that give us a pretty safe tip whether or not we are witnessing the Holy Spirit. They are: fearlessness, power, love, and self-control.

You may recall that Jonathan Edwards said that the one thing that Satan cannot produce in us is a love for the glory of God. He can bring about many things, but not that. He wrote this when endeavoring to show whether a person's affections have been truly set on *God* and that these feelings were motivated by *the Holy Spirit* and not the flesh. So, said Edwards, a love for the glory of God is one thing that *Satan cannot produce in a person.* Only God can make that happen.

So too when it comes to the Holy Spirit, there are four things by which you may know you have not been deceived. For some of us there may always be a lingering doubt. There may always be an apprehension that we will be caught off guard if a dove suddenly turns out to be a pigeon. What I want to submit now is what I judge to be the nearest you get to knowing for sure that you have not been deceived by strange fire.

Fearlessness

God has not given us a "spirit of fear" said Paul to the fearful young Timothy (2 Tim. 1:7, KJV). The NIV translates this "spirit of timidity," which I think misses the real meaning. A person may have a personality tendency to be timid or shy—and probably always will be. Paul is not speaking of a personality tendency. The Holy Spirit does not change our basic temperament. If you were an extrovert or sanguine when you were converted, you will be an extrovert afterward. The same would be true with melancholy, choleric, or phlegmatic type of people.

The Greek word translated "fear" is *phobos*—from which we get words such as *claustrophobia* (fear of being closed in). Second Timothy 1:7 may be put alongside Romans 8:15: "For you did not receive a spirit that makes you a slave again to fear, but you received the Spirit

of sonship. And by him we cry, 'Abba, Father.'" Paul here (
spirit of bondage—which comes from living under the M
with our loving heavenly Father. You do not need to be afr.
heavenly Father or fear you will not come up to His stanc
Father accepts us as we are, and we don't have to prove anything to
Him, unlike what many fear with their parents.

In any case, a *spirit* of fear is alien to the Holy Spirit. Dr. Lloyd-Jones
used to say, "God never oppresses us." Satan does. A spirit of fear is
a perpetual anxiety that governs a person—worrying that something
will always go wrong, that you will displease someone. You are always
looking over your shoulder. People governed by a spirit of fear have a
constant dread of disapproval. It comes down to this: the fear of man.
"Fear of man will prove to be a snare" (Prov. 29:25).

If you are obsessed with what people think of you, this is a spirit of
fear; it did not come from God, says Paul. Apparently Timothy was
governed by a spirit of fear (1 Cor. 16:10). Paul did not moralize him for
this, but merely pointed out that such an attitude did not come from
the Holy Spirit. We all have attitudes that come from the flesh, not the
Holy Spirit. Even Paul was once so depressed that he "despaired even
of life" (2 Cor. 1:8). There is not a single one of us who has not had an
off moment—a time we would die a thousand deaths for anyone to
see us. The point is, such feelings do not come from the Holy Spirit. It
certainly does not mean we are not Christians; it does not even mean
we are not spiritual or pleasing God generally. Were God to hide His
face from us—even for five minutes—most of us might get all kinds of
thoughts, attitudes that would make the angels blush.

Fearlessness is not courage. Of course one seems to have courage
when there is no fear. But you can have courage when you are scared
to death. You just press on. We have reason to believe that Martin
Luther was filled with great anxiety when he stood before the Diet of
Worms in 1521 and said, "Here I stand. I can do no other. God help me.
Amen." He was showing courage.

Fearlessness is when there is simply no fear. I wish I felt this way
every day. But I have known this—at times. There is nothing like it. It
is when the Dove comes down and the whole landscape changes, like

sunrise that reveals what was hidden in the night. Fearlessness. As the hymn "Like a River Glorious" puts it in verse two:

Hidden in the hollow of His blessed hand,
Never foe can follow, never traitor stand;
Not a surge of worry, not a shade of care,
Not a blast of hurry touch the spirit there.[2]

—FRANCES R. HAVERGAL
(1836–1879)

Fearlessness is a state of mind that can only be achieved by the Holy Spirit. You can't work it up. You *can* work up courage. But you can't make yourself feel no fear. If you have it, admit it; just say, "I'm afraid. I'm anxious. I'm nervous. I don't know what is happening." It is no disgrace to feel like that. But when the Holy Spirit comes down, *all fear is gone.* At least for then. It may not last forever. But when this calm sets in, you know God has come. It's the real thing. Only the Holy Spirit can bring this about.

One reason the devil cannot produce fearlessness is that he is full of fear himself. He is the embodiment of fear. He is running scared sixty seconds a minute, sixty minutes an hour. He knows that his time is short (Rev. 12:12). The next time Satan reminds you of your past, remind him of his future. All those who oppose us—mark it down—are the ones who are afraid. "Do not fear what they fear" (1 Pet. 3:14). So if you have been given the grace of fearlessness, you have an inner strength for which there is no natural explanation.

Total fearlessness is what Peter had on the Day of Pentecost. No fear. He was not the slightest bit bothered by thousands of intimidating Jews around him—some of them high ranking. It was what he later felt when he said to the Sadducees, "Whether it is right in the sight of God to listen to you rather than to God, you must judge, for we cannot but speak of what we have seen and heard" (Acts 4:19–20, ESV). It was what Peter and John felt when they left the Sanhedrin having to pinch themselves that they were chosen to suffer the shame of Jesus's name (Acts 5:41). It is what Elijah felt when God swore an oath to him: he knew there would be no rain unless God said so (1 Kings 17:1–2). It is what he experienced on the top of Mount Carmel when poking fun at the desperation of the false prophets (1 Kings 18:27).

When you have no fear, you do not need to raise your voice. You will not panic if you think you are losing an argument or lacking the exact words. The greatest freedom is having nothing to prove. This freedom—fearlessness—can only be produced by the Holy Spirit. When this fearlessness has set in, you know it is the Holy Spirit and not you. And when you find yourself governed by fear, accept the plain truth: God did not give you that fear.

The flesh or the devil can never manufacture this fearlessness.

These things said, the word *fear* can be tricky in this discussion. In the days following Pentecost, everyone was filled with fear or awe (Acts 2:43). Strange as it may seem, the same Holy Spirit who imparts utter fearlessness in a person can simultaneously impart an astonishing awe of God. Indeed, the greater the measure of the Spirit in us, the greater will be our genuine fear of God. You will respect God and His Word more than ever. Never forget that the "eternal gospel" is a command: "Fear God and give him glory" (Rev. 14:6–7). The more I love God, the more I fear Him; the greater my measure of the Holy Spirit who instills calm and joy will be matched by the greater my desire to glorify God.

Power

Power is what Jesus promised to the disciples at Pentecost (Luke 24:49; Acts 1:8). One could argue that the first and foremost evidence of the Holy Spirit is power. The Greek word is *dunamis,* from which we get the word *dynamite.* You could say that at least two things were working in Peter at Pentecost: an absence of fear and the presence of power. Fearlessness would not have been enough. It would not do for Peter to exult to those around him and say, "Guess what—I have absolutely no fear of all these people around me." So what? He would need *power.*

Peter's power at Pentecost consisted in two things:

1. The exact words to say. Clearly manifested that day was a fulfillment of Jesus's promise that we are to take no

thought what to say but it will be "given" to us what to say; it will be the "spirit of your Father speaking through you" (Matt. 10:19–20).

2. The Holy Spirit working effectually in His hearers. When Peter finished preaching, the crowds weren't arguing back. No one was scoffing. No one was laughing. They had one question: "What shall we do?" (Acts 2:37). They were prepared to do whatever Peter suggested. He told them what to do—"Repent and be baptized" (v. 38). Three thousand were converted on the same day (v. 41).

Peter had no time to get his thoughts together before he addressed the crowd on the Day of Pentecost. He had no time to prepare a sermon. He had no idea he would be speaking. But when the Spirit came down and the crowds gathered, he knew he should speak. He also knew exactly what to say. The Holy Spirit brought to his remembrance what he should say (John 14:26). This is the anointing of the Spirit. It is not something you can work up, plan for, or aim for. It is there or it isn't.

And it may not last forever. Indeed, some years later when he did not want to be seen sitting with Gentiles—but excused himself when he saw Jews coming—the cowardly old Peter was on display. "Before certain men came from James, [Peter] used to eat with the Gentiles. But when they arrived, he began to draw back and separate himself from the Gentiles because he was afraid of those who belonged to the circumcision group" (Gal. 2:12). This was not Peter's most glorious moment. Paul rebuked him before everybody (v. 11). The same Peter who denied Jesus before a Galilean servant girl (Matt. 26:69–70) more or less resurfaced. It is not unlike Elijah, who had extraordinary power on Mount Carmel but ran for his life when threatened the next day by Queen Jezebel (1 Kings 19:2–3).

No matter what degree of power may be given us for a moment of need, let no one ever think he or she has *arrived* and will always have such power and boldness. We are all as weak as baby kittens before people if God does not supply the power. He can give it or withhold it.

He can give mercy or withhold it. "I will have mercy on whom I will have mercy, and I will have compassion on whom I will have compassion" (Rom. 9:15). This means that God was showing mercy and compassion to Peter at Pentecost. And yet not for Peter's sake, but for the spreading of the gospel. Whenever God uses us powerfully or chooses to display His authority in us, it is not for us. It is for those around us who need what we have to say. This should keep us from becoming smug and self-righteous. The moment we think we have arrived—and have an irrevocable anointing of *dunamis*—God will look down from heaven and say, "Really?," and let us show our weakness and be embarrassed before people and the highest heavens.

This power can be in great measure, and it may come in small measure. Peter had it in great measure for a good while, not only at Pentecost but also before the Sadducees days later. After the forty-year-old crippled man was instantaneously healed, Peter used the platform not to call attention to himself but to preach the gospel (Acts 3:1–26). Thousands more were converted. This power was on display when Peter severely warned Ananias and Sapphira before they were struck dead for lying to the Holy Spirit (Acts 5:1–10). The power of the Holy Spirit later resulted in a rather bizarre vision given to Peter in Joppa. It led to the conversion of Cornelius and to Peter's being given an extraordinary new perspective regarding Gentiles (Acts 10). Power—clearly outside of Peter's hands—was further on display when he miraculously escaped from prison, with angels going before him and opening iron doors (Acts 12:6–10).

All the gifts of the Holy Spirit show God's power—whether with wisdom, healing, or prophecy. It is the same Holy Spirit. He can do what appears to us as spectacular. It is as easy for Him to cure cancer as it is to heal a headache.

Whereas you cannot successfully imitate fearlessness, it is possible for unscrupulous ministers to assimilate what would seem to some as power. This is why some famous faith healers don't want the ushers to bring people in wheelchairs down to the front before everyone— putting the evangelist on the spot. They would far prefer to pray for people with less ostensible illnesses and have them fall down—which may be impressive to the undiscerning. The person who falls may or may not be healed, but the claim is almost always made that they were healed. People cheer and stomp and shout, "Praise the Lord," without giving it another thought. The gift of discernment is needed when it comes to preachers claiming power, for people can be so gullible. I fear this of myself, this being one of the reasons I myself have been deceived at times. A pigeon can look like a dove.

The power manifested in the Book of Acts was not doubted. "'What are we going to do with these men?' they asked. 'Everyone living in Jerusalem knows that they have done an outstanding miracle, and we cannot deny it'" (Acts 4:16). But sadly, most claims made nowadays for extraordinary healing have a way of remaining under a cloud. When you get to the bottom of it—whether it be ABC News investigating or sincere Christians trying to find out what really happened, it is almost always *not* what the faith healers claimed.

I honestly don't think that was always the case. I have reason to believe that in the years 1949–1951 people were miraculously, supernaturally healed. I have watched videos of Oral Roberts in the early 1950s that truly show remarkable healings. But they eventually subsided and virtually came to an end. As I said in the previous chapter, Oral Roberts talked about his *old anointing*, which since passed behind a cloud, perhaps awaiting another day when God would do something different.

People understandably love to laugh at reports of people falling on the floor and laughing their heads off. But we might laugh a little less if we were present during the high-water-mark moments of the Great Awakening, the Cane Ridge Revival—not to mention what it was like on the Day of Pentecost when people were accused of being drunk! My own first reaction to people falling and laughing at London's Holy Trinity Brompton Church of England was, "Yuck." I did not believe such to be of God. I find this sort of thing offensive to my fingertips. And if I am totally candid, I didn't want this strange phenomenon to be of God because if it was *truly* of God, it would have come to Westminster Chapel first! But it didn't. What the *Sunday Telegraph* called the "Toronto Blessing" spread to London and found a home at the prestigious Holy Trinity Brompton. I warned my congregation against this. Then later I had to climb down.

Here—in part—was what happened. Ken Costa, church warden of Holy Trinity Brompton (Church of England) and one of London's most respected bankers, asked to see me. A few years before he had claimed that my book *God Meant It for Good* had impacted him.[3] So we already had a relationship. Knowing what was going on at HTB, I sent him four sermons I preached on 1 John 4:1–4 (about testing the spirits to see what is of God and what is false), thinking this might help him work through his grave concern that "something rather unusual has happened at Holy Trinity and I need some guidance." I met with him for lunch, armed to put him straight regarding what I decided was certainly strange fire that broke out in his Anglican church.

I was not prepared for what followed. Ken had read my sermons on 1 John 4:1–4. He was obviously not worried now and also had no desire to convince me of anything. He only wanted the truth. As I prepared to sort him out, I began to feel that I was the one who needed sorting out. I knew he had an enormous stature among the top people of Parliament, the leading businessmen and bankers of London, and I discerned he was obviously prepared to lose his reputation in front of them. I could see before my eyes that Ken Costa had obviously been deeply touched by God. Strange fire could not do this. His life had been changed. I have rarely met a layman with a heart after God like this man. He would not call what happened at HTB *revival* but only *God's feather*—a light touch.

Ken's spirit shook me rigid. For the first time I began to fear that I was on the wrong side of the issue. He was so full of joy and with the most profound reference for Holy Scripture. I immediately phoned Louise and asked her to pray for me. "I have a feeling I have been wrong about this matter," I said to her. I cannot stress how much a sense of the fear of God came on me—that I was ominously in the exact same tradition of people who *opposed* the Great Awakening in Edwards's day and the Welsh Revival. For days I was sobered. I did not want to be on the wrong side. I suggested that our deacons go with me to a midweek time of prayer at HTB. Some went to observe, some volunteered to be prayed for. The Spirit of God began touching some of them! I did the only honorable thing I could think of: I publicly climbed down at Westminster Chapel and stated I had been wrong. My reputation would never be quite the same after that, but I never looked back. After a while HTB became like a sister church to Westminster Chapel.

Parallel with the influence of Ken Costa was yet another incident I could not put out of my mind. Bob Cheeseman, a pastor I had not met, had just returned from Toronto. He was at Westminster Chapel for a minister's meeting. The glow on his face persuaded me to ask him to pray for me. But one of my closest friends—a Reformed Baptist pastor—also came to my vestry for coffee. As it happens, both men knew each other—pastors from Richmond, a suburb of London. As Bob began to pray for me, my Reformed Baptist friend walked over and said, "I'll let him pray for me too." Here's the significant thing: my beloved friend had no idea what Toronto meant. Had he known, he would almost certainly not have let himself be prayed for. As Bob began praying, my friend Gerald Coates knocked on the door. I invited Gerald to join in prayer. As Bob and Gerald prayed for me, I felt singularly nothing. But my friend, not knowing what was happening to him, fell facedown on the red carpet in my old vestry. He lay there for almost ten minutes. That sobered me to no end.

Here are two scriptures that come to mind: (1) God's ways are higher than our ways (Isa. 55:8–9), and (2) He chooses the foolish things of the world to confound the wise (1 Cor. 1:27–28). It is easy to make fun of things like this. A loving caution: don't do it. You have no idea what you may be criticizing. Never forget that nobody dreamed at the time that Jesus dying on a cross on Good Friday was God's way of saving the world. The crucifixion in some ways could have appeared as distasteful, disgusting, and ridiculous then, just as falling down and laughing does now. Like it or not, God seems to love showing up in a manner that takes the most learned and sophisticated off guard.

The power of the Holy Spirit cannot be successfully duplicated. If a person is supernaturally changed and given a love for God's glory, *God* did it. If a person is truly healed, *God* did it—whoever prayed for the healing. Moreover, if God gives words that are so filled with truth that the opposition cannot gainsay—as when Stephen's enemies "could not stand up against his wisdom or the Spirit by whom he spoke" (Acts 6:10), that is Holy Spirit power.

Whenever power defies a natural explanation that sets people free, it is not what the flesh or the devil did.

Love

. The third thing Paul mentioned to Timothy is that God has given us the spirit of love, not a spirit of fear. Perfect love casts out fear (1 John 4:18). As light makes darkness disappear, so love makes fear go away. According to Paul's list in Galatians, the first fruit of the Spirit is love (Gal. 5:22–23). I think a case can be made that if you truly have the unfeigned fruit of love, the other fruit will follow: joy, peace, patience, kindness, goodness, faithfulness, gentleness, and self-control.

This is *agape* love, which is self-giving and unselfish, caring about others. It is described in beautiful detail in 1 Corinthians 13. This love goes right against nature. When we have been hurt, maligned, lied about, or treated unfairly, the most natural feeling in the world is to get even—to see the other person punished. Perfect love casts out fear; fear has to do with punishment (1 John 4:18). You want to throw the book at your offender. You pray that God will get that rascal. That is what the imprecatory psalms encourage us to do, do they not? But Jesus comes along and says, "Love your enemies, do good to those who hate you, bless those who curse you, pray for those who mistreat you" (Luke 6:27–28).

Agape love is as alien to our nature as is *dunamis* power. When there is true *agape* love, however, it is proof of the Holy Spirit. The flesh can't demonstrate *agape* love. The heart is deceitful above all things and incurably wicked (Jer. 17:9). The devil can't manifest *agape* love. He is full of hate, a murderer from the beginning (John 8:44). Only the Holy Spirit can love. And because we have the Holy Spirit, we can love. The onus is on us to prove it to those around us who are longing to see Christians behave like this.

Love "keeps no record of wrongs," said Paul (1 Cor. 13:5). Why do we keep records? To prove we paid our bills. Why do we keep a record of wrongs? To use it against an enemy—or one's spouse—when it comes in handy. Love tears up that record of wrongs so that their bad comment or deed can never be told again. One of the saddest statistics to emerge in recent years is that the proportion of Christian marriages ending in divorce are little different from those marriages where the couple are not Christians. What an embarrassing testimony for the Christian faith—at least in America.

When I am in Durban, South Africa, I always find myself thinking about Mahatma Gandhi, who lived there a good while. It is well known there that Gandhi seriously considered Christianity as a way forward for himself. The more he read the teachings of Jesus, the more intrigued he became—until he began to meet Christians in that area. The world will never know what might have been—if only Mahatma Gandhi had run into Spirit-filled Christians who demonstrated total forgiveness and praying for their enemies. That is what Gandhi was looking for. His famous quote—it makes me want to weep: "I like your Christ; I don't like your Christians. Your Christians are so unlike your Christ."

I suspect there is a horrible absence of the kind of Christian living needed today to keep marriages together. *Eros* love may cause a man and a woman to want to get married, but it is not the love that will sustain the marriage. *Agape* love must parallel (but not replace) *eros* love sooner than later, or the marriage is doomed. If our marriages are to survive the long haul, we certainly must have a love that keeps no record of wrongs.

God has not given us a spirit of fear but of love—which means every Christian has it within his or her grasp the need to forgive—totally. Total forgiveness is an act of the will. You don't wait for God to knock you down. You obey Jesus's teachings. *You just do it.* When Paul says God has given us this love, it means we are without excuse. I'm sorry, but that is our responsibility, which any Christian can make happen. We can all do it. It may be the hardest thing in the world to do (and it is), but it is what lies within our grasp because we have the Holy Spirit (Rom. 8:9).

These four proofs of the Spirit that God has given us—fearlessness, power, love, self-control—are equally divided. The first two only God can make happen: fearlessness and power. The last two—love and self-control—are within our grasp to do. The proof of the Holy Spirit is fearlessness and power; the proof of the Holy Spirit *equally* is love and self-control. These *prove* the Holy Spirit is at work in you.

I am ashamed to admit that I went for many years—over half of my Christian life—before my Romanian friend Josif Tson said to me, "RT, you must totally forgive them. Until you totally forgive them, you will be in chains." It is the greatest word anybody ever spoke to me. It transformed me. But it was something I had to make happen. It wasn't a matter of saying, "Lord, You supply the grace and I will forgive them." No. That is the big cop-out, the reason (alas) many Christians today are filled with bitterness and will go to their graves like that. Such doesn't mean they aren't saved. It means they will be saved by fire and lose any reward that could have been theirs (1 Cor. 3:14–15).

Do you have this love? Only God can give it. But you have to show it. Total forgiveness is a choice—and act of the will.

How do I know I have totally forgiven? When I don't tell anybody what they did to me. When I stop letting anybody be afraid or nervous around me. When I stop pointing the finger and making another feel guilty. When I let them save face rather than rubbing their noses in it. When I protect people from their darkest secret. When I keep doing it—day after day and even year after year. Finally, total forgiveness reaches its zenith—and ultimate expression—when I sincerely pray for the person who has been unjust. I don't merely say, "Dear Lord, I commit them to You." No. It is when you pray from your heart that God will bless them, prosper them, and keep them from getting caught. Oh, dear. But yes, that's total forgiveness. (For those who want to go into this more deeply, see my *Total Forgiveness*—published by Charisma House).[4]

Do you not want to wait until the judgment seat of Christ to see how God Himself will handle this? I wouldn't miss it for the world, and neither would I want to mess things up by vindicating myself here below.

When you do these things, you show the proof of the Holy Spirit.

Self-control

The Greek word translated "self-control" in 2 Timothy 1:7 is *sophronismou*. It is translated "sound mind" in the King James Version. There is a sense in which that is a reasonable translation. But the word is more aptly to be translated self-discipline or self-control. In the last (but not least) of his list of the fruit of the Spirit in Galatians 5:23 Paul uses the word *egkrates*—self-control or self-discipline. In the ancient Hellenistic world it referred to the power or lordship that one has over himself. It meant superiority over every desire, especially to food, sex, and the use of the tongue.

Like love—an act of the will—so too is self-control. One may wish that the fruit of the Spirit guarantee a spontaneous joy, peace, patience, and so forth, but that is not the case. God has given us not a spirit of fear but self-control. And because we have the Holy Spirit, we can demonstrate self-control. Indeed, the proof of the Holy Spirit is not the exercise of the gifts of the Spirit but self-control. The onus is on us to show we have the Holy Spirit not by speaking in tongues but mastery over our bodies.

Food. We live in Tennessee—the heart of the Bible Belt, but also the second-highest state for obesity. It is scandalous. In much the same way Christians dismiss their bitterness and unforgiveness, so too do an alarming number of Christians who are vastly overweight. I have yet to run into a minister who will tackle the problem. On one occasion the pastor's subject was "Fat Christians." I thought, "Oh, good." But he was lamenting how Christians are overfed spiritually but do not win their neighbors. It was a good sermon but did not touch the problem of obesity.

Self-control is what we have in the Holy Spirit. But we must exercise it. It means watching our intake of food and drink—not only for our personal health but also our testimony. When I was at Westminster Chapel, we allowed a choir from America to give us a concert. They were great singers. But the first thing our people noticed (and almost the only thing) was the obese people who were singing. Although obesity is fast on its way to England, the immediate thought of many of our people was, "Don't these people exercise any self-control?"

Sex. There is nothing that brings disgrace upon the name of our Savior like adultery in His church. Sadly it is happening all the time. Ministers showing lack of self-control regarding sex are being found out in every denomination weekly. I wish I could report that one's theology has a direct effect on the person's personal life. But having crossed denominational and theological lines many times, I can safely say sadly there is no correlation with regard to one's doctrine and self-control. The Reformed churches have the same proportion of fallen ministers as Pentecostals and charismatics. One could argue that the latter should have the best and cleanest record owing to their claim to be Spirit-filled. But this is not the case. The scandals among TV ministers prove not that they are filled with the Holy Spirit, but rather lack self-control.

The baptism with the Holy Spirit—however you define it—certainly gives us an impetus to glorify God and live a holy life. And in the days of afterglow after initially being Spirit-filled, perhaps one is less vulnerable to temptation. But sooner or later we all come down from the mountain of glory and have to come to grips with our sinful nature. It is *then through self-control* that we demonstrate we have the Holy Spirit.

Control of the tongue. "We all stumble in many ways," said James. I am so glad he said that. It makes me feel better. "If anyone is never at fault in what he says, he is a perfect man, able to keep his whole body in check" (James 3:2). The truth is, we aren't perfect; no one is, and none will ever be in this present life. That is what glorification is for.

But James does give us a check list by which we may know the difference between wisdom from "above" and wisdom from "below." The wisdom from below is harboring bitter envy and selfish ambition in our hearts. This brings us back to the issue of *agape* love. In a sense we have come full circle. You will recall that whereas fearlessness and power are out of our hands—only God can make these happen—love and self-control are put firmly in our hands. This is because we have been entrusted with the Holy Spirit. If He remains *ungrieved* in us, we may be sure we will not displease the Lord or bring disgrace upon Christ's name. The wisdom that comes from "above," then, is "first of all pure; then peace-loving, considerate, submissive, full of mercy and good fruit, impartial and sincere" (James 3:17).

Self-control brings honor and glory to God. What is more, people admire self-control. No one looks up to a person filled with bitterness, one who cannot control his or her tongue, appetite, or sexual urges. If we claim to have the Holy Spirit—and want the Holy Spirit to be given the respect due Him—we should care about Him enough that we discipline our tongues and our bodies.

I don't know of course how long I have to preach and write books. I know one thing: I want to end well, to finish well. If I practice what I have preached in this book, I will. So will you.

During my years at Westminster Chapel I almost dreaded returning to America without having been a phenomenal success—as my predecessors Dr. G. Campbell Morgan and Dr. Martyn Lloyd-Jones enjoyed. I feared I would have no ministry over here at all, knowing as I do how much Americans are impressed with success. And yet I have been abundantly blessed, being given a ministry that has gone right around the world. In much the same way, I have had some apprehension in writing this book as I realize there would be those readers who might be more inclined to take the sort of risks I took had I enjoyed the phenomenal success I so desired. But hopefully that would be a superficial, even worldly, motivation for you.

My closing word to you therefore is this. If your heart yearns for God more than anything in the world, don't give up. And if you see the slightest way forward by which you can demonstrate the courage of your desires, take full advantage of this. *Don't wait for God to knock you down.* Delight yourself in the Lord, and He will give you the desires of your heart (Ps. 37:4). I can honestly say to you that I have no regrets about my ministry at Westminster Chapel during those twenty-five years. None. I would make every single decision I made all over again. Why? I followed the principle of John 5:44, seeking not your praise but

God's. Am I disappointed I had no more success? Of course. I wanted to see revival. But that phenomenon is out of my hands. There is no possibility of ultimate disappointment when your highest goal is to know you pleased the Father.

Chapter Thirteen

ISAAC

And Abraham said to God, "If only Ishmael might live under your blessing!" Then God said, "Yes, but your wife Sarah will bear you a son, and you will call him Isaac. I will establish my covenant with him as an everlasting covenant for his descendants after him. And as for Ishmael, I have heard you: I will surely bless him; I will make him fruitful and will greatly increase his numbers."

—GENESIS 17:18–20

When the Word and Spirit come together, there will be the biggest movement of the Holy Spirit that the nation, and indeed the world, has ever seen.[1]

—SMITH WIGGLESWORTH
(1859–1947)

WHEN I WAS PASTOR (AGE NINETEEN) OF THE CHURCH OF THE Nazarene in Palmer, Tennessee, I will never forget the day my dad first heard me preach there. I had prepared carefully a sermon on prophecy and eschatology. I had it all figured out—the signs of the times, the Rapture, the Great Tribulation, the Antichrist, the mark of the beast, the millennium, and how things would wind up at the final judgment. I was keen to get my father's reaction to this fantastic sermon I just preached. Silence. A couple hours later he said to me, "Son, let me give you some advice from the man I named you after. Dr. R. T. Williams always said to pastors and preachers, 'Young men, stay away from the subject of prophecy. Let the old men do that. They won't be around to see their mistakes.'" That put me in my place.

But now that I am old, I might get away with the things I say in this chapter! And yet I believe with all my heart what I forecast in this chapter to be true and will come to pass.

In October 1992 some of us held the first Word and Spirit Conference at Wembley Conference Centre in London. Lyndon Bowring chaired the meeting. Graham Kendrick introduced his new hymn, which he wrote for us, "Jesus Restore to Us Again"—showing the need for the Word and Spirit to come together. I gave an address that got me into more trouble than any talk or sermon I gave in my entire life—before or since. Perhaps I should have seen it coming, but I didn't. I had no idea it would be so controversial.

A few days before that conference, I asked a friend in England a question: "If you were told that the charismatic movement is either Ishmael or Isaac, which would you say it is?"

He thought for a moment and said, "Isaac."

I then asked him, "What if I were to tell you that I believe the charismatic movement is Ishmael?"

"Oh, no, I hope not," he said.

I pointed out to him that his reaction was the same as Abraham's when told that Isaac, not Ishmael, was to be the promised son. "O that Ishmael might live before thee!," Abraham immediately said to God (Gen. 17:18, KJV).

Ishmael was part of God's plan. When he was born, Abraham assumed this is what God must have had in mind. He was from Abraham's loins; he was male. "True, he did not come from Sarah. But if this is what God had in mind, it is OK," thought Abraham.

The Pentecostal and charismatic movements are part of God's plan. Their influence in the world is incalculable. But as Ishmael was the forerunner to Isaac, so this vast movement that has emphasized the person and manifest presence of the Holy Spirit has set the stage for what is coming next.

ISAAC IS COMING

For thirteen years Abraham truly believed that Ishmael was *the* promised son that had been promised to him. It began when Abraham worried about not having an offspring. "Sovereign LORD, what can you give me since I remain childless and the one who will inherit my estate is Eliezer of Damascus?...You have given me no children; so a servant in my household will be my heir." The Lord replied, "This man will not be your heir, but a son who coming from your own body will be your heir." God took Abraham outside his tent and said, "Look up at the heavens and count the stars—if indeed you can count them." Then the Lord added, "So shall your offspring be" (Gen. 15:2–6). Abraham might have said, "Nonsense. Do you really expect me to believe that? I don't believe that." But no. Abraham "believed the LORD" (v. 7). The result of Abraham's belief was that he was counted righteous in God's sight. That account became Paul's chief illustration for his doctrine of justification by faith alone. (See Romans 4.)

But as Abraham got older, and Sarah was apparently barren, she suggested that Abraham sleep with her maidservant Hagar to help that promise along. He did. Ishmael was born (Gen. 16:15). Abraham was eighty-six years old when Hagar bore him Ishmael. It fit the promise. As I said, Ishmael was a male child from Abraham's body. So fair enough. No, it wasn't what Abraham expected when he first heard the Lord's promise. He believed Sarah would be the mother of his son. But since Ishmael was born, although Hagar was the natural mother, and it was certainly his own seed, he accepted it and lived with this for the next thirteen years.

Then one day God interrupted Abraham's life with what was now an unwelcome word: Ishmael is *not* to be the link to the seed that would be as numerable as the stars in the heavens. Sarah, aged ninety, would conceive and bear Abraham the son with whom the covenant would be established. But not to worry; Ishmael was indeed part of God's plan, and he too is blessed. But the covenant would be established with Isaac (Gen. 17:21).

When Abraham first heard this word from God, he fell facedown and laughed (v. 17). When Sarah later heard the word, she too laughed (Gen. 18:12). Within a year Sarah became pregnant in her old age (ninety) and gave Abraham a son in his old age (one hundred). Abraham called the son, Isaac. Isaac means, "laughter" or "he laughs."

That is the background for the talk I gave at the Wembley Conference Centre. The point I made was: *Isaac is coming.* It will be a demonstration of what happens when the Word and Spirit come together. The simultaneous combination will result in spontaneous combustion. I believe that what is coming down the road will be greater than any movement of the Holy Spirit ever seen since Pentecost. It will cross denominational, geographical, cultural, and theological lines. The glory of the Lord will cover the earth as the waters cover the sea. As the promise to Isaac was a hundred times greater than the promise to Ishmael, so what is coming will be a hundred times greater than anything we have ever seen. As for Ishmael, we haven't yet seen what God is going to do with his seed. I believe Muslims will be converted by the millions before it is over.

I truly thought this Wembley message would be welcomed. It was not. At the close you could almost hear a pin drop. I offended many charismatic leaders in the place. It also offended non-charismatic evangelicals because I said that with some well-known exceptions, "most of the churches in England worth their salt are charismatic." Moreover, the great hymns of this generation have overwhelmingly been written by well-known charismatics—such as Graham Kendrick, Chris Bowater, and others. Indeed, I had (for some) too many good things to say about charismatics that night.

Of course I understand how some charismatic leaders were offended by my word. Some still are somewhat hurt, having given their lives and reputations for a movement that has been largely despised by traditional churches. I don't blame them. I think of my friend Charles Carrin, who not only lost his church, his comfortable income, and beautiful home in one of the best parts of Atlanta, but also his credentials and retirement—all for the charismatic movement.

That said, the future for Pentecostals and charismatics is brighter than ever. They are the ones who should be the primary beneficiaries of the coming movement of the Holy Spirit, a move that I believe will be the greatest in the history of the Christian church. I put it that way because I predict that countless conservative evangelicals will equally be a part of the great revival that is coming. It is when the Word and Spirit come together.

Do not forget too that Ishmael was given a great promise—namely, that his seed would mean millions. I doubt many would have dreamed that what began in Azusa Street in 1906 plus what was first known as the glossolalia movement would mushroom as it has. Consider the success of the charismatic movement. Look at third world Christianity. Consider the television and radio ministries. Nearly all of them are Pentecostal or charismatic.

The Midnight Cry

At that time the kingdom of heaven will be like ten virgins who took their lamps and went out to meet the bridegroom. Five of them were foolish and five were wise. The foolish ones took their lamps but did not take any oil with them. The wise, however, took oil in jars along with their lamps. The bridegroom was a long time in coming, and they all become drowsy and fell asleep.

At midnight [Greek, "middle of the night"] the cry rang out: "Here's the bridegroom! Come out to meet him!" Then all the virgins woke up and trimmed their lamps. The foolish ones said to the wise, "Give us some of your oil; our lamps are going out."

"No," they replied, "there may not be enough for both us and you. Instead, go to those who sell oil and buy some for yourselves." But while they were on their way to buy the oil, the bridegroom arrived. The virgins who were ready went in with him to the wedding banquet. And the door was shut.

Later the others also came. "Sir! Sir!" they said. "Open the door for us!" But he replied, "I tell you the truth, I don't know you." Therefore keep watch, because you do not know the day or the hour.

—MATTHEW 25:1–13

Jesus gave this parable for several reasons. First, to describe the condition of the church generally in the very last days—that the church would be asleep. Second, the church generally would be made up of two types: those who were wise—who pursue their inheritance by taking oil in their lamps; and those who were foolish—who blow away their inheritance by taking no extra oil in their lamps. Third, there would be a cry in the middle of the night (not twelve o'clock midnight but in the middle of the night when people are sleeping): "Here's the bridegroom! Come out and meet him!"

It is my view that the cry in the middle of the night will usher in the next and final great move of God on the earth. It is when the Word and the Spirit come together simultaneously. This message will wake up the wise and foolish. The entire church will be awakened. But the foolish will not be allowed to enjoy the great move of God.

Jesus builds this parable on the ancient Middle Eastern wedding, which was vastly different from our weddings today. The marriage did not take place in a synagogue or church but in the groom's home. The groom would go to the house of the bride and bring her back to his home. But the bride had no idea when the bridegroom would call on her. Strange as it may seem to us, sometimes the groom would go to her home in the middle of the night. Jesus implies that the cry will come when the church is in a deep sleep. However, a rule with all parables, don't try to make them stand evenly on all four legs; get the main point. For further study, see my *The Parables of Jesus*.[2]

I believe the church is asleep at the present time. We don't know we were asleep until we wake up. We do things in our dreams we would not do when wide awake. Likewise the church is involved in things it would have nothing to do with if awake. Also, the foolish hate the sound of an alarm, but the wise will welcome the wake-up call.

This cry in the middle of the night I believe to be a move of the Holy Spirit—call it Isaac—*prior* to the Second Coming. The main thing is this: I believe that a great movement of the Holy Spirit is coming. I believe it is coming very, very soon. I hope to be alive when it comes. If I die first, I promise you: it will come.

I had no idea when I gave that message at the Wembley Conference Centre in 1992 that forty-five years earlier—in 1947, just three months before he died—Smith Wigglesworth (1859–1947) gave the following prophecy. Although he speaks in a British context, what he says equally fits the same period and development in America. Here is what it says:

> During the next few decades there will be two distinct moves of the Holy Spirit across the church in Great Britain. The first move will affect every church that is open to receive it and will be characterized by a restoration of the baptism and gifts of the Holy Spirit. The second move of the Holy Spirit will result in people leaving historic churches and planting new churches. In the duration of each of these moves, the people who are involved will say, "This is the great revival." But the Lord says "No, neither is the great revival but both are steps towards it." When the new church phase is on the wane, there will be evidenced in the churches something that has not been seen before: a coming together of those with an emphasis on the Word and those with an emphasis on the Spirit. When the Word and the Spirit come together, there will be the biggest movement of the Holy Spirit that the nation, and indeed the world, has ever seen. It will mark the beginning of a revival that will eclipse anything that has been witnessed within these shores, even the Wesleyan and the Welsh revivals of former years. The outpouring of God's Spirit will flow over from the UK to the mainland of Europe and from there will begin a missionary move to the ends of the earth.[3]

Even so, come Holy Spirit.

May the blessing of God the Father, God the Son, and God the Holy Spirit rest upon you, now and evermore. Amen.

Appendix

FIRE

⌇

They saw what seemed to be tongues of fire that separated and came to rest on each of them.

—ACTS 2:3

His word is in my heart like a fire,
  a fire shut up in my bones.
I am weary of holding it in;
  indeed, I cannot.

—JEREMIAH 20:9

We are told to let our light shine, and if it does, we don't need to tell anybody it does. Lighthouses don't fire cannons to call attention to their shining; they just shine.

—D. L. MOODY
(1837–1899)

THERE ARE BASICALLY FOUR KINDS OF FIRE IN THE BIBLE: natural fire, supernatural fire, strange fire, and poetic or symbolic fire. The word *fire* appears 520 times in the Bible. All fire mentioned in the Bible, except for the strange or unauthorized fire, is holy fire. Even the natural fire used in the sacrifices was to honor God.

177

The prophet Elijah was led to stand on a mountain in the presence of the Lord because the Lord was about to pass by. Then a great and powerful wind tore the mountains apart and shattered the rocks, but, "the LORD was not in the wind. After the wind there was an earthquake, but the LORD was not in the earthquake. After the earthquake came a fire, but the LORD was not in the fire" (1 Kings 19:11–12).

It seems rather surprising that the Lord was not in the fire. After all, fire was the most common way God had manifested Himself in ancient times up till then, including with Elijah. God had not manifested Himself through an earthquake up to that time. But He certainly had used wind to bring judgment to show His power—three times (Exod. 10:13; 14:21; Num. 11:31). And God used fire many times. So it would seem predictable that He would show up through fire. But instead God showed up in a "gentle whisper" (1 Kings 19:12—"still small voice," KJV; "low whisper," ESV). This demonstrates how God is predictably unpredictable. When you think you know exactly how He will manifest Himself, you find out how wrong you were.

The first time the word *fire* appears in the Bible is in Genesis 19:24. It is supernatural fire and used of God to punish Sodom and Gomorrah for its decadence: "The LORD rained down burning sulfur on Sodom and Gomorrah...out of the heavens" (Gen. 19:24). The last time the word *fire* appears in Scripture is also supernatural fire, and it too refers to punishment: "But the cowardly, the unbelieving, the vile, the murderers, the sexually immoral, those who practice the magic arts, the idolaters and all liars—their place will be the fiery lake of burning sulfur. This is the second death" (Rev. 21:8).

The first reference to natural fire in the Bible is when Abraham was prepared to offer Isaac as a sacrifice: "Abraham took the wood for the burnt offering and placed it on his son Isaac, and he himself carried the fire and the knife" (Gen. 22:6). There was nothing supernatural about this fire. It was natural fire, also anticipating fire that would be used in the Mosaic sacrificial system some four hundred years later. As for the last time natural fire is used in the New Testament, it is not so easy to determine. It partly depends on one's interpretation of the Book of Revelation. For example, is the great prostitute burned with natural fire or supernatural fire—"She will be consumed by fire, for mighty is the Lord God who judges her" (Rev. 18:8)?

There are multitudinous uses of natural fire. The basic uses are obvious. Fire consumes. Fire provides heat and light. The heat also purifies, burning out impurities; it can even test the genuineness of silver or gold. Paul said that on the last day supernatural fire would test the quality of one's work (1 Cor. 3:11–15). God used supernatural fire to demonstrate His justice and vengeance.

PURIFICATION AND NATURAL FIRE

Why did Abraham carry fire with him when he was preparing to sacrifice Isaac? It is because God told Abraham to offer his son as a burnt offering (Gen. 22:2). Abraham fully intended to slay his son, then offer him as a burnt sacrifice. Under the sacrificial system later, the animal was slain and then its blood was used for atonement. But why the need for *fire* when the Levitical priesthood was instituted? Partly to ensure there was no blood left if the burnt sacrifices were to be eaten. But sometimes they were totally consumed and simply given to God.

Natural fire with reference to all sacrifices was for purification. It burns away what is undesirable. In a word: fire was required whether the sacrifice would be eaten or totally consumed for the Lord. On the night of Passover Moses commanded all the people to take a lamb without defect, take some of its blood, and put it on the sides and tops of the doorframes of the houses where they were to eat the lambs. That same night they were to eat the meat roasted over the fire. If some of the meat was left till morning, they had to burn it (Exod. 12:8–10). God would then send the death angel and strike down every firstborn to bring judgment on all the gods of Egypt. Then came one of the most significant and memorable words in all Holy Writ: "When I see the blood, I will pass over you" (Exod. 12:13).

FIRE AND GOD'S VENGEANCE

When Aaron foolishly led the children of Israel to make a golden calf, Moses commanded it to be burned. Moses was angry when he came down from the mountain and discovered what they had done. "He took the calf they had made and burned it in the fire; then he ground it to powder, scattered it on the water and made the Israelites drink it" (Exod. 32:20).

God commanded the people of Israel—when they entered Canaan— to "break down their altars, smash their sacred stones and burn their Asherah poles in the fire; cut down the idols of their gods and wipe out their names from those places" (Deut. 12:3). This commandment was honored generations later when King Josiah ordered Hilkiah the priest to remove all the articles made for Baal and Asherah from the temple. "He burned them outside Jerusalem in the fields of the Kidron Valley" (2 Kings 23:4).

Three Hebrews—named Shadrach, Meshach, and Abednego— defied the decree of King Nebuchadnezzar by refusing to bow down to the image he had set up (Dan. 3:16–18). They were cast into the furnace of fire as punishment. This was natural fire. In fact, the king ordered the furnace to be heated seven times hotter than usual. The three men were thrown into the blazing furnace. The flames even killed the soldiers who threw the men into the furnace. Although the three Hebrews were "firmly tied" when they were put into the fire, they were seen *walking*—"unbound and unharmed" with a fourth man who had joined them. It was natural fire; only the rope that tied them was burned (Dan. 3:25). The fire served to vindicate the three Hebrews.

THE POWER AND PRESENCE OF GOD IN SUPERNATURAL FIRE

Supernatural fire was a visible manifestation of the power of God. Whether at Sinai, Mount Carmel, or when tongues of fire appeared upon the disciples on the Day of Pentecost, it showed God's manifest presence and power. Supernatural fire always produced an awe in the hearts of the people whenever it was manifested. It revealed the glory of God. It was also the clear indication that God Himself—no counterfeit spirit—was at work. It showed too that God was on His people's case, sending a convincing signal that something very significant was at hand. But supernatural fire also often indicated the anger of God, showing His punishment for sin—whether at Sinai or retribution for strange fire. God does not waste the appearances of supernatural fire. When supernatural fire is manifested, it is no small thing.

Angels

"He makes winds his messengers, flames of fire his servants" (Ps. 104:4). This is quoted in Hebrews 1:7. God uses angels to create supernatural fire. Angels are the explanation for the examples of supernatural fire shown below.

The burning bush

One day when Moses was tending sheep, an angel of the Lord appeared to him in flames of fire from within a bush. This was not natural fire; it was supernatural. Moses saw that though the bush was on fire, "it did not burn up" (Exod. 3:2). He was told to take off his shoes; he was on holy ground (v. 5).

The plagues on Egypt

The next time supernatural power was used, it was during the plagues God sent upon Egypt when Pharaoh's heart was hardened.

> When Moses stretched out his staff toward the sky, the LORD sent thunder and hail, and lightning flashed down to the ground. So the LORD rained hail on the land of Egypt; hail fell and lightning flashed back and forth. It was the worst storm in all the land of Egypt since it had become a nation.
>
> —EXODUS 9:23–24

The pillar of fire

At this stage there appeared what would be one of the most wonderful, thrilling, glorious, and comforting manifestations of the glory of God in the Old Testament. While the children of Israel were preparing to cross the Red Sea on dry land—with the Egyptians pursuing them, "the LORD went ahead of them in a pillar of cloud to guide them on their way and by night *a pillar of fire to give them light,* so that they could travel by day or night. Neither the pillar of cloud by day nor the pillar of fire by night left its place in front of the people" (Exod. 13:21–22, emphasis added). This supernatural fire gave Israel both infallible guidance and total protection from the enemy. When they crossed the Red Sea during the last watch of the night, "the LORD looked down from the pillar of fire and cloud at the Egyptian army and threw it into confusion" (Exod. 14:24). This phenomenon became the standard witness for the next forty years that God was on Israel's side.

> Glorious things of thee are spoken,
> Zion, city of our God!
> He whose word cannot be broken,
> Formed thee for His own abode....
>
> Round each habitation hovering,
> See the cloud and fire appear!
> For a glory and a covering,
> Showing that the Lord is near....[1]

—JOHN NEWTON
(1725–1807)

Mount Sinai

Moses prepared the Israelites to get ready for God to show up. They were to consecrate themselves because the Lord promised to "come down on Mount Sinai in the sight of all the people" (Exod. 19:11). They were also warned not to go up the mountain or even touch the foot of it. There came thunder and lightning, with a thick cloud over the mountain and a very loud trumpet blast. Everyone trembled. The people stood at the foot of the mountain. It was covered with smoke, "because the LORD descended on it in fire. The smoke billowed up from it like smoke from a furnace, and the whole mountain trembled violently" (v. 18). Moses later reminded the people that the mountain "blazed with fire to the very heavens" and that the Ten Commandments were spoken to them "out of the fire" (Deut. 4:11–13, 33, 36). This resulted in a great fear of God. The people were "afraid of the fire" (Deut. 5:5). "This great fire will consume us, and we will die if we hear the voice of the LORD our God any longer. For what mortal man has ever heard the voice of the living God speaking out of fire, as we have, and survived?" (vv. 25–26). The further consequence of this was that the people said, "We will listen and obey," a pledge to do whatever God said (v. 27). The writer of the Epistle to the Hebrews referred to this, but noting that Christians today have not come to a mountain that is "burning with fire" (Heb. 12:18). He nevertheless admonished them to worship God "with reverence and awe" (v. 28). For as Moses had first stated, "God is a consuming fire" (Deut. 4:24; Heb. 12:29).

Supernatural fire that consumed Nadab and Abihu

These two men had offered strange or unauthorized fire before the Lord, contrary to His command. "So fire came out from the presence of the LORD and consumed them, and they died before the LORD" (Lev. 10:2).

When the people complained

The Israelites complained about their hardships in the hearing of the Lord. When He heard them, His anger was aroused. "Then fire from the LORD burned among them and consumed some of the outskirts of the camp. When the people cried out to Moses, he prayed to the LORD and the fire died down. So that place was called Taberah, because fire from the LORD had burned among them" (Num. 11:1–3). Sometime after the aforementioned event involving Korah and his followers rebelling against Moses's leadership, Moses was vindicated when "fire came out from the LORD and consumed the 250 men" (Num. 16:35). These occasions are a grim reminder of how much God abhors grumbling. Paul cautioned: "Do not grumble" (1 Cor. 10:10).

A sign to Gideon

An angel of the Lord appeared to Gideon. As Gideon was preparing a meal, "fire flared from the rock, consuming the meat and the bread. And the angel of the LORD disappeared" (Judg. 6:21). This sign indicated that Gideon had been chosen to lead Israel at a critical moment.

A sign to King David

When David bought the land on which the threshing floor of Araunah the Jebusite was located, David built an altar to the Lord. There he sacrificed burnt offerings and fellowship offerings. He called on the Lord. The Lord answered him "with fire from heaven on the altar of burnt offering" (1 Chron. 21:26). This was a sign that David's sin of numbering the people had been forgiven.

A seal on Solomon's temple

Building a temple to the Lord was David's idea. But he was not allowed to build it. This privilege and responsibility fell to Solomon. His prayer of dedication is one of the great prayers of Holy Scripture. (See 2 Chronicles 6:12–42.) When King Solomon finished praying, "fire came down from heaven and consumed the burnt offering and the sacrifices, and the glory of the LORD filled the temple" (2 Chron. 7:1). The fire was a seal of God's approval on the temple. The priests could not enter the temple because the glory of the Lord filled it. When all the people "saw the fire coming down and the glory of the LORD above the temple, they knelt on the pavement with their faces to the ground, and they worshiped and gave thanks to the Lord, saying, 'He is good; his love endures forever'" (vv. 1–3).

Elijah and supernatural fire

We saw at the beginning of this chapter that when the Lord promised to show Himself to Elijah on the mountain that "the LORD was not in the fire" (1 Kings 19:12). God sometimes repeats Himself; sometimes He doesn't. In any case, Elijah's finest hour was when he confronted the prophets of Baal and made a proposition: the God who answers by fire is the true God. The false prophets agreed. They also failed to bring down fire by their silly ritual and shouts. When they gave up, Elijah prayed. As soon as he prayed, "the fire of the LORD fell and burned up the sacrifice, the wood, the stones and the soil, and also licked up the water in the trench. When all the people saw this, they fell prostrate and cried, 'The LORD—he is God! The LORD—he is God!'" (1 Kings 18:38–39).

On a different occasion Elijah made a similar proposition—this time with a captain, that if Elijah was truly a man of God, "'May fire come down from heaven and consume you and your fifty men!' Then fire fell from heaven and consumed the captain and his men" (2 Kings 1:10–15). This happened a second time. But when it might have happened a third time, a captain fell on his knees before Elijah and begged that this not happen and no more fire from heaven came (vv. 13–14).

Finally, on the day Elijah was to be taken, Elisha (Elijah's chosen successor) had begged for a "double portion" of Elijah's spirit. Elijah agreed upon condition that Elisha saw him when he was taken. As they were walking along and talking, "suddenly a chariot of fire and horses of fire appeared and separated the two of them, and Elijah went up to heaven in a whirlwind" (2 Kings 2:11).

Supernatural fire as protection

Elisha prayed that his servant would see there was nothing to fear. His servant was afraid of King Aram, the enemy of Israel. "Don't be afraid," the prophet told him. "Those who are with us are more than those who are with them." To prove this, the Lord opened the servant's eyes. "He looked and saw the hills full of horses and chariots of fire all around Elisha" (2 Kings 6:16–17).

An angel told the prophet Zechariah that Jerusalem would be a "city without walls" because of the great number of men and livestock in it. Then the Lord said, "I myself will be a wall of fire around it" and "its glory within" (Zech. 2:4–5). I often borrow from this expression when I pray for protection for my family and those I may feel especially need this kind of support.

The Holy Spirit's fire

John the Baptist said that Jesus would baptize with the Holy Spirit "and fire." His "winnowing fork is in his hand, and he will clear his threshing floor, gathering the wheat into his barn and burning up the chaff with unquenchable fire" (Matt. 3:11–12; see also Luke 3:16–17). On the Day of Pentecost as the Holy Spirit fell, "they saw what seemed to be tongues of fire that separated and came to rest on each of them" (Acts 2:3). Peter quoted from Joel to explain what was going on, adding,

"I will show wonders in the heavens and on the earth, blood and fire and billows of smoke" (Joel 2:30; Acts 2:19).

Supernatural fire at the Second Coming of Jesus and final judgment

Just as Isaiah prophesied the death of God's Messiah (Isa. 53), so he also foresaw our Lord's Second Coming. "See, the LORD is coming with fire, and his chariots are like a whirlwind; he will bring down his anger with fury, and his rebuke with flames of fire. For with fire and with his sword the LORD will execute judgment upon all men" (Isa. 66:15–16). As Paul said, the Lord Jesus will be "revealed from heaven in blazing fire with his powerful angels. He will punish those who do not know God and do not obey the gospel of our Lord Jesus. They will be punished with everlasting destruction and shut out from the presence of the Lord and from the majesty of his power on the day he comes to be glorified in his holy people and to be marveled at among all those who have believed" (2 Thess. 1:7–10).

As noted above, Paul said that the Judgment Day will bring to light whether a Christian will receive a reward at that time. "The Day will bring it to light. It will be revealed with fire, and the fire will test the quality of each man's work. If what he has built survives, he will receive a reward. If it is burned up, he will suffer loss; he himself will be saved, but only as one escaping through the flames" (1 Cor. 3:13–15).

Peter said that the present heavens and earth are "reserved for fire, being kept for the day of judgment and destruction of the ungodly" (2 Pet. 3:7). He added that the day of God will bring about "the destruction of the heavens by fire, and the elements will melt in the heat" (v. 12). There are some who believe Peter was talking about nuclear war; if so, he would not be speaking of supernatural fire.

The fire of hell

"Anyone who says, 'You fool!' will be in danger of the fire of hell" (Matt. 5:22). "It is better for you to enter life maimed or crippled than to have two hands or two feet and be thrown into eternal fire. And if your eye causes you to sin, gouge it out and throw it away. It is better for you to enter life with one eye than to have two eyes and be thrown into the fire of hell" (Matt. 18:8–9). "In hell, where he was in torment, he looked up and saw Abraham far away, with Lazarus by his side. So he called to him, 'Father Abraham, have pity on me and send Lazarus to dip the tip of his finger in water and cool my tongue, because I am in agony in this fire'" (Luke 16:23–24). "The tongue…corrupts the whole person, sets the whole course of his life on fire, and is itself set on fire by hell" (James 3:6).

The Book of Revelation

It is not always easy to tell what is symbolic and what is supernatural in this book. Fire that is connected to punishment would appear to be supernatural fire. "He will be tormented with burning sulfur in the presence of the holy angels and the Lamb. And the smoke of their torment will rise for ever and ever" (Rev. 14:10–11). "The two of them were thrown alive into the fiery lake of burning sulfur" (Rev. 19:20). "And the devil, who deceived them, was thrown into the lake of burning sulfur, where the beast and the false prophet had been thrown. They will be tormented day and night for ever and ever" (Rev. 20:10). "Death and Hades were thrown into the lake of fire. The lake of fire is the second death. If anyone's name was not found written in the book of life, he was thrown into the lake of fire" (vv. 14–15). Near the beginning of this chapter we saw that those who were "cowardly, the unbelieving…their place will be in the fiery lake of burning sulfur. This is the second death" (Rev. 21:8).

SYMBOLIC OR POETIC FIRE

The song of Moses

> For a fire has been kindled by my wrath,
>   one that burns to the realm of the dead below.
> It will devour the earth and its harvests
>   and set afire the foundations of the mountains.
>
> —DEUTERONOMY 32:22

The psalms

On the wicked he [God] will rain
 fiery coals and burning sulfur;
 a scorching wind will be their lot.

—PSALM 11:6

Smoke rose from his nostrils;
 consuming fire came from his mouth,
 burning coals blazed out of it.

—PSALM 18:8

At the time of your appearing
 you will make them like a fiery furnace.
In his wrath the Lord will swallow them up,
 and his fire will consume them.

—PSALM 21:9

The voice of the LORD flashes forth flames of fire.

—PSALM 29:7, ESV

Our God comes and will not be silent;
 a fire devours before him,
 and around him a tempest rages.

—PSALM 50:3

Fire goes before him
 and consumes his foes on every side.

—PSALM 97:3

When you pass through the waters,
 I will be with you;
and when you pass through the rivers,
 they will not sweep over you.
When you walk through the fire,
 you will not be burned;
 the flames will not set you ablaze.

—ISAIAH 43:2

His word is in my heart like a fire,
a fire shut up in my bones.
I am weary of holding it in;
indeed, I cannot.

—JEREMIAH 20:9

Ezekiel

The prophet Ezekiel mentions fire more than fifty times, often in what would appear to be symbolic visions. A typical example is this:

I looked, and I saw a windstorm coming out of the north—an immense cloud with flashing lightning and surrounded by brilliant light. The center of the fire looked like glowing metal, and in the fire was what looked like four living creatures.

—EZEKIEL 1:4–5

Daniel

As I looked,
thrones were placed,
and the Ancient of Days took his seat;
his clothing was white as snow,
and the hair of his head like pure wool;
his throne was fiery flames;
its wheels were burning fire.

—DANIEL 7:9, ESV

His body was like beryl, his face like the appearance of lightning, his eyes like flaming torches, his arms and legs like the gleam of burnished bronze, and the sound of his words like the sound of a multitude.

—DANIEL 10:6, ESV

The prophecy concerning John the Baptist

I will send my messenger, who will prepare the way before me....But who can endure the day of his coming? Who can stand when he appears? For he will be like a refiner's fire or a launderer's soap.

—MALACHI 3:1–2

The apostle Paul

If your enemy is hungry, feed him;
    if he is thirsty, give him something to drink.
In doing this, you will heap burning coals on his head.

—ROMANS 12:20;
see also PROVERBS 25:21–23

Jesus described in the Book of Revelation

His eyes were like blazing fire. His feet were like bronze glowing in a furnace.

—REVELATION 1:14–15

I saw heaven standing open and there before me was a white horse, whose rider is called Faithful and True. With justice he judges and wages war. His eyes are like blazing fire.

—REVELATION 19:11–12

Fire in the Book of Revelation

I counsel you to buy from me gold refined in the fire.

—REVELATION 3:18

The angel took the censer, filled it with fire from the altar, and hurled it on the earth.

—REVELATION 8:5

The horses and riders I saw in my vision looked like this: Their breastplates were fiery red...out of their mouths came fire, smoke and sulfur. A third of mankind was killed by the three plagues of fire, smoke and sulfur that came out of their mouths.

—REVELATION 9:17–18

I saw another mighty angel...his legs were like fiery pillars.

—REVELATION 10:1

If anyone tries to harm them, fire comes from their mouths and devours their enemies.

—REVELATION 11:5

He performed great and miraculous signs, even causing fire to come down from heaven to earth.

—REVELATION 13:13

Still another angel, who had charge of the fire, came from the altar.

—REVELATION 14:18

I saw what looked like a sea of glass mixed with fire.

—REVELATION 15:2

The sun was given power to scorch people with fire.

—REVELATION 16:8

They will eat her flesh and burn her with fire.

—REVELATION 17:16

She will be consumed by fire.

—REVELATION 18:8

The fear of the Lord

A subsidiary purpose of the use of fire was to instill an abiding fear of the Lord when it came to the worship of God. When natural fire was used, there was to be a holy fear of God. When this appeared to diminish—as in the case of the offering of unauthorized fire, God stepped in to revive the fear of God in holy things (Lev. 10:3–20). One of the immediate results of the sin of Nadab and Abihu in offering strange fire before the Lord was that Moses was required to *teach* the fear of the Lord to all who remained.

Supernatural fire—whether to show God's vengeance or merely His power—would almost certainly bring this fear without having to be taught it. But the writer of the Hebrews reminded the people that God Himself is a consuming fire, and warned them never to forget this. They must never—ever—outgrow approaching God with reverence and fear.

We must *pray* for the fire of God to fall on us today. But we must equally be faithful to *teach* the fear of God to be instilled in us today.

It is my opinion that the greatest absence in the church today is the fear of God.

NOTES

From the Foreword by Jack Hayford

1. "To understand the significance of this phenomenon, it is important to know that Dr. R. T. Kendall embraces the doctrinal tradition and positions of Reformed theology. Though ridiculed by some peers in that circle because of his openness and commitment to teach, preach, and minister the truth, experience, and lifestyle of New Testament leaders and believers in Acts and the Epistles, he stands firm for the charismatic/Pentecostal testimony. He, just as many others of Reformed theological tradition (as well as other sectors of the larger global church), came to a place of recognizing the truth that 'Jesus Christ is the same, yesterday, today, and forever' truly means *now*!"

2. "I want to urge that *Holy Fire* be read, studied, and utilized by we who lead; that we consider the book as a graciously written, charitably communicated witness and resource for fellow leaders. Many who have been influenced to withdraw from pursuing the truth of Jesus as our 'baptizer with the Holy Spirit' may be assisted to renew their convictions and zeal. Others who have been either intimidated or misinformed (or even offended by the arrogance or biblical recklessness of self-righteous charismatics) are increasingly 'hungering and thirsting after righteousness.' They are looking deeper into the well where the rivers of living water flow with Holy Spirit–begotten purity and power. The hour of redemption's history into which we are all now plunged is an hour awaking more and more fellow servants of Christ to our desperate need for New Testament power.

"This realism is probing at the roots of fear and pride and beginning to uproot the vanity born of incomplete views and prejudiced theology concerning the Holy Spirit's power and ministry in and through the church. My experience is that an increase is again beginning to stir those earnest enough to overthrow fear, fatalism, and passivity. A new vanguard of young leaders is just now beginning to live and lead in the light of this timeless fact: Jesus's unchanging, never-ceasing works of power, love, and ministry to and through His people today are available when and where the Holy Spirit is welcomed and unrestricted in the life of believers and the worship and ministry of congregations!"

3. "It is essential to note: as with any sector of the church, at times ungodly and wholly unworthy leaders rise and gain a following. From local

pastorates to notable media ministries one can find shameful violations of the Word and personalities lauded as 'anointed' who ignore biblical standards regarding morality, financial accountability, and biblical integrity. Pop culture themes that compromise the *whole truth* of God's Word on subjects that lead to human, financial, lifestyle, and attitudinal shoddiness are often paraded in the name of 'charismatic.' This is a tragic miscarriage of a biblically rooted word (*charismata*) and shameless rejection of the charismatic lifestyle modeled by the apostles' own first-century ministry—one lived without compromise of truth, character, behavior, or morality, and devoid of any self-serving ways.

"May it be known and affirmed here: such biblically inconsistent leaders, be they men or women, who violate God's Word—and any who follow them—are not and should not (no matter what 'signs following' are claimed) be seen or understood to be a valid definition of what charismatic or Pentecostal life or leadership is about.

"It is grieving to all who seek to live and walk in humility and holiness as members of the Spirit-filled community of believers, when there is evidence of a leader's doctrinal, ecclesiastical, moral, or financial compromise, and yet nothing of confrontation, discipline, or disapproval appear to be administered. However, truth is that this is not at all the case among the vast majority of those within the Pentecostal or charismatic community. For the most part, existing denominations and structured nondenominational networks *do* administer correction and discipline, as well as directing recovery and restoration programs where repentance is shown by the errant or fallen.

"The most flagrant cases of violation and neglect of discipline occur in the glaring instances where independent, self-directed, self-ruled, and self-governed leaders move. The absence of structures requiring accountability to fellow leaders, or the 'cronyism' of some who unite, but do so forming small circles of equally errant ministers who 'measure themselves by themselves' (2 Cor. 10:12) and smugly exercise a self-affirming tolerance and grace that refuses the legalism of critics; these are of the nature of those the Epistle of Jude identifies as 'dreamers' who 'defile the flesh, reject authority, and speak evil of dignitaries,' and as having 'gone in the way of Cain, run greedily in the error of Balaam for profit, and perished in the rebellion of Korah...for whom is reserved the blackness of darkness forever' (Jude 4-13, NKJV).

"Further, it is an egregious exercise in unkindness when categorical charges or institutional 'blackballing tactics' are leveled against charismatics as though all are given to indifference concerning Bible interpretation or moral recklessness. Even those differing theologically know full well that such broad brush treatment is a violation of facts—that the few characterize neither the values nor lifestyle of the many, i.e., charismatics who love, honor, and live for Christ, the Lord of us all—charismatic or otherwise. May God extinguish the foul incense from the 'strange fire' offered by voices among leaders at either group's altars, and may His 'holy fire' baptize us all with a fresh baptism of His unifying love, whatever our doctrinal differences."

INTRODUCTION

1. C. S. Lewis, *The Lion, the Witch and the Wardrobe* (New York: HarperCollins Publishers, 2002).

CHAPTER ONE—DISCERNING THE TIMES

1. The details of the M'Cheyne Bible Reading Plan are available at: http://www.esv.org/assets/pdfs/rp.one.year.tract.pdf.
2. William Cowper, *Poems*, vol. II (England: Manning & Lorring and E. Lincoln, 1802). Viewed online at Google Books.
3. Matthew D. Green, *Understanding the Fivefold Ministry* (Lake Mary, FL: Charisma House, 2005), 161.
4. "And Can It Be?" by Charles Wesley. Public domain.
5. "When I Survey the Wondrous Cross" by Isaac Watts. Public domain.
6. "God Moves in a Mysterious Way" by William Cowper. Public domain.
7. "How Sweet the Name of Jesus Sounds" by John Newton. Public domain.
8. "O for a Heart to Praise My God," by Charles Wesley. Public domain.

CHAPTER TWO—WHAT EVERY CHRISTIAN
SHOULD KNOW ABOUT THE HOLY SPIRIT

1. D. James Kennedy, *Evangelism Explosion*, 4th edition (Wheaton, IL: Tyndale House Publishers, 1996).
2. "Holy Spirit, Truth Divine" by Samuel Longfellow. Public domain.
3. "Holy Ghost, Dispel Our Sadness" by Paul Gerhardt. Public domain.
4. "Lord God, the Holy Ghost" by James Montgomery. Public domain.
5. "Spirit of God, Descend Upon My Heart" by George Croly. Public domain.
6. R. T. Kendall, *Why Jesus Died* (Oxford, England: Monarch Books, 2011).
7. "Oh, for a Thousand Tongues to Sing" by Charles Wesley. Public domain.

CHAPTER THREE—THE IMMEDIATE AND DIRECT
TESTIMONY OF THE HOLY SPIRIT

1. This is a typical phrase used by Jack Taylor, with whom I preach often.
2. Oxford University's Doctor of Philosophy degree.

3. John Calvin, *Institutes of the Christian Religion, 1536 Edition* trans. Ford Lewis Battles (Grand Rapids, MI: Wm. B. Eerdmans Publishing Company, 1995).

4. John Cotton, *A Treatise of the Covenant of Grace… 1662* (Ann Arbor, MI: EEBO Editions, ProQuest, 2011).

5. As quoted in John Norton, *Memoir of John Cotton* (Boston: Perkins and Marvin, 1834).

6. D. Martyn Lloyd-Jones, *God's Ultimate Purpose: An Exposition of Ephesians 1* (Grand Rapids, MI: Baker Books, 1978).

7. Ibid., 271.

8. Ibid., 275.

9. Ibid., 267.

10. Ibid., 268.

11. Ibid., 269.

12. Ibid., 248–249.

13. Ibid., 269.

14. Ibid., 274.

15. Ibid., 271.

CHAPTER FOUR—THE OATH AND THE STIGMA

1. R. T. Kendall, *These Are the Days of Elijah* (Grand Rapids, MI: Chosen Books, 2013).

CHAPTER SIX—THE DOVE

1. R. T. Kendall, *The Sensitivity of the Spirit* (Lake Mary, FL: Charisma House, 2002).

2. "Sweet Hour of Prayer" by William Walford. Public domain.

3. R. T. Kendall, *God Gives Second Chances* (Lake Mary, FL: Charisma House, 2008).

4. R. T. Kendall, *Tithing* (Grand Rapids, MI: Zondervan, 1983).

CHAPTER SEVEN—MY PERSONAL TESTIMONY

1. R. T. Kendall and David Rosen, *The Christian and the Pharisee* (New York: FaithWords, 2007).

CHAPTER EIGHT—CESSATIONISM

1. Charles Carrin, *On Whose Authority?* (Boyton Beach, FL: Charles Carrin Ministries, n.d.). Copies available through Charles Carrin Ministries at: www.CharlesCarrinMinistries.com.

2. "A Mighty Fortress Is Our God" by Martin Luther. Public domain.

3. John Calvin, *Institutes of Christian Religion* (Peabody, MA: Hendrickson Publishers, Inc., 2008), 958. Viewed online at Google Books.

4. Ibid.

5. These remarks from Colin Dye were included in a personal letter to the author.

CHAPTER NINE—THE CONSEQUENCES OF CESSATIONISM

1. This statement from Rolfe Barnard is from a sermon the author has heard many times.

2. As quoted in J. I. Packer, *Evangelism and the Sovereignty of God* (Downers Grove, IL: InterVarsity Press, 2012), 37. Viewed online at Google Books.

3. R. T. Kendall, *Just Love* (Lake Mary, FL: Christian Focus, 1969).

4. Jack Deere, *Surprised by the Power of the Spirit* (Grand Rapids, MI: Zondervan, 1996).

CHAPTER TEN—THE BAPTISM WITH THE HOLY SPIRIT

1. Henry T. Blackaby and Melvin D. Blackaby, *Experiencing the Spirit* (Colorado Springs, CO: Multnomah Books, 2009).

CHAPTER ELEVEN—GIFTS OF THE SPIRIT

1. Brother Yun and Paul Hattaway, *The Heavenly Man* (Peabody, MA: Hendrickson Publishers, 2009).

2. Wayne Grudem, *The Gift of Prophecy in the New Testament and Today* (Wheaton, IL: Crossway, 2000); *Systematic Theology* (Grand Rapids, MI: Zondervan, 1995).

CHAPTER TWELVE—THE ULTIMATE PROOF OF THE HOLY SPIRIT

1. This quote is widely attributed to Mahatma Gandhi, but no direct source is available.

2. "Like a River Glorious" by Frances R. Havergal. Public domain.

3. R. T. Kendall, *God Meant It for Good* (St. Louis, MO: Morningstar Publishers, 2009).

4. R. T. Kendall, *Total Forgiveness* (Lake Mary, FL: Charisma House, 2007).

CHAPTER THIRTEEN—ISAAC

1. Smith Wigglesworth gave this prophecy in 1947.

2. R. T. Kendall, *The Parables of Jesus* (Peabody, MA: Chosen Books, 2008).

3. Smith Wigglesworth gave this prophecy in 1947.

APPENDIX—FIRE

1. "Glorious Things of Thee Are Spoken," by John Newton. Public domain.

SCRIPTURE INDEX

INDEX

CONTINUE ALONG THE ROAD TO FORGIVENESS

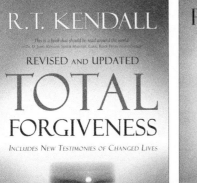
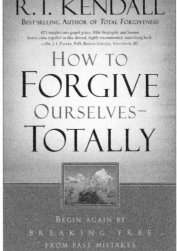
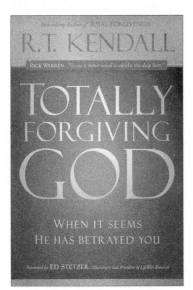

Books By R.T. Kendall

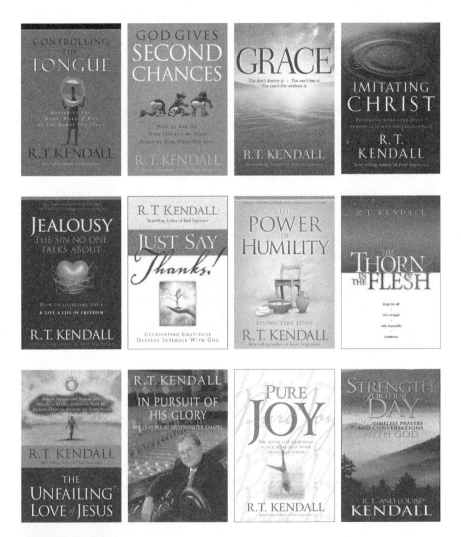

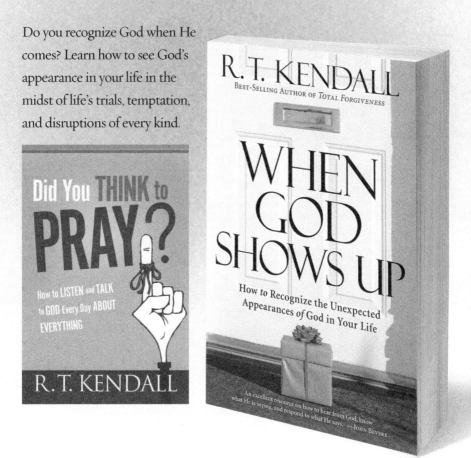